YESTERDAYS
OF AN ARTIST-MONK

YESTERDAYS
OF AN ARTIST-MONK

BY

DOM WILLIBRORD VERKADE, O.S.B.

Angelico Press

For information, address:
Angelico Press, Ltd.
169 Monitor St.
Brooklyn, NY 11222
www.angelicopress.com

ppb: 979-8-88677-052-0
cloth: 979-8-88677-053-7

Cover design by
Julian Kwasniewski

CONTENTS

YESTERDAYS
OF AN ARTIST–MONK

❧

CHILDHOOD

I WAS born on the 18th of September, 1868, in Zaandam, in the vicinity of Amsterdam, about a quarter of an hour after my twin brother had seen the light. We were not baptized, for my father belonged to the sect of the Mennonites, who do not practise infant baptism. When we were born, two little girls had already arrived, one of whom was a child of my father's first marriage. After us were born four other children, a girl and three boys, so that finally there were eight of us brothers and sisters, three girls and five boys. I was somewhat stronger than my twin brother. Yet we were both healthy and sturdy, and when we were called to do our military service we had attained the considerable height of about six feet. We were named after our two grandfathers; my twin brother receiving the name of Erich, and I that of John, although usually called in short Jan. We lived at first on the Dam, a high embankment. From the windows of our house we looked out upon a small harbour, where many river-boats lay at anchor. The street in front of our home was very lively, as boatmen, longshoremen, factory hands, peasants and citizens gathered there to transact business or to discuss the news of the day. Many wagons also passed, loaded with casks, sacks and wood, and thus the activity of an important little commercial and manufacturing town unrolled itself daily before our eyes. My father had a manufactory of oil. As very small boys, we already knew the way thither, and thus from childhood had an opportunity to develop our powers of observation, and soon became two very wide-awake lads.

Up to our eighteenth year, when the exigencies of life forced us to go our different ways, we twins were inseparable. We formed practically one heart and one soul and even one head, for what one thought the other usually had to think also. We had indeed in the course of these years one friend or another in common, yet we were perfectly satisfied with each other's society.

As a child, I believed in God. I knew that He sees everything and that He is merciful and forgives all; but also that He punishes if one does not change for the better, and that He answers our prayers. Like other children I often prayed that this or that act of mine might not be discovered, that the teacher might that day omit to call me up to recite, and other such things. Frequently my prayer was answered.

These fundamental truths and much of what Jesus Christ had spoken, taught and done, I learned through conversations with my parents and the servants, and through the general instruction given in school without, however, having ever been taught precisely about prayer and religion.

CHILDHOOD

The only prayer at home, common to us all, was grace at table. Then we boys said simply and briefly: "Lord, bless this food! Amen." As far as I can recollect, the servant girl taught us also an evening and a morning prayer, but I must have soon forgotten them. I memorized the "Our Father" with some difficulty. I often heard people talk of Jesus Christ, the Redeemer, as the Son of God, who died for our sins, and also about the kingdom of God, and of mortal sin and grace, but I never could understand it all. To this there must have also been added the idea that Jesus Christ is "God of God, Light of Light, and true God of true God." I kept my faith in God until my fifteenth year, but after that time it became ever darker in my heart, till finally I believed in God no more.

I STILL remember very well one hour in the little garden behind our house on the *Gedempte Gracht* (the filled moat) in Zaandam, near the heap of sand, where we used to play. It was there that I for the first time wondered where I came from. I thought of the heavens and the stars, and in the obscurity of my unconscious life I asked myself whether I could not remember the moment when I began to exist: "I was certainly present there." But no, I could recollect nothing, absolutely nothing, and my thoughts always lost themselves in the profound darkness of the unknown. This darkness had for me, however, something awe-inspiring in it. After one timid attempt to ask others about my origin, I gave up making any further inquiries, for I perceived at once that people would not tell me the whole truth.

[3]

YESTERDAYS OF AN ARTIST–MONK

I no longer know the circumstances exactly, but I think it happened at a time when I had cut my finger deeply, and had received a severe reproof for doing so; but certain it is that, small as I was, I then blasphemed God in my anger shamefully, because He was to blame for it all, and because He, the Almighty, could and ought to have prevented it. I did this in a corner of my bedroom, to which I had hastened. Soon after I had the feeling of having done something monstrous, and was surprised that God had not revenged Himself on me, and that He still let me live. It is true, I did not expressly beg for forgiveness; nevertheless I felt remorse.

Not far from our house lived a poor, sickly young woman, named Mina. She was entirely bowed over by sickness, and her head inclined strongly towards the left shoulder. I observed her often with sympathetic curiosity. Her features were distorted with pain. The boys in the street often shouted after her: " Mina, hold your head straight," because they knew she would then become angry and rail at them. It always made my heart ache to see that. Yet once I could not resist the temptation, and I also cried out: " Mina, hold your head straight! " The poor woman flew into a rage. For a long time I felt the full wickedness of my act, and I subsequently often thought of this Mina whenever, still as a boy, I heard the Lord's beatitudes read aloud.

There are two saints' festivals in Holland which Protestantism has not been able to eradicate: *Sintermaarten* and

CHILDHOOD

Sinterklaas, the festivals of St. Martin and St. Nicholas. They were retained for the children; " for theirs is the kingdom of heaven." On the evening before St. Martin's, boys and girls march through the streets with turnips, radishes or large potatoes, the inside of which has been scooped out to hold a lighted candle; sometimes they have also coloured paper lanterns. In this way they sing little songs before the doors of the richer citizens or their own relatives. One of these songs runs as follows:

> *Here there lives a wealthy man,*
> *He will give much, for he can;*
> *He has got a lot to give,*
> *Long may he live!*

Of course we twins did not lag behind in this fun, and sang ourselves hoarse. I often wondered who this St. Martin could be. The name had for me something so intimate and genuine in it. Also whenever my mother spoke of the "Martin's Tower" in the city of Groningen, I always thought in that connection of something indescribable. Later St. Martin came again into my life, as we shall see.

In Holland when one sees a work which has required much patience for its execution, one says, " That is a monk's work." This expression had for me an inexpressible charm. Although in my youthful days I was very impatient, I nevertheless gladly performed certain tasks, which needed much patience, and this because it was a " monk's work."

[5]

YESTERDAYS OF AN ARTIST–MONK

In 1877 my father changed his residence from Zaandam to
Amsterdam. Even as children in a large city, we still enjoyed the greatest freedom. In Holland one is accustomed
to bring up the boys to be self-reliant, and does not wish to
check their innate spirit of enterprise. Hence a good deal
of my youth was spent in the streets, on the condition however, that the usual destination of our walks and wanderings should be the great zoölogical garden of the city or
the *Vondelpark*. This continual strolling about gave us, it
is true, an opportunity to perpetrate all possible boyish
tricks, but it had also a formative influence upon our characters. The sight of every sort of professional labour, such
as work at the forge, horseshoeing, lead-smelting, plumb-
ing, building, carpentering, cabinet-work, and the like, and
the mere standing for a time before all kinds of occupations,
are the most natural form of object-teaching, for which
home and school can offer only a poor equivalent. One
should think of this the more, when one speaks of the
" dangers of the streets."

At that time we had a Catholic neighbour, a woman who
came once or twice a week to mend the linen. Her name
was Truitje de Naaster. She had been brought up by sisters
in a cloister, and had herself taught there, until the law
decreed that only female teachers, who had obtained diplo-
mas might give instruction. She knew a quantity of stories,
and could relate them admirably. Hence we children were
glad to sit beside her, and listen to her, while she sewed.
Sometimes we paid a visit to Truitje in her dwelling, and

[6]

drank a little cup of coffee with her. Then she would tell us much of the parish priest, of confession, and of a well-known family, which was so strictly Catholic, and to which she also went every week to sew. One evening she took us with her to the Catholic church, on the *Singel*. A famous pulpit-orator was to preach. I accompanied her with a beating heart. I saw then for the first time, how every visitor to the church bent his knee before the high altar. Of the sermon I understood nothing. When the benediction with the Blessed Sacrament was given, Truitje told us to kneel down. We did so, but awkwardly. This time the whole ceremony made little impression upon me, and I left the church, as I had come. I have always remembered Truitje with pleasure. Thanks to her faith, she lived in an atmosphere of the supernatural and poetical, in which I always felt happy, whenever I was brought into it by her narratives.

IN those years, and subsequently as well, my twin brother and I went on Sunday to the so-called children's church. Every time a different pastor preached. First the choir sang a hymn and the preacher uttered an extempore prayer; then he delivered his sermon, and finally all the children sang a hymn. We did not object to going to the children's church, chiefly because each of us received then a ten-cent piece to put into the collection-bag. This bag, however, never got more than one cent, or perhaps nothing at all, for sometimes we stayed away from church altogether. Yet at the conclusion of the service we always were in evidence at the

[7]

door and asked one of our comrades who had attended service what the sermon had been about.

I can, however, say this for myself, that many a word of the preacher fell upon good soil. Often, with my eyes tightly closed and my hands piously folded, I would repeat inaudibly but faithfully after him what he prayed aloud. On one occasion the story of Esther was related to us. The preacher knew how to tell a story exceedingly well, and I still distinctly remember the words, " Strike Haman dead! " and the declaration that Esther saved the people of Israel.

Frequently I heard from the pulpit the words: " Unless you become as little children, you shall not enter into the kingdom of heaven " (Matt. xviii. 3); and I always thought, when they were spoken: " Either Jesus seems not to have known children very well, or formerly they were better than now. If He had known, how much I have already stolen, He would not have said that."

Until we were twelve years old, my twin brother and I slept in one bed. One evening we were lying beside each other thus, both on the right side. My brother had turned his back to me. I was already half asleep, when he turned around and said: " Jan, do you sometimes pray? " We had indeed, not long before, heard in the Mennonite Church on the *Singel* a sermon on prayer. I had not understood much of it, but some words had nevertheless remained in my memory, and since that time I had prayed frequently. But I did not want to confess it to my brother, and so

[8]

answered, " Are you crazy? I never pray! " My brother replied, " You pig! " and turned his back on me again.

How often I have gone by a Catholic church, and would have been so glad secretly to slip inside of it. But I knew from experience that as soon as I entered it, I should be embarrassed by people looking at me, who would perceive at once that I was not a Catholic. Therefore I dared to do so only if I saw many people going in and out of the church. Then I could quietly stand in the rear, without being stared at. I saw always the same picture: an altar enveloped in light and veiled by thick clouds of incense, and at the altar the priest with his acolytes going to and fro, while the church choir sang. Everything was very solemn and pleasing, yet also strange and wholly incomprehensible to me, a poor little fellow who, nevertheless, felt himself drawn to it irresistibly.

A near relative, who lived in our house, was undoubtedly of a deeply religious nature. As a child, she had built one day in the recess of a garret-window, hardly three feet wide, a little altar, which she adorned with white linen, little candles, flowers and two small figures of saints. I found it beautiful and made one like it, only I screened my little altar with a curtain hung before the recess, and thus had a little space for myself alone, so small, however, that I could scarcely move in it. Then I knelt down before my tiny altar, and in doing so had the feeling that I also ought to pray. But my praying did not prove very satisfactory and I soon abandoned it.

[9]

WE children also sometimes played at " Catholic church." Children like to make fun of things, and I used to put on some old clothes and play the part of priest. My elder sister then usually said: " No one can do that so well as you." Listening behind the door of a Catholic church, I had often heard its Gregorian chants, and the character of this music and especially the intervals in it had impressed themselves strongly on my mind. My brothers and sisters always broke into peals of laughter, when I let my voice intone the service in the Gregorian style. When the " service " was over, there also followed " confession." My sister then said to me: " Father, forgive me my sins! " Thereupon I answered: " Child, what have you done? " She then uttered some nonsense, on account of which I usually sent her away without " absolution," with the words: " Go away, child of the devil." At these words all my brothers and sisters broke out again in uproarious laughter, and one of them once said: " Jan is just the fellow to do that! "

One day, my twin brother and I found in the street a little Catholic prayer-book. When we opened it, we came upon the litany of Loreto and read: " Thou tower of ivory," " Thou chosen vessel of piety," " Thou golden house," " Thou morning-star," etc., " pray for us! " That provoked us to laughter, and we at once threw the " crazy stuff " into the neighbouring water. But why could I never forget this occurrence? And has the fact no significance that even today I could go to the exact place, where we found that remarkable little book? Did I perhaps even then, in spite of my contemptuous action, somewhat appreciate the lofty poetry of these noble invocations?

My twin brother and I attended a city school for sons of the "better" citizens in Amsterdam. There, from our extraordinary likeness to each other, we could play many a good trick.

At times I was also diligent and even received twice a so-called "prize for industry." But, on the whole, it must be said that we went too far. Accordingly the headmaster one day called my father to him and said: Your boys are too much indulged at home. Send them to a boarding-school, where the discipline is strict. And in fact, this is what was done. So with tearless eyes we one day took leave of our weeping mother, and our brothers and sisters, and father himself brought us to a boarding-school at Oisterwijk, a village in the province of Noord-Brabant. . . .

AT BOARDING-SCHOOL

LIFE in the boarding-school gave me a new impulse towards religion. In the morning at breakfast the Director read aloud a chapter from the Bible, and I thus became acquainted with the ancient people of Israel and with its figures of heroes and prophets. Moreover, as I have already remarked, I knew by this time many passages and utterances of the Holy Scriptures. In our school a prayer was said before and after the principal meal, and every Sunday we went to the Reformed Church. Once a week also came a preacher to give us instruction in the catechism. All the boys, however, did not take part in this, as they belonged to different sects. There were several sons of pastors among them, but they were certainly no more religiously inclined, nor did they behave any better than the other pupils. Only one of them tried to exert a good influence. It was only a little church in which we boarding-school pupils attended divine service every Sunday. There were, in fact, only about a dozen "Reformed" families in that great Catholic community. The service consisted of two hymns, a prayer by the preacher, the sermon and some concluding remarks. We sat in high box pews, so that one could read or write there by himself. To follow the sermon attentively was for me impossible; therefore, instead of listening, I usually read the Bible or some other book, or wrote a letter.

AT BOARDING-SCHOOL

EVERY week the pastor came, as I have said, to give us instruction. He usually arrived towards evening after our walk. We had a catechism, out of which we were to learn our lesson, but I almost never committed anything from it to memory and rarely listened to what the preacher said. I can remember only that the pastor talked about an Old and a New Testament, and that he spoke once of Pentecost and of the miracle of the gift of tongues. The " speaking with tongues," he explained, does not mean that Christ's disciples, after they had received the Holy Ghost, spoke and understood different languages, which they had not known before; the expression is to be explained exegetically, as meaning that they were exceedingly happy and gave expression to their joy in the liveliest manner. I thought: " Such a pastor must have studied much, before he found all that out." From that moment I had more respect for him.

IT was at this period of my life that I saw a monk for the first time. He wore a brown habit with a cowl, went barefooted, with no covering on his clean-shaven head, and had a cord about his waist. It went through me like a flash and I was quite horrified: " A penitent," I thought; " the cord about his waist is for scourging." I looked after him. The monk was going quietly on his way. Now I saw also that he had a staff in his hand and that his sandals were shod with nails. I sought some information about monks from a friend of my brother, who I thought must be able to enlighten me, for he came from the province of Noord-Brabant, where there are many monasteries.

" These monkish vermin," the youth replied, " are the terror of this population. The mendicant monks go about the country and seek places to sleep in among the peasants, plunder the poor people completely and then go on farther. If you give them nothing, they threaten you with the devil and hell."

I found it strange that the peasants permitted this, but thought: " The Catholics are, after all, so stupid." I could not forget that monkish figure and thereafter, if I saw on the road the prints of nails in the sand, I said to myself: " Again a mendicant monk has gone by here "; for in Holland it is not customary to put nails in shoes.

On one occasion during our vacation, my father took us to his birthplace Vlaardingen, a little seaport, famous for its herring fisheries. He had lived there a part of his youth and often spoke of his grandfather, who had been a lawyer and notary there and had taken the place of a father to him, for my father had never known his own father, having been born some months after the latter's death. To begin with, we visited the house of my great-grandfather, and then looked up an old servant, who had carried my father as a baby in her arms, and finally went to the cemetery where my father's parents and grandparents were buried. After a long search we found their graves. " Hats off," commanded our father, who was evidently deeply affected, though he very rarely showed emotion. There we

[14]

stood like mute dogs and quite idiotically, our hats in our hands, and knew not what to do. There is a bridge between those who go to the other world and those who remain behind — prayer. But this bridge we did not find.

WHEN I left the boarding-school, I took leave of the pastor. He said to me: "My dear boy, we have never been great friends. I hope for the best, but I fear that you will have a hard time in later life; still, as I have said, I will hope for the best. God protect you!" Then it suddenly came to me that I had often given the good man much cause for sadness, and I felt genuine remorse. "But," I thought, "so I am to have a hard time in life, am I? Not much! I have no such idea. Hang it! I'll fight my way through yet."

IN THE COMMERCIAL SCHOOL

W E were, therefore, taken home again, and from September 1883 we attended the commercial school at Amsterdam, whither my parents, after having lived for two years in the country, had returned. This institution was the most expensive of all the public intermediate schools of the city. Only the élite of the citizens was represented there. The teachers were without exception worthy men, and maintained themselves, so far as possible, strictly neutral in religious matters. There prevailed in general a good discipline during the hours of instruction, although no such penalties as extra tasks or blows were inflicted. As everywhere however, the writing and drawing teachers had much to endure.

In this school I heard for the first time " the great Church Fathers " spoken of, especially St. Augustine and also the oldest order of monks, that of the Benedictines. I was affected by this name, as if I had been introduced to some one, whom I greeted immediately as a future intimate friend. Our route in life is marked out for us in advance, and as soon as we hear the name of a great station ahead of us we start involuntarily. But very few are aware of this. All of us are born with sensitive antennae, but usually these shrivel up as our education increases, or else with time they become atrophied of themselves.

[16]

IN THE COMMERCIAL SCHOOL

In August 1884, we twins passed a portion of the summer vacation on the Mosel, near Cochem. On the way thither we visited Cologne and Trier. Already the year before, we had travelled with our father up the Rhine as far as Mainz and had, on the return journey from Coblenz, seen Kreuznach. We arrived in Cologne on a Saturday. After we had found lodging in an inn, we went to the cathedral.

It was already almost dark in the grand interior. In the left transept a few lights were burning. A chant in four parts resounded from the singers' gallery. Only the director, who conducted the music in slow measure was visible. The chant was not loud, but on the contrary sweet and tender, and stole through the lofty vaults like the wind through a forest of pines. It was a wonderfully solemn moment, and both of us were profoundly moved. I still remember that the words fell from my lips: "Truly, it is enough to make one a Catholic."

Then from the choir came the soft sound of a bell, and a priest approached us who held something in his hand. Before him walked a boy swinging a censer. Two other boys carried candles. The sound of the little bell came ever nearer. . . . "Let us go now," I said, and we poor souls fled from the Eucharistic Lord! Alas! how much we have all lost in life, because we were not willing to wait!

On the following day, the great bell of the cathedral woke us very early and when we rose some hours later, the reverberation of the bells was resounding from all the church towers. How new, surprising and delightful this was for us, who came from the north of Holland, in whose large cities the bells are rung only when a royal child is born or dies.

FROM Cologne we went to Trier. As we drove into the city, we passed by the *Porta Nigra*. I shall never forget the overpowering impression which this late classic structure made upon me. For the first time in my life I received from a specimen of architecture the sensation of something really monumental. In comparison with this, everything that I had previously seen was merely graceful, ornamental, charming, fairylike, or beautiful, even wonderful, but never to such a degree *monumental,* not even excepting the cathedral of Cologne.

While I had bought in the latter city photographs of two male heads after an old North German painter, I took with me from Trier pictures of the Porta Nigra and the Igler column, and this gave evidence of the trend of my artistic taste, a preference for the primitive and classic.

In Trier we lodged in the " Red House " on the market place, and thence went forth to see the many beautiful churches of the city. The subtle attraction which issues from the tabernacle in a Catholic church did not fail to exert its influence upon us also. We felt ourselves uplifted in those solemn spaces and left those sanctuaries of consolation full of reverence and admiration.

We also came to one church which was closed. It appeared to have been very recently built. We asked to have it opened for us, and a girl about eighteen years of age led us into the interior. Here she repeated her little speech:

[18]

IN THE COMMERCIAL SCHOOL

" This church, which belongs to the Lutheran congregation, was rebuilt some years ago, but only of bricks; it is
partly new. The organ—" But we had had enough. It
was a pretty room, furnished with many chairs and was
kept very clean, but a house of God? No; of that we had
gained quite another conception after all the visits to
churches we had previously made. We pressed a fee into
the girl's hand, and got away as soon as possible. The
words, " only of bricks," which our guide had several
times repeated, amused us greatly; and yet at home we had
seen hardly anything else than brick buildings.

My immediate ancestors on both my father's and my
mother's sides had all been lawyers or notaries. My father
alone had been an exception. He had been told that he was
too restless and lively for that profession, and that he
should rather be a merchant. The grandfather of my
mother often went hunting, yet chiefly in order to be able
secretly to paint and sketch. He left behind him many
landscape-paintings, some of which were good. My
grandfather on my father's side had wanted to become a
painter, but he was not allowed to do so. My grandfather
on my mother's side was also a man of much artistic taste
and moreover very learned. My father too sketched and
painted aquarelles in his leisure hours; indeed there was
a time when he thought that he could become a second
Mesdag; certainly an illusion, as he soon perceived. It was
no wonder, therefore, that the desire to sketch showed itself
in me also at an early age. One day a Parisian merchant

came to visit us. My father took him to the picture gallery of Amsterdam and I accompanied them. After that, I went to it almost every week and soon was very well acquainted with the Museum. I knew not only the names of the painters, but also when they had lived and to what school they had belonged, and I myself possessed a beautiful collection of engravings of their works. At that time I thought no walk too long, if I could see anything new displayed in a shop-window, and I attended all the auction sales of paintings. I went frequently also to the zoölogical garden, in order to " counterfeit " the lions, bears, camels and other animals. Once I even played truant from school a whole week, in order to sketch there. It was shortly before the Christmas vacation. In the morning I left home with my twin brother Erich and went to the zoölogical garden, while he on the contrary proceeded on his way to school. There he would say, " Jan is ill." As I remained away five or six days, it was believed. After the vacation, no one thought any more of asking for a physician's certificate, but people inquired sympathetically, " Are you better again? "

WHEN my father remarked my fondness for art, he gave me an admirable teacher. This was a young painter named Haverman. " Boys," my father often said, " I shall leave you no great fortune, it is true, but I will see to it that you have a good education. Then, however, you must stretch your hands out of your coat-sleeves and help yourselves." Even at times when he was not prospering in business, he was faithful to this principle. Thus he allowed my brother

[20]

IN THE COMMERCIAL SCHOOL

Arnold, when scarcely twenty years of age, to make a journey to America, in a year, when he had had a great deficit. Through my teacher I became acquainted with several very ambitious and clever artists. It was my greatest pleasure to visit them in their studios and watch them at their work. I began to love art more and more, and slowly the determination grew in me, also to be a painter. Nevertheless I wavered a long time. There was a severe conflict between my artistic gifts and my practical way of looking at things. To become a painter meant for me to give up the prospect of wealth and an early marriage; indeed, under certain circumstances it might mean to be half-starved. And in case my talent did not suffice to make me a good painter, what then? That was, after all, the most important question. I stood like Hercules at the parting of the ways. Thank God that, following the impulse of my heart, I then decided for the ideal in me; for thereby I laid the foundation of my future happiness.

For my father it was a disappointment that I did not go into the business which he had recently founded, yet he soon gave his consent to my choice of a vocation, and when I was halfway through the third year I left the commercial school, in order to prepare myself for the entrance-examination into the National Academy of Fine Arts in Amsterdam. I was now soon to be separated from my twin brother. I have never found a separation so hard as that.

Before closing this chapter, I must relate the following: When my twin brother and I were eighteen years of age, our father said to us one day that we ought to be confirmed in the sect of the Mennonites. "It is part of the social position of a respectable man," he said, "to be a member of some church society. If he wants to get married, for example, the first question addressed to him is, 'Of what religious communion are you?'" But I had been present, two years before, at the baptism of a near relative, and had on that occasion said to myself very positively, "I will never join in doing that." Accordingly I replied, "Father, I have no desire to repeat, parrot-like, after the domine, what he teaches." This I said with reference to the written confession of faith, which in the sect of the Mennonites one must present to the pastor, when one is confirmed; but I added: "When I am a few years older, I will make up my mind about matters of religion." With this my father was satisfied, and for the time being I troubled myself no more about questions of belief, even when, now and then, some passing event gave me occasion to do so.

AT THE ART SCHOOL

AFTER I had prepared myself for five or six months under
the instruction of my teacher, Haverman, I underwent my
examination for admission to the art school — but failed!
My father was glad of it. He liked to speak of the blessings
of adversity and of the salutary results of hindrances. But
after three more months, I presented myself again, and this
time was admitted.

The art school was not then especially flourishing. Its
curriculum was very one-sided. For two whole years one
sketched from classical plastic works, without being properly
initiated into the spirit of the ancients. This was merely the
preparation for drawing and painting from the living
model, and after the pupil had toiled at this for another
two years, he became a master-scholar, received his own
studio and began to work independently. Then, however,
he usually became aware that although he could paint all
sorts of objects from nature, he had not yet learned how
to make practical use of his ability. He resembled some one
who knew many words and rules of a language, without
being able to speak it. Hence the pupil had, after years of
study, to begin again at the beginning in order to learn
how to express himself in lines and colours. And this was
all the harder for him because his powers of imagination
and invention had become almost atrophied through the

[23]

aimless copying of nature. That is the fault of many academies. One teaches the pupils many clever devices, instead of instructing them how a work of art is produced. And this is precisely something one can learn perhaps only at the side of a master, and surely sooner if one aids him with all one's powers in his works.

For four and a half terms of six months each I toiled assiduously in the art school, not, it is true, without sometimes, even out of vacation time, studying on my own account. Then I left this institution and went to my brother-in-law in the country, a talented painter, in order to continue my studies under his guidance.

UNTIL I made my choice of a profession, I had often been wanting in seriousness, and had laid little importance on order, exactitude and punctuality. Very early in life I followed my own inclinations and did what I liked. The great freedom which my brother and I had enjoyed at home had made us, however, clever. We had become smart young fellows, unaccustomed to strict discipline, it is true, but also absolutely neither low nor vulgar. Moreover, we were on the whole honest, as well as true to ourselves. We had inherited from our father energy and a sense of justice, and from our mother a certain distinction and tender sensibility. To these there was added in me an ardent enthusiasm for the beautiful, and a great longing to make something of myself, something genuine and essentially worth while. I did not yearn for mere outward success, but had rather a profound contempt for the " stupid crowd." But I came to the study of art rather late, too late unfortunately. In the first place painting is a noble handicraft, and in order to acquire a handicraft, one must start in early to learn it. Even at fourteen it is already too late. Now I was already eighteen years old and could only sketch something from nature. Hence arose that disparity between perception and feeling on the one hand and the ability to express them on the other, under which almost all young people suffer, and which makes life for them a torment. My eye perceived the beautiful and my heart embraced it with eager joy, but I could not yet give it form. The act which alone could emancipate me, remained unaccomplished, for my hands were still too incapable.

WHAT ideals a particular age believes in, what it puts its trust in, and what it is that gives it joy, is revealed to us by literature and art. The Middle Ages believed in God, put their trust in the merits of Christ and the intercession of the Blessed Virgin and the Saints, and found joy in their festivals. Of this the cathedrals, the paintings of the Madonna, the figures of the Saints and the mystery plays all tell us.

When I was young people believed in the omnipotence of science, had confidence exclusively in human powers and merits, and rejoiced over the advancing development of technical knowledge. Hence one sought, as the highest task of art, the portrayal of modern life in a great city. There one could best follow up the triumphs of the human intellect. There one enjoyed in copious draughts the "blessing " of modern culture. And in fact what was there really more beautiful and imposing than our huge factories, with their chimneys and astonishing machines, or than our railway stations with their gigantic halls and surging crowds, or our brilliantly lighted principal streets and squares with all their rush of men and animals, automobiles, omnibuses and trains? And what could equal in interest the hunting down of *la bête humaine* in its haunts, and the portrayal of its manifold activity? Art is nothing but a "corner of nature seen through a temperament," or a bit of nature looked at with the eyes of a highly sensitive soul! To this program of the naturalists and impressionists I also had subscribed, and in order to realize it, I threw myself into the whirlpool of life. But how much sensual curiosity was, unfortunately, also involved in this!

What my own experience could not furnish me, books were to offer me. During my last vacation I had read in French the life of the painter, Jean François Millet by his friend, Sensier, a thick book with beautiful illustrations, and I had bravely overcome the difficulties which the reading of a foreign tongue at first presents. Now came in their turn the works of Daudet, Zola, Flaubert, De Goncourt and Balzac, as well as the novels of the Russians, Tourgenieff, Tolstoi and Dostojewski. Through these works of fiction I certainly gained some insight into life and art; and, however strangely it may sound, those writers actually contributed not a little to the formation of my religious knowledge, even if the tendency of their books, Dostojewski excepted, was either anti-religious or hostile to the Church — the latter because authority in religious questions was not acknowledged, and religion was left entirely to the private judgment of every individual. Both in France and Russia positive Christianity had planted its roots too deeply for it not to come to light continually in the phenomena of daily life, and in the views, habits and customs of the inhabitants of these lands. And so it occasionally breaks into view in the works of those writers, who have chosen for the material of their fiction the daily activity of these peoples. Certainly there are novels of Zola, *e.g.: L'Assommoir,* in which the human conscience seems to be annihilated, a proof that this " collector of human documents " was often an evil-minded collector, looking for what he found. But in order to do his best work, he needs always the Catholic Church as his artistic theme. Goethe also could not do otherwise than make his " Gretchen " Catholic. Think only of the prayer: —

> *Ach neige,*
> *Du Schmerzensreiche,*
> *Dein Antlitz gnädig meiner Not!*

And in Zola's *La Faute de l'Abbé Mouret,* as well as in his *Le Rêve,* in Goncourt's *Germinie Lacerteux,* and in Flaubert's *Madame Bovary,* I came upon many a passage of genuine Catholic human nature, characterized by a warmth and a comprehensive universality, such as I had never found in my Dutch environment. And seldom has the story of the resuscitation of Lazarus so affected me as when I read it in Dostojewski's *Crime and Punishment.*

BUT I extracted from these novels not only what was good, alluring and enthralling; they aroused in me also sensual desires. Indeed they increased in me the love for sensations of every sort, and soon caused me to look at the whole world through pessimistic glasses. " Virtue? " " Nonsense! " " Lofty sentiments? " " Don't be a fool." " Innocence? " " Good heavens! even the children are corrupted." Thus I often thought, and yet I was always searching for virtue, noble sentiments and purity. But I sought them almost always where they are not to be found, was of course disappointed and thereby became still more pessimistic.

In the evening a fearful spirit of unrest sometimes drove me out to wander for hours through storm and rain. There I felt better, when the fresh wind from the sea whistled through the dry branches and the rain-clouds seemed to be chasing the moon at furious speed. What did I think of during such wanderings? I cannot recall any special thoughts. In fact, I did not really think much in those years. I lived only with my eyes, and dreamed or read. I let all possible impressions sweep over me and welcomed them eagerly. I observed particularly the tone-values and colours of things; thus, for example, I asked myself with what sort of a tone-value a house detached itself against the background of the sky. I lived much also with the heroes of the books I read. Of course, now and then pleasures were experienced, but these were for the most part not worthily obtained. Hence they were not lasting, and the after-effect was sure to follow. I was never able to spend the whole night in dissipation and carousals, like some of my companions. I should have paid dearly for every excess.

If I compare my present life with that of my later youthful years, I must always exclaim: "How poor I then was! How poor I was, especially on Sunday!" For the most part I slept very late and, to the great sorrow of my mother, did not want to get up. After breakfast I went sometimes to an exhibition of pictures or to a museum. But what was there to do in the afternoon? The museums were often filled to overflowing, and there were no solitary walks. My artist friends were usually not at their studios on Sunday. Good books I did not always have, and I could not paint in Sunday clothes.

Ennui drove me then occasionally into a café, where an orchestra was playing, but there also there was seldom a place to be had. And then the roar of voices, the tobacco smoke and the smell of beer. Horrified, I fled away. About six o'clock came dinner, and then we sat the whole evening together, first with a cup of tea and later with a glass of wine or grog. One of my brothers or sisters would read the paper, another a book, another would play dominoes or chess. Our father thought of his business, or spoke of it, or conversed with a caller. Mother dispensed the tea, and knew how to fill numberless cups of it from her solitary teapot. The very youngest soon wanted to say good night,

[29]

and went to bed. It was certainly a beautiful family life, but how there rose within me the desire to do something great, and a longing in my heart for some unknown good, for which I hungered terribly!

Saturday evenings I usually went to some variety theatre or music hall, where I often had to laugh heartily and amused myself fairly well, but I could seldom repress the thought: "You were born for something better than this nonsense."

I must mention one religious recollection of that time. We academic students resolved one evening to visit a meeting of the Salvation Army, which not long before had pitched its camp in Amsterdam. We entered a large, well-filled hall. The " soldiers " and the " Hallelujah lassies " had taken places on a platform. The " major " delivered a very popular sort of sermon and at its conclusion said: " A collection will now be taken up. Many of you may have sometimes put less money into the plate than you had received from your parents, and have thus robbed God. Here you can make that good! " The supposition of the major was true of me, as I have already related. That day, however, I too made reparation. During the collection a song was sung with the refrain: " Oh, we are joyful, we are joyful." Every time this was sung, the Salvation Army soldiers clapped their hands and assumed an air of exaggerated happiness, which made on me a very painful impression. Upon the wall in huge letters were displayed the words: " God so loved the world, that He gave His only begotten Son, that whosoever believeth in Him should not

perish " (John iii. 16). The inscription affected me powerfully and moved me deeply.

ABOUT this time my father had heavy anxieties. Although
already at an advanced age, he had still recently founded a
new business, a bread and biscuit factory. This undertaking, it was true, never went really badly, but at the start
it was far from yielding what the upkeep of a big family
like ours needed in order to live in a way corresponding
to our position. In this way my father lost in the five suc-
ceeding years a large part of his fortune. Naturally this
weighed heavily on the poor man. In the evening he would
often sit for a long time in the midst of us without speaking
a word, reading the paper in silence or thoughtfully blowing out before him clouds of smoke from his cigar. We
children did not pay much attention to this and left him
to himself; but our mother went to him every now and
then and kissed him tenderly on the forehead. Then indeed
he resisted a little, and grumbled somewhat, but in reality
it pleased him. Usually, however, father would become more
lively towards ten o'clock and would begin some conversation with me. " Ah," he would exclaim, " if it were not for
this slight brittleness of the biscuits and these anxieties
about selling them again! " I listened to him as a rule
quietly, for I knew that it relieved him to speak out his
feelings. But I often grew fearfully sleepy, when it continued
almost always till half past eleven or midnight, until father
said, " I don't know what you think, but I'm going to
bed! " The rest of the family had long since done so. I

[31]

would then answer, "I must still read a short chapter," or said, "I will shut up the house and let the dog out." But as soon as I knew that father was in his bedroom, I slipped into bed.

I owe much to these conversations, for thereby I gained a knowledge of business and a good deal of practical common sense, which many painters lack.

WHEN the disgust which I felt over my still very small amount of artistic skill became too bitter, and when my nervous sensibility, stimulated to excess by life in a great city, gave me ever-increasing torments and where many an opportunity for evil threatened to bring about my moral ruin, I fled to the country. For this my father always gave me willingly both the permission and the money. He knew what I needed; for, after the death of his first wife, he had saved himself from a nervous breakdown by a journey in Switzerland. God's gift in nature (especially the forest) has always exerted a soothing and purifying effect on me. In joyful admiration of the beauty which surrounded me, which I sought to translate now into forms and colours, I became a new man. The storm-swept sea of violent emotions calmed itself and speedily subsided and my pure environment soon drew forth from their hiding places, so to speak, the shy wild creatures of my better nature — the bold stag, representing noble pride; the unicorn, emblem of purity; the timid deer, symbol of modesty; the forest pigeon, exponent of tenderness; the turtle-dove, symbolical of candour, and many others. I took great pleasure in these dear creatures, and they in turn grew also fond of me. Before my mental vision rose too at times the figure of an innocent maiden, whom I had somewhere seen. This likewise had a purifying effect upon me, and if I then recalled the preceding months, the thought involuntarily came to me, " My God, whither was I drifting? "

SUCH a flight from the great city, in 1887, during my summer vacation, brought me to Haarzuilens, in the vicinity of Utrecht. Haarzuilens is not situated on the railroad, and is only a little village, which in a semicircle enclosed an old ruined castle. The village was wholly Catholic and yet there was no church in the place. One saw indeed the dilapidated remains of an old cemetery chapel, as well as ancient gravestones, with ornamental coats-of-arms and Latin inscriptions, which testified to the piety of the former Counts of Zuylen. Around the ruined castle lay a broad moat, in which water lilies floated among great round leaves. Behind the old castle were beautiful meadows with many fruit trees. I lodged with an artist friend in a peasant inn, quite near the cemetery chapel. Our hosts were still young and had two red-headed boys. Every day we made out our own bill of fare. Very often we had pancakes with applesauce, which we both liked immensely. At table everything was very simple. The landlady would come into the sitting-room with the smoking frying-pan (there were guests there only on Sunday) and shake off the still crackling pancakes into our plates. They tasted best fresh from the stove. One of us, by turns, had to sleep on the floor, for there was only one bedstead. During the day we sketched and painted. Evenings we went out "hunting," for there were often a few hares to be found on the great castle meadow. Since this was enclosed by a wide moat and since Mr. Hare swims only when dire necessity requires him to do so, the swift-footed little creatures always ran along the moat. We knew this and arranged our plan for the hunt accordingly. Each of us was armed with a couple of stones, and if a hare was sighted, there ensued a desperate running-match. Once we really could have killed one. The poor little animal, seeing that we had cut off his retreat, had sprung into the water and hidden himself among the water plants. But we magnanimously gave him his life. After our hunt we rested usually under a pear tree, which I had hired from our landlord for that summer. It bore very good early pears. We were obliged, however, to eat them quickly, lest they should decay. Several weeks passed thus. My friend finally went away, but I remained for a fortnight more. I should have found it wearisome, if the village children had not been there. In the evenings we chatted together, or I let them sit in the swing that hung before the inn and swung them high up in the air. That was great fun.

One day I received from England from my twin brother the following telegram: "First prize, five pounds." He had passed his examination in England, as first in his class, and had received a gold medal and five pounds as a prize. He truly was in earnest. I too brought home with me good sketches and studies. When I left, the children wanted to accompany me to the railway; but I declined the proposal. It was too far for them.

EVERY vocation brings with it peculiar perils. The merchant and the functionary are protected from much danger by reason of their regular work, connected with certain specified hours, and by their anxiety to have a good name, upon which their promotion and credit depend. They are, however, almost always confined to one place, and if they ever do fall into a moral blind alley, there is often no more chance for them to save themselves. They are caught and remain caught. The painter is less supported by his work, since he, especially when he is still young and has less physical skill, is very dependent on immediate inspiration and a favourable moment. He would often like to work, but he knows not how or what to begin! This easily leads him astray into fickleness and idleness, which all too readily ally themselves with evil habits. The employment of models also, which now becomes necessary, brings certain dangers with it, and anxiety about a good name does not bother him any too much in this respect, because he knows that one overlooks much in artists. There is, however, an ideal element in him. He does not crave immoderately the good things of this world, and knows how " to abound and to be brought low, to be full and to be hungry " (Phil. ix. 2). Just as he becomes easily enthusiastic over the beautiful, so also he is very susceptible to the good and true, and he loves what is genuine. Fundamentally he is by nature almost as religious

[35]

as a woman. Finally he has a remarkable instinct for self-preservation, which tells him exactly when he must take to flight. And usually he can escape, for his vocation does not limit him always to one place. That fact has saved many artists, and myself as well.

IN HATTEM

As I have already said, in 1889, after having studied two years and a half at the Amsterdam art school, I went to my brother-in-law in the country, who resided in a little town, situated near the Vissel, a delta-outlet of the Rhine, not far from the city of Zwolle. Its name was Hattem.

In one of its principal streets I hired for a hundred and eighty gulden a year a house with three spacious rooms, besides kitchen, cellar and storeroom, procured the necessary furniture and set myself up in artist-fashion. Every morning a woman came for an hour to keep the house in order; otherwise I was alone all day. In the afternoon about one o'clock I dined at the inn. Breakfast and supper I provided for myself. The formerly fortified little city, with its surrounding walls and moats, in places still preserved, rises from twenty-five to thirty feet above the level country, and is protected from the inundations of the Vissel by a high dyke. Between this dyke and the Vissel lie the so-called "*Uiterwaarden*," a region which in winter is usually under water, but in summer furnishes the finest meadows. A quarter of an hour's distance from the dyke, further inland, the ground gradually rises and becomes always more sandy, yet affords sustenance for fine forests of beech and pines.

The well cultivated plain between the dyke and the forests is picturesquely enlivened by large detached peasants' farms, with groups of lofty trees, and by many little white-washed dwellings of labourers. On the edge of the woods is situated a gentleman's estate with a well-kept park and a large pond. The painter of landscapes finds, therefore, in Hattem a great variety of subjects. In my time also it was not difficult to procure suitable models among the population. Mothers with infants in their arms and old women and children in the national costume were quite willing to pose. I had, therefore, opportunities enough for my studies, for I could also practise painting from still life. Every day my brother-in-law came to my studio and helped me in word and deed.

I HAD left my father's house and had become a citizen of a little town. I paid taxes, wrote my name in the charity lists, was obligated to have the street in front of my house cleaned every Saturday, and soon received, like every one else in the town, a nickname, "Long Jan." I was frequently addressed thus without any bad intention or desire to tease. In the summer evenings every one sat till sundown before his house or at his door. I often joined some neighbour's family, and was always a welcome guest. The women and girls sometimes spoke of how fine it must look in my house, and only too willingly would have made their way into my "mysterious" bachelor's quarters. One summer evening their curiosity was to be satisfied.

It was customary in this little town, when any one married, to strew with white sand the path (about a yard wide) from the home of the bride to the town hall. Now the daughter of a neighbour was about to marry, and I set to work to strew the path of honour, since this duty from time immemorial had devolved upon the unmarried men and the maidens. When all was finished, I invited those who had taken part in it, about ten persons, to a cup of chocolate. Great was the curiosity. And what a surprise it was, when one entered my living-room. Everything there was in the best of order. " One could eat off the floor," one girl said. Another peeped into the sideboard: " Knives, forks, spoons, plates — Long Jan has everything fine. He needs only one thing more — a wife! " Of course my name was now soon spoken of in connection with this or that girl, but I had no thought of marrying; I was still not earning a penny, but lived only from what my father generously gave me.

OPPOSITE my house, on the other side of the street, stood a little dwelling belonging to a widow, known as "Old Tonia." This one-storied little house was much dilapidated, the roof especially being very bad. The old widow had, however, no money with which to have it repaired; indeed one did not know from what she really lived. Tonia and I were good friends. Sometimes I invited her of an evening to a cup of tea, and sketched her old face. She sat there then immovable, looked silently before her, her hands in her lap, and was glad to be in such a warm room, for in her little house it was bitterly cold, the floor being of stone and the roof full of holes.

One evening, I stood by the window and watched the

clouds, which were rolling up over Tonia's tiny dwelling. It was winter and already almost night. The street was empty; not even a cat was visible. In my room the fire was crackling and the old Frisian clock ticked busily. I was just about to draw the window-curtain and light the lamp, when my glance fell on the high chimney of Tonia's cottage. In an instant it flashed through me: "It is remarkable that for a long time I have not seen any more smoke come out of that chimney. Can it be that Tonia has no coal?" I ran across the street and entered her little house. There she sat in the dark behind the table, her spectacles on her nose. Before her lay the Bible, which she had evidently been reading. It was icy cold in her room. "Tonia, haven't you any more coal or peat?" "No." "Haven't you had anything warm to eat?" "No." "And for a long time?" She did not answer. Thereupon I brought her bread, a box full of coal and some pieces of peat. How glad I was that I had discovered her distress. Had Tonia prayed to the Father of the widows and the fatherless? I would like to have believed it positively.

NEAR Tonia's little dwelling was the butcher's shop of a Jew. He was a good-hearted, quiet man, and, to make up for it, his wife was so much the livelier. They had two children, Salomon and Miete. There was always some quarreling and wrangling going on in the house. One heard it often from a distance. But hardly was the screaming over, when father and mother, son and daughter stood already once more smiling on the doorway, and appeared

[40]

to have the greatest pleasure in one another's society. If the son was absent from home half a day, the mother would relate to everybody what the youth was doing; that Salomon had gone to fetch cattle for slaughter, or was at a wedding or elsewhere. She evidently thought of him continually and also spoke willingly of Miete. When she lay on her deathbed, she had no peace until she had once more seen her hens. So they were driven into her room, and soon after she died. There were a few other Jewish families in the town and indeed even a little synagogue and a Jewish cemetery. I have always felt a reverence for believing Jews, and in fact for every deeply felt and openly confessed conviction.

Another neighbour was the sexton of the so-called "little church." He was a clever little man, extraordinarily conversant with the Holy Scriptures. People said of him, that one needed only to quote a Bible text and he would know at once the words that followed. He was also the man who prayed for the dead, and made the funeral orations. One day my bell rang. I opened the door and there stood my neighbour before me. But in what a costume! He had a great clerical hat on, with black crape, the ends of which hung down very low, and he wore a black swallow-tail coat and knee-breeches. In his right hand he held a great handbill. He touched his hat and said, "*Mmmijnheer!*" and then read in unctuous tones from the handbill a death notice. Then he touched his hat again, repeated "*Mmmijnheer,*" made a profound bow and disappeared. It was high time, for such an irresistible fit of laughter came over me that I almost choked to death when I could give vent to it. Once I was going by the cemetery, when some one was being buried there. My neighbour was delivering a funeral oration, and I listened to it behind the dense hedge. After every fourth or fifth word came the name of Jesus Christ. More than that I did not understand.

For some months two members of the Salvation Army had been staying in Hattem. One evening I attended their meeting. It was held in the empty room of a simple peasant's dwelling. I scarcely found a place left, although all the people were standing. The Salvation Army soldier read aloud a chapter from the Bible, and thereupon began with really brilliant eloquence and touching impressiveness to influence those present, whom he conjured to be converted. " Christ," he said, " is standing at the door of the heart of every one of us; we should not turn him away, but open our hearts to Him. He wishes to be our friend and to lead us to the way of happiness," etc. I confess, that I was deeply moved as I listened, but at that time I saw in Christ only an ideal man, and so did not understand the deeper sense of the words. Also with all the high appreciation which I felt for the Salvation Army's spirit of self-sacrifice, which was known to me, I was clearly aware that it practised religion on its own account. I wished to have nothing to do with it, " for I could do that too."

There were two churches in the little town, the " great " church, and the " little " church. In the former the Re-

formed Dutch held their services; in the latter the Calvinists. In Holland today the Calvinists still occupy a strictly
dogmatic standpoint, while the Reformed Dutch, in part
at least, have for a long time no more done so. Frequently
a strange pastor preached in the great church. Then my
neighbours sometimes complained that the preacher had
again not at all adhered to the Bible. I was only once in
the great church. It was on the evening of an Advent
Sunday. The beautiful, Gothic and formerly Catholic house
of God was lighted with petroleum lamps. Men and women
sat, divided from one another, in high pews around the
pulpit. It was quite homelike in the large white-washed
room. A couple of hymns were sung and the pastor delivered a sermon on the virtues of the Virgin Mary. He
emphasized especially her humility. It was all simple and
pious, but it could not captivate me.

In the Far North the lamp is the winter's sun. While in
midsummer the twilight disappears there only after half-
past nine o'clock, in midwinter the day is already declining
at three. Often it is scarcely clear during the whole day. One
cannot paint then, at least with oil-colours. I had, therefore,
taken precautions in advance, and had drawn a strong cord
obliquely across the room. By this hung two great petroleum
lamps on two movable iron posts. One of these lamps
lighted my sketch, the other my model. Almost every winter
evening I sketched some old woman, or a mother with
her child, or a girl or a boy. When the model was gone, I
had often a couple of delightful hours. It was then as still

as death in the little city. Only now and again could one hear the clatter of the wooden shoes of a neighbour's wife, who was getting water at the creaking town-pump. After ten o'clock, came by with leisurely tread the night-watchman, droning before him in a deep, muffled voice the hour of the night. There was something uncanny in it, yet also something quieting. One is watching, while all others sleep. If the deep stillness of the night in my room was at times broken briefly by a noise from the flickering lamp, it seemed as if some one were suddenly waking up. One heard the old-fashioned peasant clock only if it changed its rhythm after a few ticks, or if it struck the hour with its clear ring. Now and then, behind the wallpaper, a little mouse would make itself audible. Sometimes a board would creak or something crackle in the stove. Even silence has its sounds, its songs and its sighs. Even immovable things live and move, swell, stretch themselves and shrink. And as the eye always sees something, and the ear always hears something, even if it is only the stillness, so the other senses are always feeling and experiencing. Whoever has his senses, does not need continually fresh excitements. Amid the commonplaces of everyday life, he can live like a king. If the objects which he possesses are old and uncouth, he admires the effect of the light, which glorifies them. If the food is unappetizing and common, he enjoys its health-giving strength; he understands the melodies of the birds and the harmonies of the wind, appreciates the softness of a meadow landscape and is refreshed by the strengthening odours emitted by plants and herbs.

[44]

IN HATTEM

From the wall in the semi-darkness the children of my brush looked down upon me, and on the easel stood my latest works, my youngest which had cost me so much care, clearly illumined by the soft light of the lamp.

I often looked up from my book and observed them again and again, mostly through thick clouds of smoke, which I blew towards them, and which quickly dispersed again, almost without having come in contact with the sketches. Then I would meditate on the future. I saw myself almost always as a silent man, working and painting quietly, without ever becoming a distinguished artist, yet as one who, once in his life, achieves something really beautiful and who, moreover, is compelled to be creatively active by the need of his own soul. Ah yes! once to produce something beautiful. Great heavens! The thought of it would drag me out of my chair, and with great strides I would pace back and forth in the spacious room. Then I would even compose sometimes an allegro, which I whistled joyously. Truly I often spent beautiful hours in my quiet room, evenings of wild presumption and the most daring hopes. Yet life has really brought me much more than I then even hoped, although many things have come to me very different from those of which I had dreamed.

Of certain extremely cheap models, which were obtainable in the little town, I have not yet spoken. These were the cows. They offered splendid material for studies, and what beautiful specimens I found on the great meadow of the municipality. In Holland cattle remain on the meadow from

May to November, day and night, perfectly free and without any herdsman. Indeed, one sees bulls there in the daytime even in winter. That, together with the abundant water, in which the clouds mirror themselves so effectively, gives to Dutch landscapes their peculiar character. Other countries seem to me sometimes empty and lifeless by comparison. Even if one occasionally sees there cattle running about, nevertheless one recognizes in them at once animals accustomed to the stable. They have not grown up with the landscape, and feel strange in it. I often spent the whole day on the municipal meadow, alternately sketching and painting. I learned the habits of the animals always better and knew exactly when they would lie down and when they would graze. If it was sunny weather, the entire herd would remain together, in order to be better able to drive away the flies. But the poor cattle could never rest on such days; but grazed badly and lay down for only a short time. One could scarcely work. But with a clouded sky the cows evidently enjoyed themselves, and grazed as if it were a pleasure. Then, if one of them lay down, one could count with certainty on the fact that the animal would remain lying there sometimes for two full hours. If the cow stood up, my study was broken off, and there was a pause.

What a pleasure then to lie among the grazing cows, and to admire their profiles, sharply outlined against the sky, to hear them breathe so deeply and eat the grass so busily, and to let oneself be quietly sniffed by them. Some were indeed far too impertinent, but a swing of the pole of my painting-chair was enough to drive them away. Or else I suddenly opened my big painter's umbrella and then they fled with leaps and bounds.

The horses had their own meadow. There the weary old nags often stood hours at a time in one place, with drooping heads and shaky legs, and dreamed of their youth, when there had been plenty of oats and few blows. That lasted until some of their young and still lively comrades came galloping by, and tormented the old ones till they gave up their dreaming. Then they would perform all kinds of antics. Some old horses threw themselves down, rolled on their backs and rocked to and fro, their legs in the air. Only the younger ones could roll entirely over; the old ones tried it, but in vain. Thereupon the horses stood again quietly together, and nipped one another in the back in the most friendly manner. All at once the group would become lively again, and gallop away. Then there would ensue a mad race over the meadow, the young horses in advance. The old ones followed as well as they could, and soon one saw their dark bodies on the narrow embankment at the edge of the meadow, one behind the other, with heads held high and flying manes, sharply outlined against the sky covered with its swiftly running clouds. A fantastic picture.

The calves too had their playground. They were a lively little crowd, and also affectionate and charming. They lived not only on grass, but each of them received every evening, before it grew dark, a pail of buttermilk with meal. The children of the little town brought it to them. It was thoroughly delightful to see the young children in the midst of the youthful animals, which always stood then in expectation in the foreground at the entrance to the meadow. Many a push and kick was given them, it is true, and many an abusive epithet uttered; for the calves had no comprehension of the distinction between mine and thine, and wanted to thrust their heads also into the pails of others. Often the sun went down blood-red behind this crowd of children and animals, and shed an enchanting light over the rustic scene. Only when the children were going homeward and the young cattle were again scattered over the mist-exhaling meadow, could I tear myself away.

One summer's day I had gone, as usual, to the great municipal meadow in order to paint the cows. As I was returning in the evening, I was caught in a thunderstorm. There were neither houses nor trees in the neighbourhood, where I could shelter myself, and I therefore sat down on the ground, opened my big painter's umbrella, rolled a cigarette, and waited quietly till the downpour should be over. Meanwhile I admired the liquid-green colour of the meadows, enlivened by the black and white spots of the cows, the fine cobalt-blue of the apparently limitless horizon and the tender play of hues, from creamy-white to deep gray, revealed in the ever new combinations of the masses of clouds.

All at once a young man, about thirty years of age, stood before me. Hidden behind my painter's umbrella, I had not noticed him before. After we had exchanged greetings,

IN HATTEM

I invited him to take a place beside me until the rain should cease. He did so. I made a cigarette for him, and we began to talk. He told me that he was a farm-hand and in search of work, since he unfortunately had lost his place. " Why? " " Well," he replied, " that is a long story. I had been already almost ten years in the same service. It suited me well, and my master was satisfied with me. I lived very quietly, but once in a while, two or three times a year, something always gets hold of me, and then I go to the tavern and come home drunk." I asked him, "How much do you drink then, four or five glasses of grog? " " Oh," he said smiling, " even fifteen; I could never get drunk on four or five glasses. So I came home last Wednesday, pretty full. There was a row, and I smashed everything in the room. Then of course I had to go. Perhaps the police will get me yet. God punishes wrongdoing even in this world." I shrugged my shoulders. The man looked at me and said, " Don't you believe that? " I answered, "Is there then a God at all? " Then he said: " When I was still a boy of seventeen or eighteen years, I also doubted that, but now I know for sure that there is a God. You can be quite certain, sir, that there is a God. Believe me, it is absolutely certain, absolutely certain." The rain had ceased, and the stranger stood up and took his leave. I remained a quarter of an hour more under the umbrella. The landscape was really so wonderfully beautiful.

To this day the words of that simple rustic echo in my heart, and I shall never forget the man who uttered them. They were spoken also with such perfect ingenuousness and profound conviction, that not merely the unknown, penitent sinner himself, but also all the beauty of nature which surrounded me, seemed to cry out to me: "There is a God!"

I was now at an age when presumption, self-conceit and therewith the depreciation of others are so universal in young people that one could almost think that they are one of the "minor evils" permitted by God. I can explain to myself now very clearly whence this phenomenon comes. From about the sixteenth to the twenty-first year one makes such important intellectually progressive steps that one thinks he can with certainty conclude, "At thirty I shall be a very famous man, something quite different from this or that blockhead." One has not yet found out by experience that this capacity for development diminishes with increasing years, just as the body also, at a certain time, grows no more in height, though perhaps in breadth. Another cause of youthful conceit is the fact that a young man values himself then according to his *efforts*, while others appraise him according to the *results* of those efforts. Yet what would youth be without a little presumption and self-conceit? I fear it would have less strength and less power of attraction. For does it not always stir an old man to enthusiasm again and often draw from him a joyous smile, to see a young man rush forward with the greatest self-confidence through thick and thin, to carry out his convictions, although these have perhaps been too insufficiently considered and too little clarified by experience? And are not self-assurance

[50]

and presumption usually followed by depression and de-spondency and a gnawing pain of dissatisfaction with one's own work, and is not that dissatisfaction, in the case of healthy, vigorous souls, a spur to further development?

THE following letter from me, written in the autumn of 1890, may explain more clearly what has just been said:

MY DEAR ——,

If you had not gone with me to Hattem, and shown to me and B. your studies, which pleased us so much, you would now have been sitting brooding over that stupid criticism of X. Do you know I am awfully glad that you write me you had a happy time here with me? You are the first man who has perceived that there has been some change in me this year, even if everything that I paint is rubbish. You are the first also who feels about a book (*Mes Haines* by Zola), precisely as I do, and goes into raptures over it. Our friend K. would only say that he had read it atten-tively, and T. also does not understand it. Apropos, I think T. will want to "mother" you a little now and then. Don't submit to it. Yes, painting, this vile yet noble art of painting, this continual bother with those devilish colours that will never become bright enough; this accursed making of pic-tures with a brush, is a fine business, but it is also a dread-ful drudgery! One is chained, do you hear, yes, *riveted* to that female called *art*. Art-production is the attempt to create something more beautiful than what the world can offer. You ought to see the daubs that I turn out. I believe

[51]

I shall begin again with making dots or with some similar technique, for ordinary painting begins to bore me. I shall go to Paris this winter, and study all the new styles of painting. I'll send you another fine book, as soon as you have returned *Mes Haines*. I don't want to be deprived of all my good books at once. I must have some consolation. Apropos, will you tell X. that he should give up painting, and say to him also, please, that you laugh at his criticism. Oh, this crazy hide-and-go-seek playing with modern French art, and this way of representing it precisely as if those Frenchmen were all merely " systemizing asses." Do not those artists find a great intellectual delight in the combination of their colours, and will not their analytical method give them the same happiness that others find in their more passionate style of daubing? If X. and Co. had seen more of the *Vingt* group, he would not have made use of such a common expression to you. Well, after all, let him go on babbling; *paint* he never can, never. Did any one ever see more stupid, idiotic stuff than he produces? "

IN the second year of my residence in Hattem I read some books, which enlightened me on many religious questions. The first was *My Confessions* by Tolstoi, in which he describes and justifies his return to positive faith. I still remember well with what antipathy I read the words that nothing in the world, not even artistic work, can wholly satisfy permanently. Up to that time art had completely satisfied me. It was for me wife, child, wealth, joy and contentment, in a word, my God. Today I recognize my

[52]

folly in this respect, but I must nevertheless maintain that this absolute devotion to the beautiful was in my youth a great blessing to me. My love for the ideal urged me always to strive for the best in the sphere of the beautiful, and thus I early acquired that decision of character, which unhesitatingly chooses a higher good, as soon as such a good is seen.

From the lips of so great an artist as Tolstoi I had now to learn that there was something still higher and more consoling than art. "Well," I reflected, "the man is getting old; he may think so, for all I care! If he finds peace in religion, well and good."

The second book, which brought me much that was new was *A Rebours*, by Huysmans. I read this novel with genuine delight. No wonder! In many painters and poets a tendency to degeneracy sometimes shows itself at the beginning of their twenties. Although they do not precisely sink to moral depravity, one can yet frequently observe in them a craze for new sensations, as well as a longing for unusual surroundings, which stand in vivid contrast to the natural life of a student of that age. Now Huysmans gives in his novel the story of a man, worn out by low debauchery, who withdraws completely from the world and lives for a long time a solitary life, which is full of singularities and abnormal indulgences, and who finally, after he has successively tried every kind of enjoyment, and when everything disgusts him, sees his last refuge in the faith of his youth, without at first, however, being able to believe. In this book I heard for the first time some one who had nevertheless seen a great deal of the world and

[53]

doubtless possessed a great knowledge of men speak with sincere reverence of the Jesuits. Des Esseintes, the hero of *A Rebours* (Huysmans himself) " still remembered the paternal yoke of the Jesuits, who had surrounded the child with an effective yet quiet watchfulness, tried to make him happy, allowed him walks, and took advantage of all festive occasions to add spice to his meals by giving him cakes or a glass of wine, or by taking him on an excursion to the woods. A paternal yoke, which did not seek to oppress the pupil, but rather to lead him, and to treat him as an adult, and yet to pet him, as a child. He remembered the impressive voices of these gifted men and the inimitable tone of conviction, with which they spoke." I read, moreover, of his admiration for the old Church: " He saw, as in a panorama, her influence upon humanity in the most different epochs of man's history; he pictured her to himself sublime and solitary, as she proclaims to men the horrors of life and the cruelty of fate and preaches patience, penitence and self-renunciation. He saw her heal all the afflicted by pointing them to the bleeding wounds of Christ; he saw her renew the divine prophecies, and promise to those who mourn the best part of paradise; he saw her summon men to suffer and to offer up to God, as a burnt-offering, distress, affliction and pain. To the oppressed and suffering she showed herself as sympathetic as a mother, but threatening towards tyrants and oppressors."

Especially attractive to me was a criticism of the great Church Fathers among the later Latinists, and a series of subsequent Catholic writers, like De Maistre, Veuillot,

IN HATTEM

Lacordaire, Hello, and in particular Barbey d'Aurevilly. Even if I did not always trust the judgment of Huysmans, I was yet certain that it could not possibly be a question here of anything stupid or foolish in what evoked his admiration; "Catholic" and "stupid" had, however, always been preached to me, as two things which were perfectly identical. So it came about that I had advanced an important step nearer to the Catholic Church, after reading *A Rebours*.

The third literary circle of acquaintances which I then made were the works of Baudelaire and Verlaine, although the latter's *Sagesse* I was to read only at a later date.

These writers also brought me nearer to the Catholic Church, since what is good and beautiful in their books is an emanation of Catholic culture.

It is evident that my education was exclusively modern. Of Homer, Aeschylus, Shakespeare, Goethe, and Schiller I knew scarcely more than the names. When I subsequently read the Gospels, the Epistles of St. Paul and the writings of St. Augustine, St. Gertrude or St. Teresa, or enjoyed a liturgical form of prayer, like the office of the first Sunday in Advent or of *Corpus Christi*, the words sometimes fell from my lips: "On what coarse intellectual pabulum, on what dog's food you were reared!"

THE fact that nothing great is ever achieved without an acceleration of the rhythm of life, tempts many painters (I say this from my own experience) to bring about this acceleration artificially, not only by means of alcohol or similar intoxicating stimulants, but also through inflaming the

imagination by rapid and nervous creation, through excit-
ing the passions, such as rage and anger, and through enthusiasm, stimulated to madness by powerful sensations.
They think that " one can then work better." This is, however, doing violence to the noblest powers in us. It is a
substitute for true inspiration, which is a gift from heaven.
It is often also a lazy practice, by which one tries to avoid
the trouble of persevering effort and hard labour. The con-
sequences are ruinous. For whoever overworks his head
will reap sterility, and the tired children of an overstrained
heart are hardness and lack of sympathy. But where there
is no sympathy, there is also no joy, and where joy is wanting, happiness too is absent. Hardness repels and isolates
more and more, and isolation leads to unproductive intro-
spection and stupid brooding, and this to stunted growth
and self-destruction. Yet today I know that " no one by
taking thought can add even one cubit to his stature " (Luke
xii. 25), and this is also true of mental gifts.

" SOLITUDE is for the mind what diet is for the body," says
Vauvenargues somewhere. This is perfectly correct, and
every thinking man feels at times the need of solitude. But
in the long run it is injurious to the young. They are not
yet sufficiently well endowed spiritually to fill their solitude
with life, and are still too incapable of keeping always busy.
If then ennui assails them, they abandon themselves to
indolence, or seek consolation in the first best thing they
meet with, however worthless, intellectually, it may be.
So it was with me. Because my solitude became oppressive,

IN HATTEM

I sought the company of farm-hands and took part in their rough sports. Soon I went about, dressed like them, and gradually acquired their uncouth manners and coarse modes of speech. It amused me to be taken for a genuine peasant boor, and I was delighted when educated people expressed surprise at my behaviour. My parents probably often debated how best to counteract my transformation into a country lout, for, when I one day asked my father to allow me to spend two months in Paris, he gave his consent at once, and on this occasion said to my twin brother that he was heartily glad that I was going again into a different environment.

So, one day in February 1891, I packed my few belongings, and, by way of Brussels, where I saw for a second time an exhibition of the *Vingts,* travelled to Paris, which I already knew so well from the biographies of painters and the novels of Zola, Goncourt, Daudet, and others.

IN THE FRENCH CAPITAL

Now at last I was to see it, the great world-capital, in which I can truly say I had lived a portion of my youth, before ever having set foot in its streets. I had a presentiment of what this city would mean for my development, as man and painter, and I knew that for me a new life was beginning. I arrived at the *Gare du Nord* at eight o'clock in the evening. A young merchant, to whom I had been recommended, met me there. Already the first impression was intoxicating. This glorious, noisy animation, this throng of people, this life on a grand scale, captivated me at once. It was *la vie moderne,* theme of the latest art.

The young merchant took me to a hotel, in which I hired a room for a month. It was in the Rue Maubeuge, near the grand boulevards. We took our dinner in a Duval restaurant, but I found this establishment much too exclusive, and the young merchant and his brother who had joined us considered it far too proper and well-behaved. I determined to go my own way the very next day.

On the following morning, punctually at nine o'clock, I was already standing in front of the Louvre, and as soon as it was opened, made a thorough inspection of its great halls. The impression I received was like a powerful blow. For the first time I beheld plastic art in its entirety, as it had developed from that of Egypt and Assyria to our own modern achievements. In the afternoon I went to the Luxembourg Museum to see the " Olympia " of Manet. I stood with delight for a long time before this picture, though I passed by the conventional art of Jérome, Cabanel and Bouguereau with profound contempt.

Paris was glorious, but I was alone! I could speak with no one, though my heart was overflowing with emotion. I asked my way frequently, it is true, even when I knew it perfectly, merely to practise my French and I chatted with every one who sat beside me on the omnibuses, yet to unburden my heart was impossible.

ON the following day, I visited the Goupil gallery, and saw for the first time the originals of Dégas, Monet, Pissaro, Renoir and other impressionists whom I had long known by name. I lunched at a famous restaurant in Montmartre, where I hoped to meet a Hollander whom I knew. In vain. I therefore took the omnibus to Montparnasse, in order to pay a visit to a Dutch painter, named De Haan, to whom I brought a letter of introduction. I found the small, hunchbacked man in a scantily furnished room. On the hearth, however, burned a feeble wood-fire, a luxury in Paris for a painter. My compatriot was very amiable, and began at once to speak of his friend, the artist Gauguin, with whom he had lived and painted a long time in Brittany. He said that he too was then in Paris, and that I could see him that evening at dinner. After he had talked at some length about modern painting, he took me to a small restaurant in the

YESTERDAYS OF AN ARTIST–MONK

Rue de la grande Chaumière, opposite the *atelier* of Colorossi. Gauguin, whom I recognized immediately from De Haan's description, was at the moment of our entrance intent on eating his soup. He lifted his eyes with a look which seemed to say: "What sort of a blockhead is De Haan bringing me this time?" The artist made the impression of a man of fifty years, who had known difficult moments in life, but had always met his fate courageously. He had long, black hair, which grew far down over his forehead, and wore a short, thin beard, which nevertheless left visible a thick-lipped but determined mouth and the greater part of his yellowish-brown cheeks. His heavy eyelids drooped over his gray eyes and gave his countenance an expression of weariness; but a strongly marked, aquiline nose somewhat effaced this impression, and indicated sagacity and energy.

I was introduced to the master and the other table-companions, mostly foreign artists, and ate my soup. Gauguin was very reticent, and soon rose and took his departure. When he was gone, De Haan spoke for some time of his friend's art, for the elucidation of which he sketched on the top of the marble table all sorts of compositions. I returned home in high spirits, but how I found the way thither by myself, in a walk of about an hour, astonishes me still. Henceforth I dined every evening in the little restaurant of "Madame Charlotte," as its owner was called. True, it was a long walk thither, but after four o'clock the museums were closed, and I did not know then what else to do. How often I lost my way in returning home!

IN THE FRENCH CAPITAL

It was generally very late before I left the restaurant, and omnibuses were by that time no longer running, and cabmen demanded double fare at night. Once, after I had wandered about for an hour, I found myself at the same place from which I had started. When I reached home at last, I was so tired that I threw myself on the bed, with my clothes on, and slept a couple of hours before I undressed.

I HAVE always considered it a great piece of fortune that I came to Paris precisely at the time when a strong reaction against realism and naturalism in both art and literature was setting in. It is true, this so-called " symbolical " movement was too weak to gain ascendency over men's minds and, in spite of it, our generation, in the majority of its representatives, has always remained realistic and naturalistic. In order to prepare the way for a new school of art, there is needed precisely a definite aim and an extraordinary amount of creative talent. Mere recognition of defects in the existing school of art is not enough. There was wanting in symbolism a definite objective, and so the new movement lost itself in obscurity. Its exponents, the symbolists, did not oppose the living force of brutal reality, with its absorbing and often touching human element, the omnipotence of a higher reality. What made the younger generation of poets and painters hostile to realism and naturalism was in most instances merely a vague idea of a higher reality. In fact, it was not even that, but only a tendency towards the mysterious and unusual, as well as towards

[61]

revery, a mental luxury, which too frequently received its incentive only from sensual desires. Therefore the symbolists really occupied no higher standpoint than the realists and the naturalists, and moreover could never claim for themselves even remarkable creative talent. Nevertheless the new movement became for many, as it did for me, a means of passing over into a radically different state of mind. For even no definite reality could be connected with the favourite expressions of the symbolists, "the beyond," "mystery" and "symbol"; nevertheless these words coincided with some imperative needs of the human heart, which does not allow itself to be fed continually on what is merely finite. Certainly these words caused a spiritual awakening, and kindled in many a soul estranged from God a little flame, destined to illumine the pathway to eternal light.

ALTHOUGH my compatriot De Haan spoke often of his friend Gauguin, he mentioned no less frequently Gauguin's pupil, Paul Sérusier. I soon became acquainted with this young man, whom I must describe fully, since he contributed largely to my religious and artistic development. The son of prosperous parents, Sérusier devoted himself first to business, and subsequently to art. Endowed with high philosophical gifts, he loved to meditate on metaphysical questions and to discuss them. He had been educated in a college conducted by secular priests, and always spoke of his former teachers with high appreciation and reverence. It is true, when I knew him, he had

broken with the Catholic Church and had turned his attention to theosophy, but at heart he remained attached to
Catholicism, and associated much with priests and monks.
Sérusier was really the chief apostle of the painter Gauguin,
about whom I shall have something to say later. No one
had so thoroughly grasped the sound principles of the art
of this pioneer. In the private school for painters, " Julian,"
he had succeeded in interesting a group of young artists in
his master's ideas. In a short time they formed a circle of
friends, which held its weekly meetings on Saturday afternoons in the studio of one of its members, Paul Ranson.
These friends called themselves " nabis," that is, " prophets,"
half in jest, but also half in earnest, for they really wanted
in word and deed to be the heralds of a new tendency in art.
I also now became, through Sérusier, a pupil of Gauguin,
and as such was admitted into the circle of the " nabis."

Through the Hollander, De Haan, I became acquainted also with the literary representatives of symbolism. They met every Saturday evening in the Café Voltaire, opposite the Odeon Theatre. In a great city like Paris
it is impossible to make oneself known, unless several
individuals unite and form a circle of friends, which
groups itself about some prominent personality. In pro-
portion as it succeeds in bringing this personality into the
foreground, the whole group also acquires importance.
Although the poet Mallarmé well deserves to be mentioned
as a symbolist of the first rank, it was another, the Greek,
Jean Moréas (originally Papadiamantopulos), who was put
forward to make the public at large acquainted with the

[63]

existence of symbolism. Jean Moréas had already made some renown for himself in the literary world, and at the beginning of 1891 had published a new volume of poems, called *Le Pèlerin Passionné*. On this occasion a banquet was given in his honour, at which Mallarmé presided, and which was much spoken of. From that day on the existence of symbolism was an openly recognized fact, and for some time the name of Moréas was on every lip. Even the usually quiet *bourgeoisie* were interested in this remarkable phenomenon, and tried to get a glimpse of Moréas in the Café Voltaire. The meetings which took place there really did one's heart good. Many art problems were discussed and debated without bitterness or pretense. The champions of symbolism found in such intimate intercourse happy moments of relaxation. Moréas felt himself to be the king of them all, and was for some time, at least outwardly, recognized as such. But in reality every one of the young poets felt himself a king, as was made evident by the literary circular letter of inquiry which Jules Huret got up in the spring of 1891, and the results of which he published in the *Echo de Paris.*

Moréas himself was speedily dethroned when the symbolistic movement became more and more recognized in literature. He was, however, just the man to play the rôle of king. He had a naïve admiration of himself, and trod the boards with amazing assurance. "I have talent." "I will restore the Romance languages." "Since Ronsard nothing really good has been done." "Ronsard and I." "That is stupid, be silent." These were words frequently heard from him. One Saturday evening I was about to write a letter in the Café Voltaire, when Moréas entered, accompanied by two disciples. Straight as an arrow, with his head held high, and with his strong, black moustache twisted up fiercely, he looked over the circle of friends through his monocle, extended two fingers to this one and that one with a faint smile, and sat down opposite me. "Pierre," said the poet, "bring me *La France* and some ink." Moréas glanced at the newspaper. Suddenly he cried out: "What's this? A poem by Jules Lemaitre? Enough!" And to the indignation of the people present he flung the newspaper and its holder far away from him. Pierre, the waiter, silently picked it up. "Pierre," said Moréas, "give it to me again. I will read aloud the unnatural nonsense of this ass." Then in a fearful voice he declaimed two stanzas. Suddenly Charles Morice, who was exasperated by the vociferation of Moréas, threw into his face the matches which were on the café table, and which in France were rather expensive. Moréas was infuriated, but he said with dignity, "I forbid you to repeat this jest." Pierre, who played his part admirably in this scene, came running up and said: "Monsieur Morice, I beg you to be more careful of the property of the Café Voltaire." "Hush, Pierre," replied Moréas, "pick the matches up again." Then he asked me: "Are you writing poetry?" "No," I answered, "I am writing home." "Has your father sent you money, or are you asking for some?" "He has sent me money," I said. Whereupon Moréas remarked pleasantly, "What a good father! Good fathers are rare." Thus Moréas

[65]

could also be very kind and affable. Usually he went away early, for as "king" he had also to show himself elsewhere.

Sometimes the poet Paul Verlaine likewise made his appearance there. He was a tall figure, with a neglected exterior. His head resembled that of a Silenus. He usually fell into a controversy almost immediately with some exponent of symbolism, for this designation he could not endure. It was to him too vague and misty. "What then does it really mean, this symbolism, symbolism?" one heard him ask over and over again. "Nothing, absolutely nothing," he would continue; "now I am a degenerate, and that is at least something definite, I am a degenerate." People let him talk. The poor man had at that time fallen already very low, even mentally. Other prominent representatives of symbolism who appeared regularly on Saturday evenings in the Café Voltaire were Albert Aurier, a fine man with a highly interesting, sphinx-like head; also the already-mentioned critic Charles Morice, who at that time looked so astonishingly like the portrait of Francis I in the Louvre, painted by Titian; and the fantastic Julian Leclerq, with his long, out-streaming Papuan hair, riding boots and short vest with a jabot; and finally the poet Adolphe Retté, who subsequently found the way to the Catholic Church, and who has described his conversion in an interesting book, *Du Diable à Dieu*. I passed many pleasurable hours in this literary circle, and whenever I now recall those Saturday evenings, the brilliant life which scintillated from them thrills me once again.

[66]

IN THE FRENCH CAPITAL

I HAVE already said that, through the instrumentality of Paul Sérusier, the chief apostle of Gauguin, I too became the latter's pupil. After I had looked about me in Paris for some ten days, I begged Sérusier to let me paint some still-life pictures in his studio. I longed in some way to turn to account all the new things that I had seen and heard in Paris. In painting this still-life, I adopted completely the theories and counsels of Gauguin. One was quite surprised at the results that I obtained from the very first day. When I occasionally showed my work to Gauguin, he expressed himself as satisfied with it, but warned me against my manual dexterity, which could easily degenerate into tricks and artifices. Gauguin hated, in painting, the slavish copying of nature, and at the time when I knew him, stood already to some extent in opposition to impressionism. It is true, he also proceeded from the perception of the senses, but he taught that the impression of nature must be wedded to the artistic perception, which chooses, arranges, simplifies and composes. The painter ought not to rest, until the child of his imagination, which his intellect has begotten in a union of love with reality, shall have been born again, to the joy of all who behold it, in a more perfect form. A work of art, therefore, involves the necessity of two births, a birth in mind and a birth in matter. The latter, however, can have a fortunate issue, only through the application of the eternal laws of artistic representation, which intuition or the experience of ourselves and others teach us. And if Gauguin insisted on a logical development of the composition, on a harmonious apportionment of the light and dark spots of colour, and on a simplification of forms and proportions so as to produce a powerful, eloquent figure (to which the suppression of the contrasts of light and shadow should contribute), and if, as a genuine colourist, he held firmly to luminous, clearly defined, circumscribed colours, he showed thereby that he was acquainted with the most important means of expression in painting, and had diligently studied the teachings of the artists of all ages. Of *number*, " the most perfect of the prototypes in the mind of the Creator " and " the noblest trace discoverable in creation which leads to wisdom," one never heard him speak, yet he unconsciously made use of their spiritualizing force.*

This artist " often left much to be desired in his private life in respect to self-control and a consistent mode of living, but in art he tolerated no disorder." He was passionately fond of clearness and simplicity. Very clever himself, he would warn others, as I have already pointed out, against too great technical skill, for it destroys genuine deep feeling, and corrupts artistic honesty. Hence he was always referring to the first beginnings of art in the different peoples, in which a still young and fundamentally honest will to produce art struggles for expression, and in which the utmost effort is always made to satisfy their inward longing for beauty. Gauguin sought for conformity to law

* How wholly different in this respect are the so-called primitive productions of many modern artists, who reflect only laziness, clumsiness and self-conceit, and make the impression of having, as the painter Thron Prikker once said, " originated between the enjoyment of a demi-tasse and an ice-cream."

in the art of all periods, and taught his pupils once more to appreciate and understand the old masters, whom the generation of open-air artists and dottists had considered "antiquated." He also restored the composition of a picture to its proper place, and taught with Goethe that the artist first of all shows his strength in the limitation of his materials. Hence he allowed his pupils at first the use of only five or six colours, Prussian blue, madder-lake, cinnabar, chrome-yellow or cadmium, yellow ochre and white. Yet, with all that, he welcomed marked individuality, which sees in all the means of art only *means* after all.

Before my sojourn in Paris I had, in the practice of my art, abandoned myself almost entirely to the promptings of my temperament, not to say of my moods. Now it was my duty to use circumspection. Up to that time I had pursued the ever-changing appearances of things, like a boy chasing butterflies. Now I was taught that my mind was the guiding principle in the phenomena which present themselves in nature. Thus the practice of my art led me to self-communion. I derived a new support from it. It made me more sincere and honest, because more circumspect. If I have sometimes, especially in my later years, indulged too much in theorizing, and thus through excessive caution have checked my inspiration, this may have impaired the productiveness of my creative work, yet I hope I have thereby deepened the character of my creations, and have kept fresh to the present time my love for labour. "For only prudence can conserve our forces against the day of old age."

[69]

YESTERDAYS OF AN ARTIST–MONK

ONE day Sérusier said to me: "Let us go this afternoon to Saint Germain, and call on the Nabi Denis; you do not know him yet." "What does he paint?" I asked. "You will see," replied Sérusier; "Denis is a genuine symbolist."

The environs of Paris present some of the most beautiful landscapes that I have ever seen. The region, in which the charming little city of Saint Germain-en-Laye is situated, reminds one wholly of Italy, especially of Tuscany, only its splendour of colouring seems to me even more intense and vivid than that of Etruria.

It was three o'clock in the afternoon when we knocked at the door of the studio of the Nabi Denis. A young man, scarcely twenty years of age, admitted us. He was, like most Frenchmen, only medium sized. A youthful beard framed his full, red cheeks. Thick dark-brown hair fell over a noble forehead; beneath shone two maidenly pure and childlike friendly eyes. He resembled a young girl, who had never left her mother's side, and his works also made the same impression. But though they were certainly youthful productions, they were already very mature. They bore the stamp of a rich, chaste and innocently joyous imagination, and gave proof of an already highly developed sense of colour. Among them were several works of a religious character. Almost without exception they portrayed in an exalted form that joyful piety, which comes to expression, for example, so beneficently in the Catholic Church at the celebration of a first communion. Beside this highly gifted young man I felt myself very insignificant. I have seldom been so profoundly conscious of the narrowness and defectiveness of my education. I divined instinctively how greatly his faith had enriched this youthful artist who, as Sérusier told me, had grown up as a believing Catholic, and at a very early age had already passed a brilliant examination in philosophy for admission to the university.

We inspected thoroughly the works of the Nabi Denis, and then took a walk outside of the little city. It was a glorious day in spring, the time when the buds are swelling from their sheathes, but have not yet freed themselves; when the moss-grown trunks seem to writhe out of the copper-coloured earth, and the boughs and twigs outline themselves blood-red against the blue sky. Nature is then full of promise, and announces the coming splendour of the blossoms, which she will soon unfold. How this picture of nature harmonized with the paintings of the noble youth, Nabi Denis, whose works also promised an approaching spring, magnificent in its wealth of bloom. Frequently, during our walk, motifs for landscape-paintings presented themselves, of which the young artist had already happily made use in his pictures, not by a servile copy of their external appearance, but by a clear apprehension and a skilful embodiment of their spiritual significance.

The day was drawing to a close. The colours of the trees and soil glowed ever more intensely. I can still see the little river Laye, winding like an emerald-blue ribbon between the deeply orange-coloured hills. I still can see in the mysterious shadows of a little wood the many-hued farewell of the setting sun light up some slender trunks of trees. Every beginning of what has brought us something great in life can never be forgotten. So is it with this day, which gave to me one of my dearest friends.

As I have already mentioned, the circle of the *nabis* (or better of the *nebiim,* as the plural of the word is properly expressed), met every Saturday afternoon in the studio of the painter, Paul Ranson. When I made his acquaintance he had been married already several years. His wife, a vivacious little French woman, looked after her guests in an amiable spirit of comradeship, and refreshed them with sandwiches and beer.

The nabi, Paul Sérusier, whom the reader already knows, also appeared there regularly. A short, thick-set man, with long blond hair and a red beard, and more German than French in his appearance, he reminded one of the jolly bachelor in the well-known painting by Manet, *Le Bon Bock.* Ranson, who gave to each of the nabis some distinguishing nickname, called him "the nabi with the golden beard." He christened me the "obelisk-like nabi." Another faithful guest was Edward Vuillard. French to the core, and even of the type of a Saint Francis de Sales, whom he strikingly resembled, Vuillard was a fine man, with a delicate consideration for others, which he never displayed immoderatly through fear of seeming insincere. We all loved his clever remarks, and gladly listened to his stimulating conversation. Vuillard's friend, Pierre Bonnard, called the "Japanese nabi" because his pictures at that time reminded one of the art of the Japanese, was also a regular visitor. He too was a genuine Frenchman, extraordinarily gifted, but too sensible to make his superiority felt. He knew how to conceal his brilliant talents under an almost boyish demeanour. Like Vuillard, he loved the intuitive, the almost sportive method of creative work, which nevertheless is controlled, as it were, from a distance, by a superior artistic will. A self-tormenting struggle for advancement was utterly foreign to him. He had a great aversion to all ability acquired merely by manual assiduity, which never awakens enthusiasm. It is true, his own pictures, like those of the other nabis also, were oftener happy improvisations than finished productions, but they are among the best that French art has given us in the last forty years.

Closely allied in thought and effort to Vuillard and Bonnard, as the third member of that little group, must be mentioned the Nabi Xavier Roussel, the son of a well-known Paris physician. Roussel was a man of great ability in the domain of classical form and composition. He might be called an impressionistic Claude Lorraine. Unfortunately his delicate health often prevented him from following the powerful impulses of his temperament, and he was frequently obliged to lay aside his brush. Yet he would then have recourse to charcoal or a pastel crayon, both of which he handled masterfully. Maurice Denis, " the nabi of the beautiful icons," could not come to the meetings of the nabis regularly, since he lived, as I have already mentioned, in the somewhat distant Saint Germain. But it gave us all immense pleasure whenever he did come, for Denis was precisely what the French call *un bon camarade,* a loyal friend. Hence every one of us rejoiced over the early

[73]

success which he achieved. Whenever Denis was one of the circle of friends, his serious, religious turn of mind almost always brought about a discussion of philosophical questions. In these I took no part, for only at some later date did I want to reflect on such things.

Our host, Ranson, was a clever man, a native of Southern France. His father, a former deputy, was a Protestant, but Ranson himself was a theosophist. His style of painting, as regards form, inclined to the official and academical, rather than to the new, so-called symbolistic, school, but objectively it was allied to it. Hence he was never able to attain the success which the other nabis gained, and in consequence our dear friend was often disheartened. Like almost all Frenchmen, he could write charmingly, and I have in my possession letters from him, which in point of style have a high value, and which always evince the great love and admiration that he felt for his friends. Unfortunately he died at an early age.

These young men, Sérusier, Denis, Vuillard, Bonnard, Roussel and Ranson, formed the nucleus of the circle. There were, however, other members, among whom I should mention in particular the Nabi Pierre Hermant, a musician, who will be spoken of later, and Nabi Casilis, whom Ranson gave the beautiful name of " the Nabi Ben Kallyre Casilis," because he had been for a short time an Orientalist. The Nabi Casilis had already adopted several vocations, but had given them up, one after the other. In one only was he immovable, the art of friendship. He had set before him, as his life-task, to serve others, and in so doing often assumed the most unpleasant duties. If any one needed something done, he went to Casilis, who at once attended to it. A devoted son, he lived with his mother on a small income, left him by his father. Yet, with all this, Casilis was not happy, although always cheerful and amiable, when one saw him. Once he said to me, " If you walk behind my coffin some day, say to yourself quietly, ' Here is one who is content.' "

I cannot illustrate how precious these meetings were for us nabis better than in the words of Saint Augustine, who says of the circle of friends of his maturer youth in Carthage: " We talked and jested with one another, showed one another all sorts of kindnesses, rejoiced together over the works of fine literature (and art), made sport of one another, and exchanged compliments. Sometimes we also contradicted one another, yet without bitterness, but as a man occasionally wavers even in his own mind. If a case of dissension ever arose, as a rarity, it was the spicy exception to the harmony usually prevailing. Each of us was in turn the teacher and the pupil of the other. We missed those who were absent, and we welcomed joyously those who came. These and similar signs of reciprocal love, which the heart reveals through the countenance, the speech, the eyes and a thousand charms of manner, weld souls together, so that out of many there is finally formed but one."

JOHANNES JÖRGENSEN has very strikingly portrayed the peculiar intellectual movement which arose at the commence-

ment of the nineties of the last century, and had in Paris
its most characteristic representatives. He says: "Toward
the end of the nineteenth century a mystical movement
went through the world. Brunetière's remark at that time
about the bankruptcy of science is to be understood as
being uttered in opposition to that belief in the omnipotence
of science, which prevailed in Europe after the middle of
that century. In circles which had broken decisively with
the Christian tradition, because it was for them too miracu-
lous, it happened that all at once all sorts of old superstitions
awoke again. Tables danced, spirits revealed themselves by
means of the stump of a pencil and two slates, ghosts
rapped with the legs of chairs and creaked in old bureaus,
and all possible nursery tales were under new names cur-
rent again in society. In all this the reaction against naturalism announced itself. It showed itself in a distrust of
science, and as an impulse in literature to free itself from
realism and objectivism, and as a tendency towards the
subjective, the romantic and fantastic, in a word towards
what is meant by the French expression, *le rêve*. The
French schools of poetry of those years must be explained
by this romantic state of mind, symbolism in all its varieties. Such a mental attitude in Europe made possible the
success of Maeterlinck and Verlaine's and Mallarmé's
world-wide fame. In Paris all these tendencies and movements, all these propensities to the hidden, the mysterious,
the forbidden, the weird and the wonderful met and col-
lided furiously, as in a spiritual whirlpool. Like spectres
also, issuing from their graves, astrology and occultism,

[76]

fortune-telling and the calling up of spirits, magic and alchemy came forth from their remote hiding-places and mingled in the universal commotion."

AFTER this exposition of the spirit of the age, no one will be surprised to learn that also among us nabis the occultism and magical arts, of which Johannes Jörgensen speaks, enjoyed a certain esteem, all the more because Ranson and Sérusier were in the circle of friends the representatives of a theosophy marked by a flavour of Orientalism.

Since at times I saw Sérusier almost every day, I was little by little initiated into this sphere of thought, a fact which was not without importance in its bearing on my religious development. As my friend was in painting the apostle of Gauguin, so he was at that time also in philosophy the apostle of Edward Schuré, who, in a book (*Les Grands Initiés*) which appeared about 1890, had stated his religious views. To this book I shall subsequently refer again.

The doctrine which Sérusier proclaimed corresponded to the anti-realistic tendency of the period. Some of his fundamental thoughts were the following: " It is certain that we cannot know the truth without a general acquaintance with the world perceptible to the senses, yet truth has its seat above all in the intellectual power and the spiritual life of the soul. The key of the universe is, before all else, *the soul*. That is, a part of the great universal soul, which has been evolved in the world. The soul is a veiled light. If it is neglected, it becomes darkened and finally is extinguished.

But if one pours into the soul the holy oil of love, it leaps into flame and becomes an ever-burning lamp. What is called progress; that is, the history of the world and humanity, is nothing else than the evolution in time and space of the first cause and of the final cause. Man is a little world in himself; he is the divine instrument which unites within itself all the elements and forces of nature. He is the living image of the universal soul, of the ever-active Spirit. Since he unites in his body all the laws of evolution and in fact all nature, he rises above the latter, in order, through his self-consciousness and freedom, to enter into the infinite kingdom of the Spirit. The divine life in us is a series of continually repeated deaths, by which the spirit divests itself of its imperfections, and is ever drawn more powerfully by the divine attraction and by the sun of the divine Spirit and of love. The higher spiritual life is developed in two ways, through revelation and through intuition, or divination. Revelation can come to us directly from God, or can be imparted through our initiation into the mysteries. By profound study and continuous application man can open for himself the way to the supernatural, and can make himself capable of advancing in it. In fact, through contact with the Absolute he can attain to supreme truth by the contemplation of God. Hence one should rise from matter, as the flame springs upward from the wood that it consumes. The rebirth and remodeling of the physical, moral and intellectual ego is possible only through the simultaneous exercise of the will, the intuition and the reason. The soul has senses, which at present sleep, and

[78]

these must be awakened by intuition. All great religions have an exoteric and an esoteric history. The first is accessible to all; the second only to the initiated and to those who possess the gift of divination. The initiated find their way to a knowledge of the secret forces of nature and utilize them, and thus give to others the impression of working miracles."

Sérusier spoke frequently also of the mysteries of numbers. "Numbers," he said, "represent the eternal Word, the rhythm and the instrument of divinity." Sometimes, too, he spoke of the astral body and the astral light, and taught likewise the doctrine of the reïncarnation of the soul, and of its ascent through a series of successive existencies to the Absolute. To "recollect yourself" was one of his favourite expressions. If at first the reasoning of my friend left me rather indifferent (for only later did I make most of his views my own), it nevertheless soon effected a radical change in me. At the end of a month I had already acquired the conviction that there was a higher reality than that which we perceive with our senses, and quite imperceptibly I came again to believe in the existence of the soul and its immortality in some form or other. In what kind of a form was not clear to me, and for the time being this was also a matter of perfect indifference; for, even if, through my intimate association with Sérusier, my intellectual activity had been newly awakened, this did not at first incline me in the least to a pious life. I shared the religious dilettantism of the period. That was all. Moreover I was assailed in the great metropolis by so

[79]

much that excited my sensual curiosity, that I did many things, which I today strongly condemn, even from a merely natural and social standpoint, but which I then regarded as excusable, especially in Paris, and above all in the Latin Quarter where most of the students reside.

THERE are people, whom one has known only a short time, yet whom one loves through an entire lifetime; people, whose venerable forms continually rise in memory before us, surrounded by an aureole of admiration. Such a one was "Father Tanguy." Father Tanguy had a small shop in the Rue Clausel, where he sold artists' materials, principally colours. In addition to this, he carried on a small art business. There were no pictures of recognized artists to be found in his shop, but for the most part only those before which, at the expositions, people stand laughing boisterously, or pass by with scorn and ridicule. They were such works as those of the great impressionists Cézanne, Pissaro, Monet, van Gogh and others, of whom Father Tanguy was the humble friend. With what love and reverence he spoke of them, especially of Pissaro and of van Gogh, "the most charitable man he had ever known." How he loved the paintings which he was nevertheless obliged to sell. How often he was inconsolable, if again "such a beautiful specimen" had left his shop, and almost always at a ridiculously cheap price. He would have liked best to have acquired it himself, in order to enjoy it always. Tanguy was, however, poor, like the great painters, whose works he loved. And even when some of these artists subsequently became famous and obtained high prices for their productions, Tanguy remained poor, for then their paintings fell into the hands of the richer art-dealers. Tanguy was also our friend, the friend of the nabis, looked after their colours and frames, and exhibited their first works. This noble man has always remained dear to me. At his death he left a collection of paintings worth certainly five thousand pounds, but he would never have sold them for that price, unless compelled to do so.

ALREADY at the time when I made the acquaintance of the painter Paul Gauguin, he had conceived the idea of establishing himself on the island of Tahiti in the South Seas. In order to carry out this plan, the artist of course needed money. He had therefore determined to hold a public auction of about thirty paintings and studies, which he had made on the island of Martinique and in Brittany. This auction turned out to be relatively a great success for Gauguin. For a week he was the hero of the day, as the poet Jean Moréas had been a short time before. Gauguin had not anticipated such a success, yet he did not abandon his resolve, though perhaps not without an inward conflict. Before his departure, a banquet was given in his honour, on March 23, 1891, in the Café Voltaire, at which I was present. I cannot here relate any further details concerning it. For the story I am writing it is only important to mention that on this occasion I made the acquaint-

ance of the Jewish painter from Copenhagen, Mogens
Ballin.

My stay in France pleased me more and more. Hence I
determined not to return immediately to Holland. Still the
question was whither should I go. I could not remain in
Paris, for my means were insufficient for that. Moreover I
longed for regular work, which for many reasons was impossible for me in the great city. A way out of the dilemma
was soon found. My friend Sérusier often spoke of beautiful Brittany, and told me, among other things, how fabu-
lously cheaply one could live there. He said that he was
going there again this summer, and advised me to accompany him. He knew a place, he said, with splendid surroundings, Huelgoat by name, where one could be lodged
well and cheaply and where no painter had thus far gained
a foothold. I gladly accepted the proposal, but what was
I to do with my household effects in Hattem? Now that
I had lived for some weeks in Paris free as a bird, I found
the possession of furniture and other domestic encum-
brances a burdensome hindrance. "Away with the stuff,"
I thought; "I will not for the present be bound to any one
place." Accordingly, I drew up a great deed of gift, and
freed myself of all that I did not absolutely need. My sister
with her husband and child moved into my house, which
by a singular coincidence she found newly furnished. The
dwelling of my neighbour had been destroyed by fire, and
I had thereby suffered some damage from water, but I
received money enough from the insurance to put my

[82]

rooms into good condition again. Now I was once more a free man. A small trunk contained all my possessions. I had no more cares, and felt myself therefore exuberantly happy.

DURING my sojourn in Paris I had visited churches very rarely. Once I glanced at the Church of *La Madeleine,* and went twice to St. Sulpice, where Delacroix had painted a side-chapel. I was also two or three times in the time-honoured cathedral of Notre Dame. One Sunday, attracted by the booming of the great bell, I was present there at the last part of the Mass. A soprano voice was singing the *Agnus Dei.* I have never forgotten it, and can still hear it, whenever I think of Notre Dame. To the consecration and elevation of the Host at the altar I gave little attention. I was, moreover, at some distance from it, and at that time had still no idea what the Mass was or signified.

One other recollection of Notre Dame I must also mention here. It was on Good Friday, shortly before my departure for Brittany. One saw many people going into the church, although no bells were sounding. Something still and oppressive brooded over Paris. The weather was cool and foggy. I had at that time a good friend. She was one of those poor creatures, of whom there are so many in Paris. Left absolutely alone in the world, and now and then weak in the severe struggle for existence, she was nevertheless incapable of throwing herself quite away, and in her heart there was always the longing for a better self. I had become acquainted with her in a studio, where she was posing as a model, although her real occupation was that of dressing dolls. She posed as a model only when she had no work. Sometimes, of an evening, I would invite her to dinner, and in return she would listen to me with great patience and correct my mistakes in speaking French. On that Good Friday, she said to me, "Today I must go to church." I asked her why; for otherwise, so far as I knew, she seldom went to church. "Because it is Good Friday," she replied; "even if one doesn't go to church all the rest of the year, on this day one must go." I accompanied her to Notre Dame. A friend, who helped her sew on the dolls' clothes, went with us. We entered the old cathedral. Both women stepped to the basin of holy water, and made the sign of the cross. Then they disappeared behind the great columns of the nave, while I remained standing in the background near the door. The sound of soft, subdued singing came from the choir. Perhaps the *Tenebrae* was being sung. After about ten minutes my companions returned. I was still standing there, deeply affected. "But, Monsieur Jean" (I was called thus by every one), "how queer you look," said my friend, "so queer! What is the matter with you all of a sudden?" Subsequently, in the little restaurant of Madame Charlotte, she asked again what really had been the matter with me. The landlady, who heard it, helped me out by saying: "The divine service always makes an impression on artists."

ONE evening I visited a public dance-hall, the *Bal Bullier* in the Latin Quarter. The reader may outline for himself

[84]

a picture of this arena of reckless amusement, if he thinks it necessary. Today I can no more describe things of that sort. But at that time I found pleasure in such exuberant gaiety, as I still can be amused by the antics of a colt or the hop, skip and jump of a child. Now, however, every excess of merriment that I see saddens me, for I know that it will be followed by a reaction, and usually by a bad sort of reaction, which does not render the heart better, but rather hardens it. I do not wish to make what I today condemn attractive, but on the other hand I will not too loudly censure what once gave me pleasure. When one is not a saint, like St. Augustine, it is better to pass over certain aberrations in silence.

As I threaded my way through the dancing couples, my gaze fell upon a bench, on which was seated a young man alone. I was about to take a place beside him, when he rose and greeted me. It was the Dane, Mogens Ballin, whose acquaintance I had made at the Gauguin banquet.

Mogens Ballin was a handsome man; very well formed, of normal height, he resembled, with his black beard, dark eyes, full lips and somewhat thick but boldly outlined nose, a Chaldean king, such as one sees on Assyrian reliefs. After we had exchanged a few polite words, I asked him, " Do you like this hopping about? " Mogens Ballin made a grimace of despair and said: " Oh, how bored I am! I have got enough of Paris. I have been here since the autumn of 1889, and have painted almost nothing. One cannot settle down to work here." " I have been here only two months," I answered, "but I am also already surfeited with

Paris. It is as you say, one cannot work quietly in all this bustle. But I am going soon to Brittany with Sérusier (·whom he also knew), and hope to paint some good pictures there." " Would you not like to take me with you? " asked Ballin, " I would like immensely to go along with you."

To tell the truth, it did not exactly please me to go to Brittany with some one whom I knew so little, yet I answered that, as far as I was concerned, there was no objection, but that I must first speak with Sérusier, and ask him whether he also was willing. When I told Sérusier of the Dane's wish, he said at once: " If Ballin shares our views of art, I have nothing against it. Perhaps he will also make a good nabi some day."

Soon after this second meeting I saw Ballin again. It was on the evening of April 4, 1891, when Gauguin left Paris for Tahiti. Only a few friends had gathered at the *Gare de Lyon*. I remember, besides Ballin, only Sérusier, Charles Morice and another writer. After he had embraced us, Gauguin disappeared in the express train. He was visibly affected.*

When the train had left the station we, his friends, went our way together at first in silence. Then Charles Morice broke out in loud self-reproaches, saying: " Gauguin is right; what can we ever become here? We are throwing our time away in this horrible Paris. Ah! if I could

* Gauguin has written of his experiences in Tahiti in two very different works: — one a romantic story in the little book, *Noa-Noa*, the other a picture of overwhelming realism in his dramatic letters.

only go away too!" "Come with us," said Sérusier, "with Ballin, Verkade and me to beautiful Brittany." Charles Morice was silent. He probably saw no possibility of doing so.

On another evening, I lost my way again as I was returning home, and suddenly found myself standing on the broad square of the *Panthéon,* before the former Church of St. Geneviève, now the Temple of Fame. It was nearly midnight. From there I knew almost certainly my way home, but nevertheless I looked about me for some one who could give me precise information. No one was visible, and so I raised my eyes towards the mighty summit of the *Panthéon* and to its glorious cupola with its lofty cross. Great clouds were rushing by it. Then I peered to right and left into the yawning darkness on the other side of the square. Just at that moment there emerged from a narrow street on the right a tall man, wearing a large hat and a long fluttering cloak, and groping his way along the house-fronts, muttering something in his slow advance. I recognized that silhouette. It was that of the poet Paul Verlaine, who, like myself, was seeking his way home.

If I rarely entered a church in Paris, so much the oftener did I visit the Louvre. That was then my house of God. In my long wanderings through its magnificent galleries I was always amazed at the monumental art of the Egyptians and Assyrians, admired the perfect beauty of the Greek sculptures and remained speechless before the *Gio-*

conda of Leonardo. I was delighted, however, with the simple paintings of the Italian *Primitivi*. In the little hall adjoining the *Salon Carré,* I always remained a long time, riveted. There I could not gaze enough. In that room hung the great altar-piece by Fra Angelico, " The Coronation of the Holy Virgin," with the ravishingly beautiful figures of the saints. There also was enthroned the Madonna of Mantegna, with Saint Sebastian and other saints. There too I found the expressive, boyish profile of John the Baptist by an unknown artist, and finally the portrait of that good old man, with the large nose, to whom a beautiful boy looks up lovingly, a masterpiece by Girlandajo. These were then, together with the two frescoes of Botticelli, at the head of the staircase of exit, my favourites. My heart remained always true to them, even if my reason willingly conceded the superiority of other works.

At the beginning of the nineties, a war cry rang from one studio to another: " Away with easel-pictures! away with that unnecessary piece of furniture! " Painting was to come again into the service of all the arts, and not be an end in itself. " The work of the painter begins where that of the architect is considered finished. Hence let us have walls, that we may paint them over. No more perspective! The wall must remain a plain surface, and must not be broken by the presentation of limitless horizons. There are no paintings, but only decorations."

This program, somewhat hasty in its conception, which was better adapted to decorative art than to painting, appears to have been a rule which the Italian *Primitivi* adopted, and therefore they now formed the centre of interest for the artists. I, however, did not admire in them merely the monumental character of their compositions, in spite of the small extent of their works, but above all I admired their directness in portraying their perceptions. Already at that time I had an inkling of the fact that their art was not so much a product of aesthetic observation and technical effort, as modern painting almost always is, but the spontaneous expression of spiritual life. The thought which impressed itself upon me at every visit to the Louvre was that, without religion, there is no really great art, and that all great art has stood in the service of religion. This perception drove me, therefore, to seek a religious philosophy of life.

THE day came when Ballin and I were to travel down to Brittany. Sérusier could not yet go with us, but we two could not any longer endure life in Paris. We had no studio of our own and no models, and as for me, I did not have the money necessary to remain there longer. Our goal for the moment was Pont-Aven, the Barbizon of Brittany. Just as the so-called School of Fontainebleau issued from the latter place, so from the little village near the southern coast of the Breton country went forth the artistic movement which Paul Gauguin and Emile Bernard initiated and which became known as the " School of Pont-Aven " or the " School of the Synthetists." There Sérusier was to meet us later and conduct us thence to Huelgoat.

As I remarked at the beginning of this chapter, I had

[89]

come to Paris in an interesting period. Of course Paris has been repeatedly the scene of more important artistic and intellectual movements, but there was also then " something great on foot." A conflict was being waged for artistic values, which had been for some years despised and forgotten, but which no great artistic epoch has ever entirely despised or forgotten. We nabis also were in the fight, and this brought us, as a reward, the joy of creative work, that blessing which always descends upon the champions of a justified aspiration. I still feel the influence of that blessing, for one is sustained one's whole life long by the impulses which one has received in youth. During my stay in Paris the peasant-boor in me had quickly disappeared and given place to a well-mannered man. My disposition, which in Hattem had grown coarse, had now become again much more refined and, what was more important, I believed again in an immortal soul.

After I had dined for the last time in the little restaurant of Madame Charlotte, and had taken leave of the friends and acquaintances I had made there, I drove to the St. Lazare station, where Mogens Ballin was awaiting me.

BRITTANY

THERE is something unique in the reserve and tenderness characteristic of the love with which a young man seeks to win the heart of the playmate of his youth. There is also, if one may make the comparison, something touching and unique in the reserve and intimate tenderness with which almighty God seeks to gain the love of a human being. The young man has always treasured in his heart a love for the friend of his childhood, even though, as he grew older, he may have been separated from her, and though fate may have led him into distant lands. But, one day, he returns to his early home, and sees once more the friend of his youth. She has become a beautiful maiden, though perhaps a little superficial and selfish. Nevertheless he loves her, and surrounds her constantly with delicate attentions. Sometimes he lets fall a good word or two, which germinate in the soul of his friend, without her being aware of it; or he slips into her hands a few good books. Little by little she becomes a different person. Then for a time he ceases his visits. The young girl becomes singularly uneasy; she does not know what is the matter with her, but she is conscious of a longing in her heart, and is dissatisfied with what once gave her pleasure. She asks herself if the absence of the young man can be the cause of all this, but smiles at such foolishness. Certainly he is a fine young fellow, good enough for a poor girl, who might otherwise have no chance to marry, but for *her* — absurd.

One day, however, the young man appears again. At sight of him, she blushes, and her heart beats faster. He is again so agreeable, so respectful, so devoted. Now she is glad whenever he comes, and one day she has to acknowledge to herself that she loves him. Yet she is really frightened at the thought, and at first resists this new emotion. " No, no," she exclaims, " I will not yet bind myself; I am still too young; I wish to enjoy life a little before settling down."

The serious duties of a wife and mother also alarm her. Belong exclusively to *one?* She seeks again her old girlfriends and is unusually gay in their society. But scarcely does she find herself alone, when that peculiar sadness once more comes over her, and with it the longing for a permanent love and the noblest of joys. Finally she resists no longer, gives up the struggle, and is ineffably happy in her pure young love. The history of this young maiden is the story of my own experiences in " holy " Brittany.

WE arrived at Quimperlé at nine o'clock in the morning, after an unpleasant journey. The railway carriage, in which we had with difficulty found places, had remained filled till the very end of the route. We had scarcely been able to sleep at all, or even to talk with each other, as otherwise we should have disturbed our fellow-passengers, some of whom slept. At Quimperlé we had to wait a few hours till the departure of the post-wagon, which was to convey us to our destination. We made use of this time to stroll through the environs of the pretty little city.

The first impression that Brittany made upon me was both delightful and solemn. The rolling country, into which we children of the great city had been suddenly transplanted after an almost sleepless night, was so jubilant with happiness, and yet so sacredly still and full of God, that it reminded me of a nun, who in her bridal costume goes to the altar to become the spouse of Christ. The green pasture lands, the cultivated fields, the blossoming fruit trees and the purling streamlets, the musical dialect and joyous life of the people, dressed in their tasteful national costume, the triumphal crowing of cocks, the pure air, the subdued sighing of the wind, and the charming effect of all this spiritual tenderness and purity, of which we had long been deprived, was so powerful and yet so sweet and winning, that only a bending of the knee in adoration would have been the proper outward expression of what my soul felt at that hour. But I was still too proud to kneel, and my impulse to adore did not yet know whither to direct itself. Nevertheless I had come into the country where I was destined to learn how both to kneel and to fold my hands again in prayer.

In the afternoon the post-wagon brought us from Quimperlé to Pont-Aven, where we took lodging in the inn of Madame Gloanek. We paid there for room and board seventy-five francs per month. We were not the only guests. Several painters and some local functionaries were also present at the evening meal. Many pictures adorned the walls of the dining-room. Even the panels of the doors and cupboards were decorated with paintings, some from the hand of Gauguin. We were very gay at table, and the food was excellent and abundant.

The large village, with its ancient, characteristic slate-roofed houses, lies in a little indentation of the valley beside the swiftly flowing Aven, whose water turns many neighbouring mills. Steep hills enclose the region, and winding paths along their slopes lead to a fruitful plateau with chapels, peasants' cottages and clumps of trees. At a moderate altitude one perceives towards the south, penetrating far into the land from the sea, a little bay into which the Aven flows. Unfortunately this inlet is now choked with sand.

This magnificent landscape incited us at once to joyful work, and soon picture succeeded picture on the walls of my room. My friend Sérusier was pleasantly surprised when he arrived some three weeks after us. We still remained for a time in Pont-Aven, for the concourse of painters was not yet too great.

Among the memories of Pont-Aven, which I still cherish, are the solemn processions of the month of May, the month of Mary. They are the natural accessories of its streets and squares. Every Sunday, after Vespers, the children, maidens, women and men marched through the village, attired in their pretty costumes, reciting prayers in unison, or singing a religious hymn. In advance of them were borne the cross

[94]

and the banner of the Blessed Virgin. The women and girls, besides a great, white head-dress, wore dark-blue jackets and skirts, ornamented with trimmings and facings of black velvet, as well as variously coloured shawls and aprons. The men were also dressed in dark-blue clothes, trimmed with velvet, and carried in their hands hats with long ribbons. While the solemn procession passed reverently on, the church bells made the air resound with their joyous peals. Heaven and earth rejoiced; mountains and trees were glad, all nature applauded the pious action, and I as well, for all my life long I have paid homage to whatever is essentially noble, without letting myself be disconcerted by the remarks of cold intellectuals or fault-finding critics. It seems to me that I have always been conscious of the fact that the truly great does not lose its nobility, even when the intellectually small and the weak of will are unjust to it, or when the evil-minded seek to drag it in the mire.

Indeed what grander spectacle is there than that of men, women and children, united in one sentiment, invoking and praising God? And in every such procession are there not revealed harmony, solidarity, dignity, grace, order and rhythm — all ennobling things?

ONE morning, Ballin, Chamaillard, Séguin and I were sitting on a bench in front of our inn. Chamaillard was really a lawyer, but intercourse with painters, especially with Gauguin, had little by little made of him also a painter. Séguin too was an artist. He had seen a still-life picture of mine in the rooms of a friend in Paris, and when I was introduced to him, he asked me, whether I was the painter of that beautiful work. On my replying in the affirmative, he seized my hand and said pathetically, " Then, Monsieur, you are very able." I was ass enough, of course, to be greatly flattered by this praise. Chamaillard used to read aloud to us poems from the *Sagesse* of Paul Verlaine. A Breton by birth, he clung with his whole soul to the faith of his ancestors. He once read to us the marvellously beautiful sonnet, " My God has said to me: My son, you must love Me ":

Mon Dieu m'a dit: Mon Fils, il faut m'aimer. Tu vois
Mon flanc percé, mon coeur qui rayonne et qui saigne,
Et mes pieds offensés que Madeleine baigne
De larmes, et mes bras douloureux sous le poids

De tes péchés, et mes mains! Et tu vois la croix,
Tu vois les clous, le fiel, l'éponge, et tout t'enseigne
A n'aimer en ce monde amer où la chair regne,
Que ma chair et mon sang, ma parole et ma voix.

Ne t'ai-je pas aimé jusqu'à la mort moi-même,
O mon frère en mon Père, o mon fils en l'Esprit,
Et n'ai-je pas souffert, comme c'était écrit?

N'ai-je pas sangloté ton angoisse suprême,
Et n'ai-je pas sué la sueur de tes nuits,
Lamentable ami qui me cherches où je suis? "

BRITTANY

AND then another sonnet with the words:

.   .   .

Laisse aller l'ignorance indécise
De ton coeur vers les bras ouverts de mon Eglise,
Comme la guêpe vole au lis épanoui.

Approche-toi de mon oreille. Epanches-y
l'humiliation d'une brave franchise.
Dis-moi tout sans un mot d'orgueil ou de reprise
Et m'offre le bouquet d'un repentir choisi.

Puis franchement et simplement viens à ma table
Et je t'y bénirai d'un repas délectable,
Auquel l'ange n'aura lui-même qu'assisté,

Et tu boiras le Vin de la Vigne immuable
Dont la force, dont la douceur, dont la bonté
Feront germer ton sang à l'immortabilité.

At intervals, while Chamaillard was reading, he pointed out in a few words the Catholic and dogmatic meaning of these sonnets, with the beauty of which he was delighted, and from which, in his opinion, the sublimest truths shone forth in clearest light. I felt, however, extremely ill at ease, like one who walks alone by night through a dark forest. What the Breton read to me was, in spite of his explanation, so obscure I became even suspicious, and looked at him often furtively, with the thought, " Does he really believe what he says? "

YESTERDAYS OF AN ARTIST–MONK

LIKE a wanderer who, walking whither and how he likes, suddenly halts before a door and asks to be admitted, so God knocks at the door of our heart and asks us to open it to Him. One evening, Sérusier, Ballin and I were standing in the twilight of the dining-room of Mother Gloanek's inn, silently blowing away the little clouds of smoke of our cigarettes, when all at once Sérusier said: "In our meetings of the nabis in Ranson's atelier we have sometimes spoken of philosophical and religious subjects; did that please you?" I no longer remember what Ballin answered, but I replied: "I have certainly made up my mind to consider questions of religion seriously at some time, but until now I have bothered myself very little about philosophy and religion. A God certainly must exist, but I can form no clear idea of Him." Seating himself, Sérusier continued: "Have you ever reflected that creatures are not all equally perfect, although every species is so in itself? A plant has a higher form of life than a rock, and the animal a higher form than the plant. Man, as a spiritual as well as a material being, is again far superior to the animal. Can there not be, then, something higher than man? Does it not seem to you almost imperative that there should be still other creatures, which are incorporeal, pure spirits, creatures, whom we call angels?" "Certainly," I answered, "that seems to me very probable." "Well then," continued Sérusier, "does not this consideration bring us to a Being, who is more perfect than the most perfect creature, to a Being who, so to speak, stands at the top of a ladder which, in a series of progressive steps towards perfection in His creatures, rises from them to Himself, to God?"

In his reasoning, Sérusier (whether consciously or unconsciously, I do not know), did not distinguish clearly between absolute being and created being, but from that hour I believed in God, as the best and most perfect entity conceivable. I believed, for my will accepted the enlightenment which God so kindly sent me through my friend. And my heart trembled and began its upward flight, even though still timidly, towards this sublimest and most perfect Being, who had suddenly been revealed to me, and whose light was never more to be extinguished in my soul.

I HAVE already had a great predilection for gardens which are enclosed with hedges, fences or walls, preferring generally everything that is secluded and cloistered. Visions of such sheltered gardens rise continually before me in my recollections, such as the little garden of our neighbour, which I saw as a child, two other gardens in Zaandam, that of my grandfather in Wedde, and many more. In the same way one such garden at Pont-Aven has remained indelibly fixed in my memory. One day, from a more elevated road, I looked down into this walled enclosure. It lay in the rear of an uninhabited house, whose weather-beaten, pale-blue shutters were closed. The garden appeared to have run wild and, by a romantic coincidence, there was grazing in it a snow-white horse. I have never seen anything which so nearly realised my youthful conception of the sleeping beauty, as this snow-white horse in the abandoned garden.

This scene and the processions and a beautiful little country chapel form my most precious recollections of Pont-Aven; and even now I still retain this special fondness for what is enclosed, untainted, unprofaned.

At the beginning of June Sérusier, Ballin and I left charming Pont-Aven. A carriage brought us to Huelgoat, situated in the heart of the Department of Finisterre. In some places our route led us through mountainous regions, where we passed many beautiful little churches. The Gothic tradition of art maintained itself in Brittany, as well as in England, far into the nineteenth century. It was indeed never wholly interrupted, as numerous buildings, sculptures in stone, and wood-carvings prove. Whenever we came to some such interesting structure, we alighted and inspected it carefully. The kind of piety peculiar to any country expresses itself in the principal subject of its artistic monuments. Italy is the land of the Madonna with the Child, Germany that of the Mother of Sorrows and of Christ on the Mount of Olives, and Brittany the land of Calvaries, or representations of the crucifixion.

In Chateauneuf-du-Faou, where Sérusier lived in later years, we dined, and then continued our journey. Towards sunset we reached Huelgoat, where to our great surprise we met in the inn a friend from Paris, the painter Rasetti with wife and child. On the following day we inspected the locality thoroughly. Huelgoat is a rather imposing town, characterised especially by one extremely long street and a large market place. It lies hemmed in between a deep ravine and a great lake, whose waters with a rush and roar plunge down from a considerable height near the exit of the village; then, forming a brook, the torrent hastens on and disappears for a long distance under huge granite blocks fantastically heaped on one another. While on the other side of the ravine rise lofty, forest-covered mountains, the lake is enclosed by barren hills of only moderate elevation. As a painter, Huelgoat never quite satisfied me. If my gaze rested on the wall of densely wooded mountains, I felt depressed, and if it wandered over the lake and the denuded hills, I was bored. Moreover what every one finds beautiful is seldom worth painting, and what delights the tourist often does not appeal to the artist; for the painter aspires to be a prophet of artistic perception, and wishes to reveal hidden, not universally recognized beauty. In fact, is it ever really possible to copy what is acknowledged by everybody to be beautiful, without disfiguring it?

Notwithstanding all this, Huelgoat pleased me fairly well at first, particularly after I had discovered in our vicinity a large farm, where were a lot of happy children, who soon became my models. The pure and mystical features of a fifteen-year-old peasant girl inspired me to paint my first Madonna-picture. One day she asked me why I did not go to Mass on Sunday. "I pray in my own way," I answered. Whereupon she replied very decisively, "Your mouth does not look as if it prayed." Seldom has a remark gone so to my heart as this reproach from the lips of that pious girl.

I did not lodge at the inn, where we had alighted on

our arrival, but with private people, and I had at first a room from which I could overlook the entire length of the market place. Sometimes in the afternoon I heard there a plaintive song. It was the Psalm *De Profundis,* sung in the second choral tone, on the occasion of the funeral of some little boy or girl.

On two Sundays, the thirty-first of May and the seventh of June, I saw beneath my window the procession of *Corpus Christi* pass along between the houses, which were richly decorated, and the lower stories of which were hung with white linen cloths. At the ringing of little bells every one knelt twice. It reminded me of a field of wheat, when the wind blows gently over it, and all the slender stalks incline their heads. Only the priest who bore the Blessed Sacrament beneath the canopy, remained standing and gave the benediction with the monstrance.

Twenty-three years later, I was myself to bear the Blessed Sacrament, on the festival of *Corpus Christi,* through a village in the Black Forest, and from four altars adorned with flowers and lights beneath the open sky to bestow the benediction on the kneeling multitude.

My friend Sérusier often spoke to me of a book by Balzac, *Seraphita,* in which the author develops the theosophy of the Swedish philosopher, Swedenborg. How far Balzac's exposition of Swedenborg's ideas is correct, I cannot judge, but it is certain that he knows how, with all the force of his incomparable style, to transport the reader into a supernatural world, into a sphere which fills the heart with a deep longing. For the existence of such a world he brings forward arguments, strong enough to convince every thinking and unprejudiced man. It is true, the greatest errors are also mingled with these arguments, and his human beings become pure spirits, angels, and perform other similar impossibilities; but I accepted these with the same satisfaction with which I absorbed the real part of the book.

Of all the books which I had ever read, *Seraphita* was the first in which one speaks of God with enthusiasm as the supreme Good. The ardent words with which the power of prayer is there described, impelled me mightily to try this indispensable means of attaining blessedness with God. In fact, the expressions of Balzac remind one of the most beautiful words that Christian mystics have ever uttered about prayer, and he undoubtedly gained his inspiration from their writings. Thus, by the reading of his *Seraphita* I drank for the first time from the fountain of Christian mysticism.

ONE day I said to myself, " Really I must go to Mass once here," and on the following Sunday I carried out my resolution. I rose early, and with a group of young peasants entered the right transept through a side door. We were all men there without exception, standing closely pressed together, for there were no chairs or benches. The women were kneeling in the nave, some of them on prie-dieus. An old priest, bowed with years, advanced to the altar. I had never seen him before, but I knew of him. He lived a very retired life, though he still read Mass. That was his only priestly duty. The general care of souls he was no longer able to attend to. But with what touching beauty he celebrated the Mass. There he stood in an aureole of colours, above him the brilliantly illumined stained-glass windows, and before him on the oaken altar the festal flowers and the candelabra blazing with lighted candles. There he stood in his white, gold-embroidered vestment, his pale hands raised in prayer, as if transfigured. To right and left he passed before the altar, with dignity and solemnity. Several times he turned towards the people with outstretched and uplifted arms, uttering words of prayer which I did not understand; and each time his casual glance passed lightly over the believers and found its way to the distant corners of the edifice. Suddenly a bell was rung. All the men knelt down, most of them on one knee, while one or two spread their handkerchiefs on the pavement. I reflected for a moment. There was a severe conflict in my soul. What, *I* kneel down? My pride protested with all its force against such a humiliation. But I towered to such a fearful height above all the others. I could not do otherwise, and I knelt down with the rest, but only on one knee. How long I knelt there I do not know, perhaps through the entire Canon of the Mass. It seemed to me very long, for it hurt me horribly. At last the men stood up, and I with them. But I was no longer the same person as before. I was already half Catholic. My pride was broken; I had knelt.

On a second occasion I went to early Mass in Huelgoat, together with a brother of Paul Sérusier. This time also I stood among the young peasants. Again I knelt at the moment of the elevation of the Host, and again I was made most uncomfortable in doing so, although I had laid my handkerchief under my knee. Another celebrant read the Mass that day, not the old priest, and I did not experience so strong an impression as the first time. Yet all day long, especially during the forenoon, I was tormented by a terrible unrest, which I could neither explain nor dispel, although I wandered about in the forest a long while, in order to get rid of it. " How pale you look! " exclaimed my friend Sérusier in astonishment, when he saw me at noon.

AFTER having lived about a month on the market place, I hired a room in a little villa, from which I had a view of the ravine and the dark mountains. It was midsummer, and the place was becoming constantly more monotonous and less attractive. The heat, too, was often oppressive and the heavy air of the valley almost suffocating.

On the way to faith one needs usually time and tranquillity. The obsession of our modern feverish activity makes it difficult to find God. For many persons an illness is, in this respect, a great blessing, for it takes them out of their occupations and business cares, and gives them time for reflection.

Other means of bringing us to salvation are a sterility of the soul and a disillusionment of the heart. These take away our joy in transient things and bring spiritual distress. But such distress teaches us to pray, and often reestablishes the relation of man to God. Both of these calamities now came upon me, sickness of the body and aridity of the soul.

The former may have been caused by over-eating and too much sleep. But eating and sleeping were the only means I could find to counteract the perplexing and incomprehensible unrest in my heart, which was in evident need of an unknown " something."

I tried to work, but in vain; I read, but it wearied me; I sought to divert myself by conversation with my friends, but I found them busy or as mentally empty as myself. Ballin seemed to be going through an experience similar to mine. He shut himself up in his room almost the whole day, and lived like Des Esseintes in *A Rebours,* in clouds of perfumes and tobacco smoke. If I endeavoured to cure myself by a glass of absinthe, nature appeared to me in my state of semi-intoxication as very lovely, and I felt for an hour or two exceedingly comfortable, but subsequently I was all the more miserable and good for nothing. At table I was for the most part very talkative, and filled the strangers present with anger and amazement by my paradoxical assertions, so that Rasetti had several times to call me to order. The conceited Frenchmen often thought that what we nabis talked of among ourselves referred to them. One evening, two wine-merchants rose from the table in a perfect rage with the words, " They want to make sport of us." The days passed, and the stay in Huelgoat became always more tedious. In spite of abundant food, I grew thinner. My complexion became steadily sallower and yellower. A sort of dysentery which I had caught on a "tour of exploration" in the caves near the village, through which the torrent rushed tumultuously, exhausted me completely.

One Sunday afternoon, as I was trying to read in the little garden in front of my dwelling, two vipers, which were sunning themselves on the path of yellow sand, drove me away. "To the devil with this miserable nest of vipers!" I exclaimed, and on that very day gave notice of my departure. "Where are you going?" asked my friends. "To Pouldu," I replied.

I had intended to leave Huelgoat on the next Friday, but when Madame Toulec, in whose house I lodged, learned of this, she begged me not to travel on Friday, as that brought bad luck. I laughed at her, but she shook her head.

On Thursday evening, a "farewell" dinner was given me. The consequence was that I was too sick and miserable the next day to travel. Then Madame Toulec, accompanied by the landlady of the inn, came to my bedside, and with lifted finger and a serious face said, "Ah! Monsieur Jean, Monsieur Jean!" She put the whole blame on the tax-collector of the town, who had been present at the dinner, and she said that I was not naturally so bad, but that I had let myself be led away. Then she raised her eyes toward heaven and concluded with the words, "Monsieur Jean, God did not wish, after all, that you should travel on a Friday." Thereupon she departed in order to make for me a little onion soup, which indeed put me on my legs again.

YESTERDAYS OF AN ARTIST-MONK

AT noon on the following day; that is, on Saturday, I took leave of my friends and acquaintances, and took the post-wagon for Morlaix, a pretty little city, which I saw only in passing. From there I went by rail to Quimperlé, where I spent the night. On Sunday morning, a carriage conveyed me to Pouldu. Pouldu is situated near Pont-Aven, directly by the sea. It is not a compact village, but consists of scattered farm-houses, some of which are hidden in the depressions of the plain, while others are concealed behind thick clumps of trees, which shelter them from the strong sea-wind. The climate is very mild, and figs and almonds ripen there. The coast of Brittany is almost everywhere rocky and inaccessible, but Pouldu has a small beach.

Near this beach stood a lonesome inn, the inn of " Marie Poupée," as the owner was universally designated. Here, in the year 1890, Gauguin, Sérusier, Bernard, De Haan and Filiger spent some time, and established the reputation of the little village of Pouldu. Those painters had decorated the whole of the little dining-room of the inn with pictures. These I wanted especially to see, and besides I hoped to recover on the seashore my former vigour. When I alighted at the inn there came out to meet me a woman about thirty years of age, tall, robust and negligently dressed. Her black hair crowned her head like a helmet, and two dark eyes looked out from a harsh, energetic face. When I introduced myself as a friend of Gauguin, De Haan and Sérusier, she was visibly pleased, but regretted that she did not have one unoccupied room. I told her that there must surely still be some little place in the house, where I could

[108]

spend the night, and that I did not ask for much. At this she disappeared. Soon, however, she returned and asked me to come into the dining-room. There the painters Drahtmann and Maufra introduced themselves to me, and offered me at once in true Breton style a little glass of liqueur, which, after the experience I had recently had, I would gladly have declined. Then I dined with them. It was now agreed that I was to sleep for the present in the dining-room, until an Englishman with his aunt and niece should leave the inn, which they would soon do. Accordingly in a few days I secured a pretty little room and felt myself perfectly at home in the house of Marie Poupée, who was, it is true, somewhat untidy and had little sense of order, but who cooked admirably. Moreover the fresh sea-air did not fail to produce its invigourating effect. I breathed again, and the free and easy artist-life began once more.

THE painter Drahtmann, whom I have just mentioned, was a short, stout man, with full cheeks, closely cropped hair and beard, small oblique eyes and a large, sensual mouth. His was a very complex nature. He was a native of Alsace-Lorraine, and one of those unfortunate men who sometimes, through inherited weakness, cannot resist doing that which, being done, grieves and disgusts them unspeakably. More and more discouraged and embittered by their weakness, they finally take revenge upon themselves and society, commit the most frightful excesses, and try to drag others also with them down to ruin, with ever-increasing torment to themselves. They are men who suffer terribly,

[109]

but to no purpose, for their self-love and pride remain unbroken. Often only in their last hour do they utter from the profoundest depths of their misery that cry to God, which opens the doors of heaven to them, contrary to all expectation. Such companions can do much harm, but can also be of much value. They are usually endowed with great gifts of intellect and heart, possess much experience and have in the course of their lives felt and reflected deeply. Sometimes also they have loved much and prodigally, since they in all respects are prodigal. They give much, but they do not give wisely, for they often give what does not belong to them, and they even throw themselves away recklessly through mistaken love.

If such persons are painters, they seek in artistic creation a compensation for the discord in their souls. But since they have no reserved store of vital force, every picture which they produce leaves its creator poorer and emptier than before. This failure in perceptive power drives them then to the use of intoxicants, to alcohol, morphine or opium, because it is unbearable for them, after the exalted position in life to which their artistic genius has brought them, to feel themselves so devitalized and mentally impoverished. They want to feel the thrill of life anew, and hence they drink, make an uproar, shout and argue. Only religion, which brings to them grace and supernatural help, which leads them to humility and a knowledge of themselves, and which imparts to them the spirit of prayer, and thereby gives them strength, can save such unfortunates. That alone can confer upon them a sense of modesty, and make of them honourable workmen, who will, by a wise exercise of their limited powers and qualities, produce useful and edifying work. Drahtmann was not very productive, but I know some little paintings of his in water-colours, which are very beautiful. They are principally religious pictures with a strong suggestion of the works of the Byzantines and the Italian primitives, yet withal thoroughly individual and imbued with modern sentiment. He was by nature essentially Catholic, in the sense that no other faith would have ever suited him. Catholicism was in his blood, as it is in that of so many Frenchmen, even though they may assert that they have their own conception of religious things and seldom or never go to church. He often spoke of the Catholic Church, sometimes with affection, at other times with depreciation, but he never made an attempt to convert me to Catholicism. When he heard that I had become a Catholic, he found fault with me in a letter for doing so, saying that my Protestant faith was just as good as the Catholic. It is true, he was not aware that I had not only never been a Protestant but had belonged to no religious sect whatever. Whoever possesses no faith, based upon divine revelation, is soon lost in materialism, doubts the possibility of ever knowing the truth, and becomes either a sceptic, or else a reed, blown hither and thither by every mind of doctrine (Eph. iv. 14). The latter was my case. Drahtmann's opinions and outpourings of sentiment drove me now hither, now thither, yet fortunately more towards what was good than towards what was evil. I am at least indebted to him for many theories of life and art, which thus far have proven to be correct. He regarded me as his pupil, and showed me the affection of a master. Whether he is still living I do not know.

By the middle of October it became much too unpleasant in Pouldu. The deserted, windy beach, the wild, inhospitable coast, the dirt and disorder in the house of Marie Poupée drove me away. One morning I took leave of Drahtmann and Maufra, my landlady and her child, and was conveyed on a little two-wheeled cart to Quimperlé, and travelled thence by rail to Paris.

It was a glorious sunny Autumn day. Once more, during the journey, the romantic beauty of the Breton country revealed itself to my gaze, and the new scenes which I now beheld revived in me continually the recollection of what I had previously seen and met with. . . . How rich I had become in the last eight months, rich in so many new impressions, ideas and experiences. Of a truth, France had given me much. I said to myself, therefore, " Next year I will return, first to Paris, then to Brittany." But to what part of Brittany? I did not then know, but in any case to a place where I had not yet been. I had left the city of Vannes behind me. The country traversed by the train pleased me exceedingly. At one point we sped by three or four houses standing near the railway. Behind these I perceived two little Gothic churches quite near to each other, and above them on the slope of a hill some other dwellings. I discerned all this for only a moment, but it was sufficient to make me form the instantaneous resolve, " There is where

I will go next year." I therefore noted the name of the next station. It was Elven. Then I inquired in what Department we were, and was told that it was the Department of Morbihan. The name of the little village itself, however, I was not able to learn.

It was about half past four o'clock in the morning, when I arrived in Paris. I left my luggage at the station, because I had a desire to see the great vegetable market of the city (*les Grandes Halles*), which is in full activity only at night, near the cathedral of Notre Dame. A book by Emile Zola, *Le Ventre de Paris,* had suggested this idea to me.

Paris was still sleeping, wrapped in darkness. Only one restaurant, opposite the railway station, poured its light lavishly out into the obscurity of the night. Into this radiance stepped the figures of two gaily dressed women, whose repulsive shouting, boisterous laughter and shameless conduct struck me as a shocking outrage to the solemn stillness of the slumbering capital. The shops had closed their eyes, that is to say, their shop-windows; their iron lids had fallen over them, and not a door stood open. While those inside the houses felt themselves secure from those without, I for my part felt safer in the solitude of the streets. It gave me also a feeling of pride to be awake while the others slept. At first I saw only a few men who shared this watch with me. Here and there I met a policeman, and once two scavengers passed me, bent beneath their heavy load. I also overtook a woman who, with a slow and measured stroke, swung a huge broom, at least a yard in length, from one sidewalk to the other of a narrow street. But when, after having walked nearly half an hour, I entered the market place, I first saw how many people were awake, in order to provide for the nourishment of the sleeping city. Great arc-lamps cast their light over a throng of busy men, horses, wagons and enormous heaps of vegetables of every sort. A woman called out to me, " There is no room here for people who just dawdle about. Make yourself scarce." I laughed and obeyed. In the streets which radiate from the great, and yet too circumscribed area in all directions, a similar scene was visible; only there the most beautiful flowers, mostly chrysanthemums, displayed their wealth of colours. I strolled for a long time through these iron-framed markets with their roofs of glass, and watched the stout fish-wives (*les madames*) stride in, and open their booths, in which magnificent fish were swimming in huge tanks, and splendid fruits attracted the eye.

When my curiosity was satisfied, I went to my hotel. The night-porter was at first suspicious of a guest who asked for a room at such a questionable hour, and had no luggage with him. But he was soon satisfied.

I remained in Paris about ten days, and wanted on my way home to spend a day in Brussels. It was All Saints' Day. The church bells resounded continually, and I saw many people going to the cemeteries with funeral wreaths. This gave me a feeling of sadness, and I longed to see again my mother. Accordingly I left for Amsterdam that afternoon, after having first despatched a telegram, which read as follows: " The prodigal son is coming home this evening, please kill the fatted calf." Great was the rejoicing under the paternal roof. All thought me vastly improved, and my mother said, " Sit down at the table, my boy, the fatted calf is killed."

BACK IN HOLLAND

THE four months, which I now spent in my parents' home, had quite the character of an interlude. I hired a room where I could hang up my sketches and work quietly. When I showed an oil painting of Brittany to my mother she exclaimed, "Heavens! how ugly that is. It looks like a piece of needle-work; do not show it to your father." But my father was not at all disappointed, when he saw my studies and drawings. The novel element in them pleased him. "It is true," he said, " I do not understand your style of painting, but I see nevertheless that there is something good in it."

I ate and slept at home, and at the table liked to talk of religion and spiritual things, an echo of what I had heard and read in France. My father was much upset by this, and said, " I do not allow my children to teach me in such matters." For him theorizing and arguing were merely a pleasant way of passing the time, a kind of sport. It made little difference to him, what opinion he advocated. He preferred in general, however, merely to hear what the others said. He was a man of action, who seldom made a mistake in his business, but whose remarks did not always show deep insight or a logical mind. He resembled an artist, who relies upon a good tradition, and therefore thinks he can quietly trust everything to his talent and cleverness.

BACK IN HOLLAND

During this time I read again Balzac's *Seraphita* and the works of Edgar Allan Poe. But I scarcely painted at all. I missed the stimulus of my friends in Paris. I should have liked best to return to France directly. But my twin brother had meantime become engaged and wanted to be married in February. So I had to help in the preparations for the festivities which were to take place in honour of the bridal pair.

Even if the thought of God and faith did not entirely leave me then, it was for the time being forced into the background. The things among which we have lived for many years seem, when we visit them again, to emit the thoughts and feelings which dominated us, when we had them every day before our eyes. So it often seemed to me, that on my return to my parents' home the streets and canals of Amsterdam spoke to me only of materialism, naturalism and impressionism. Subsequently too when I, as a Benedictine monk, revisited the city scenes I knew so well, they still seemed to speak to me the same language. Even the Catholic churches had kept for me their character of strangeness. But when I walked in the darkness along the lonely canals, the thought of God often came to me with great intensity. At such times I reflected especially on His unchangeableness and fidelity, and found great consolation in the thought. Again and again I promised myself, " When I am once more in France, somewhere in Brittany and quite alone, I will not rest, till I have come to a clear understanding with myself in regard to my faith."

YESTERDAYS OF AN ARTIST-MONK

ABOUT that time I was present at a general rehearsal of
Bach's Mass in H minor in the concert-hall of Amsterdam.
I have attended in my life comparatively few concerts. So
much the deeper and more lasting, therefore, have been the
impressions which I received, whenever I have had the
good fortune to hear classical music. Endowed with a
good ear, I should have liked to learn to play the violin,
but that was not to be. The *motif* of the *Kyrie eleison* of
this Mass often recurs to me. It was a rolling and surging
of imploring supplications, a loud knocking, a persistent
invocation, an overwhelming cry for help and mercy. On
that evening, the suppliant sounds came moaning onward,
like the waves of a rising tide in spring which, though repeatedly shattered into spray, yet still approaches ever
nearer, till finally its surging billows, white with foam,
after one last, supreme exertion, sink exhausted at the bar-
rier of the dunes.

At the rendition of this Mass programs were distributed,
on which the different portions chanted, the *Kyrie, Gloria,
Credo, Sanctus* and *Agnus Dei,* were printed in Dutch and
Latin. And thus, for the first time in my life, I read, with
curiosity and close attention, during a pause in this performance, the Catholic confession of faith: *Credo in unum
Deum, Patrem omnipotentem.* . . . " I believe in *one* God,
the Father Almighty, maker of heaven and earth, of all
things visible and invisible. And in *one* Lord Jesus Christ,
the only-begotten Son of God, and born of the Father before all ages, God of God, light of light, true God of true
God. Begotten not made, consubstantial with the Father;

[118]

by whom all things were made. Who for us men and for our salvation descended from heaven; and was incarnate by the Holy Ghost of the Virgin Mary, and was made man. Was crucified also for us; suffered under Pontius Pilate and was buried. And the third day he rose again, according to the Scriptures. And ascended into heaven; sits at the right hand of the Father. And again he shall come with glory to judge the living and the dead; of whose Kingdom there shall be no end. And in the Holy Ghost, the Lord and life-giver; who proceeds from the Father and the Son. Who together with the Father and the Son is adored and conglorified; who spoke by the prophets. And *one*, holy, Catholic and Apostolic Church. I confess *one* baptism for the remission of sins. And I expect the resurrection of the dead and the life of the world to come. Amen."

How strange! While I was reading this, I approved of it and consented to every word, saying to myself, " That is the only true faith; it must be so." Yet I said this, without really believing. I did not even keep the program. Indeed I think I did not take it home with me, but left it in the concert-hall.

BUT how did it happen, that I did not smile compassionately, as other unbelievers do, when I read for the first time the Catholic confession of faith? Did I have any presentiments of what wonderful facts the words of the *Credo* proclaim, and what sublime mysteries they suggest? It may be that the artist in me was attracted by the powerful, immemorial form of the whole composition. At all events, I let the words exert their influence upon me in a simple way, and did not attribute to them at once a signification foreign to their meaning, as so many "educated" people in their ignorance do, in order then to calumniate the nonsense which they themselves have invented and which they then regard as Catholic doctrine. In this way my naturally Christian soul learned for the first time in a condensed form the entire content of the Christian doctrine. I found it sweet and pleasing, and that no doubt is why I approved of it. It is true, the doctrines of the theosophists had taken from me any repugnance to the supernatural, and since my residence in France I had become more cautious in forming my judgments, and the common remark, "Catholic and stupid are synonymous words," I had learned to despise as a low calumny. Yet the true light, that lighteth every man that cometh into the world, did not appear to me that evening in all its clearness. The mysteries of the God incarnate and of the most Holy Trinity, however clearly they are defined in the *Credo,* remained still hidden from me.

THERE are hours in our youth, the recollection of which in our maturer years makes us tremble, even though the experiences then acquired have enriched our lives and still remain indelibly impressed upon our memory. They have enriched us, it is true, but not without inflicting injury on others and not without a loss to ourselves of higher good.

If a guardian angel had not turned aside the dangers

into which I was at that time ready to plunge, what indeed would have become of me? I wished to go to the left and to run into ruin; but a loving hand barred the way, and an invisible light showed me the danger, so that I turned to the right with even a certain satisfaction, and was subsequently happy to have escaped. And if I ask myself today, "What has caused God to grant me this mercy?" I find the answer only in one weak point, this was my faith in the true, the good and the beautiful, which now and then showed itself in me by a noble act. God still found something good in me. To that He united His grace, and led me gradually to the path of light which His loving will had destined me to follow in spite of my opposition. For I was still, for the time being, like an unwilling dog, which always wants to go its own way, sniffs around everywhere and remains standing still, instead of following his master.

After my brother's wedding, my friend Sérusier visited me for a fortnight in my father's house, and at the end of February we returned together to Paris. We were in Brussels on the last day of the *Carnéval*, March 1, 1892. On that evening a friend was to have met me there, but she did not come. In reality I was heartily glad of it. On that evening my whole future was perhaps at stake.

AGAIN IN PARIS

W<small>HEN</small> I was once more in Paris, I hired a room in a hotel in the Rue de Richelieu, near the *Théâtre Français.* The great event of the first weeks was the inauguration of the *Indépendants,* an exposition of paintings without a jury of awards. Together with the " new-impressionists," the group of the nabis, Sérusier, Denis, Bonnard and Vuillard at their head, offered what was newest and most promising. I also was represented there by some of my paintings, and was always mentioned by the critics in company with my friends. Thus I achieved at that time the first little success of my life.

The following weeks were devoted to the preparations for a representation of Maeterlinck's *Les Sept Princesses,* which was to take place on Palm Sunday in the house of a counsellor of state. Since the actors were only little marionettes, Sérusier, his brother and the daughter of the director Lamoureux read the text aloud. Sérusier and Vuillard had made the decorations for the little stage, and I had painted the curtain. During the performance I also held one of the puppets. Since the counsellor of state lived in Passy, the preparations and rehearsals consumed much time; but the representation was a great success and the nabis by this incident were introduced into a wider circle of acquaintances. Every one was astonished that by these simple means such a poignant dramatic effect could be obtained.

AGAIN IN PARIS

The customary meetings of the nabis in Ranson's studio on Saturday afternoons were again very gay and stimulating. Equally so were the evenings at the rooms of the Nabi Hermant, a musician, who played to his friends compositions of Bach and Wagner on a great harmonium. His apartment was near the house of the famous painter, Meissonier, who was however not much esteemed by us. Hence in the evening, when we were returning home, we never failed to show our contempt for this " prince of firemen " (that was the title given to the representatives of the official style of painting), by some act, which on one occasion brought us into contact with a policeman, who wanted to take one of us to the station-house. When, however, we all insisted on going thither with him, he soon dismissed us with the authoritative warning, " Gentlemen, the next time behave yourselves! " He had evidently observed us already on several occasions. Thus something different was going on every day: regular visits and dancing lessons at the house of a business friend of my father, introductions into this or that circle, a rendezvous here and a soirée there, in short, a continual activity, which may have had its influence upon me as a means of acquiring social polish, but by which any real work in my profession was rendered almost impossible.

THE business friend of my father, to whose house I paid regular visits, and where I took dancing lessons, was by origin a Polish Jew. He had three daughters. They had been baptized and brought up as Catholics, but had, when

I made their acquaintance, almost completely lost their faith. When, however, the eldest daughter, a clever and amiable girl, perceived my interest in religious things, she loaned me the *Pensées* of Pascal, and advised me to read also the *Imitation of Christ,* especially the chapter " On the Wonderful Effect of the Divine Love " (Book III, chapter 5). I certainly was sensible of the literary beauty of these books, but I was still too deeply immeshed in my vague theosophical ideas, and still too little settled in my spiritual conceptions, to comprehend their contents clearly.

More decisive was a meeting with a certain Paul B. whom I had seen a few times, the previous year, in the circle of the symbolists. He was a young, but already bearded man, who was always in haste, gesticulated much and generally carried a large leather portfolio. I heard that this nabi had become a " convert " in the course of an illness which he had caught during his military service, and that he even entertained the thought of entering a religious order. I met him one evening on the boulevard, and we arranged forthwith an interview. Accordingly on the next day, I called at his apartment. We soon came to speak of religion, of the Mass and of other religious things. I told him that I did not know what the Mass was and signified. With a terribly serious face, as if he trembled before the mystery, he then began to explain the Mass in a pathetic, unctuous voice, but in doing so went to such lengths that I understood practically nothing. What he said appeared to me exaggerated, and assuredly I should not have advanced one step farther, in spite of a visit which we subsequently made together to the new Church of the Sacred Heart on Montmartre, if he had not given me a life of the Saints and a small catechism. I had to promise him to read these books, as well as the eighth chapter of the *Confessions* of Saint Augustine, which unfortunately he could not give me.

When I returned home, tired, that evening, I went to bed and began to read by the light of my candle the small catechism. As I did so, the whole doctrinal structure of the Catholic Church rose before me in its simplest form and marvellous logical accuracy. Then for the first time I read what the words *Son of God* signify, and learned also for the first time how to interpret a whole series of passages in the Gospel. I read the little book from cover to cover with the happiness of one who has discovered a great treasure. True, I did not yet believe, but I was extraordinarily glad to have become acquainted to some extent with the Catholic doctrine, and I found it much more reasonable than I had imagined it to be.

When I got up next morning, I missed my candle. Had it perhaps fallen from the little table? I looked for it even under the bed, but did not find it. Then only did I perceive that the expensive candle, which was always charged up to me in the bill at a franc, was quite burned out. I had evidently fallen asleep over my reflections on the catechism. The candle had indeed burned itself out, but in its place a new light had risen in my soul.

Palm Sunday had come, and the representation of *Les Sept Princesses* by Maeterlinck had been given. Now I was free. I resolved, therefore, to go to Brittany on the day after

[125]

Easter. Mogens Ballin had also returned to Paris and I invited him to go with me, but he wanted to remain a few weeks longer in the city. Before my departure I bought a Bible and *Les Grands Initiés* by Edward Schuré, a book which Sérusier had recommended to me. The *Confessions* of Saint Augustine I would have also gladly purchased but, after having inquired for it once in a bookshop in vain, I thought of it no more.

ONCE MORE IN BRITTANY

On the following morning, as the train was approaching Vannes, I asked a young priest, who sat opposite me in the compartment, whether he could give me any information concerning the village which was situated directly beside the railway between Vannes and Elven. He told me that it was called Saint Nolff and really formed part of a large parish, but that the village itself consisted of only a few houses. He doubted very much whether a traveller could find a lodging there. I alighted, however, at the station of Elven and went in an omnibus to the place of that name. There I breakfasted and received the same information given me by the priest, that Saint Nolff was only a tiny village, where there was no lodging for strangers. Nevertheless I would not allow myself to be dissuaded from my purpose, hired a carriage and drove thither.

Meantime it had become afternoon. When the carriage turned into the village, I saw a little Gothic church, and very near it, though detached, a Gothic chapel. Besides these there were about ten houses. That was all. The driver stopped before an inn. I told him to wait, and stepped into the general room for guests. Two elderly people were sitting in the low-ceilinged apartment, one a little old man with long, white hair, the other a stout woman bowed with years. It was a picture of cosy intimacy. They were visibly astonished to see a stranger, and inquired what I wanted. "I want to lodge with you," I said, "from three to four months." "But, Monsieur," replied the landlord, "we can offer you almost nothing." I was not discouraged. "I will pay you ninety francs a month," I answered, "and am content with little." "But, Monsieur," said my host apologetically, "we have not even a stove; we cook only with an open fire. We have indeed a room, but the meals! Really we cannot do it." I asked for something to drink, and the old people took counsel of each other. Finally the husband said, "If you are satisfied with what we can offer you, in heaven's name stay with us."

I paid the driver and was shown to my room. The old man went with me up an outside staircase, which appeared to lead to a hay-loft. I was prepared for the worst, but to my joyful surprise I came into a room which certainly had a low ceiling but was of a very good size. "*Voilà*," said the old man. "*A merveille*," I answered.

Since I had scarcely slept the night before, I first rested for a few hours, and then took a walk to explore the new region. The country around Saint Nolff has a genuine Breton character, and offers all those *motifs* which one finds almost everywhere in Brittany; moderately wide valleys, through which flow rapid streams; beautiful, well-watered meadows; hilly plateaus with peasants' houses shaded by trees; orchards surrounded by walls; narrow hollowed-out paths with stone crosses on their edges, strangely clipped trees, which rise like spectres towards the sky, and numerous chapels.

ONCE MORE IN BRITTANY

Saint Nolff is said to have been in former years the residence of Templars. But the name of its church patron, Majolus, the great abbot of Cluny, indicates rather that its former owners were the monks of Cluny. In any case the builders of the two little churches, the witnesses of my ever-increasing joy in the Christian faith, were Benedictines. I was soon to become thoroughly acquainted with this little place, and my hosts, old Conan and his wife, considered me almost as a son. A great sorrow weighed upon their hearts. A few months before my arrival, one of their sons had been fatally injured and the young wife of the second son had died. One day the mother told me about the death of her son. " I was myself to blame," she said; " he was such a good boy, lively, witty, friendly. The whole village loved him. My husband did his share of the work, and both of them got along so well together.

"One Sunday afternoon, my son took a hand in a game of bowling in front of the inn. The parish priest was looking on. All at once I had a great longing for some cherries, and I said: ' Jean, fetch me a plateful of cherries from the tree.' At first he did not want to, and protested that he was now in the very midst of the game, but finally, obliging as ever, he went. Five minutes later, he was lying under the tree. ' Let me lie here,' he said; ' bring the priest; I must die.' When he had been given the last Sacrament, they raised him carefully. His spine was broken; his life hung now only by a thread. A few days after, he died. And so it was my fate to send him to his death! " The old mother wept bitterly, and old Conan as well; but he said, in order to comfort his wife, " He had a beautiful death; he died as a Christian."

The youngest of the three daughters, Marie Perrine, the only one still at home, wept also. She was a quiet, pious, affectionate soul, always somewhat ailing, and yet so happy to be alive. She kept by preference in the background, and lived only for God and her old parents.

Shortly after my arrival, I said to my hosts that I was not a Catholic, nor even baptised, but that I esteemed and loved religion, whereupon old Conan answered, " Perhaps God has sent you here, that you may become a Catholic! " This he said with great simplicity, without in the least the air of a preacher, and therefore I did not feel at all offended by the remark, especially as the thought had already occurred to me also.

AFTER the long interruption in my work, it was a joy for me again to take up my art. I have always been fortunate in my painting when, after a period of excitement in some great city, I have withdrawn into solitude. A wearisome illness nevertheless confined me for some time to my room and to the immediate vicinity of the house, but I was already so far advanced in my religious life, that I accepted this as a penance.

A blessed peace came over me. The stormy agitation of the previous year at Huelgoat had ceased. One evening I went into the church, knelt for a few moments on a *prie-dieu,* gazed at the coloured windows above the altar, and felt myself, as the only visitor, happy in the thought of God, the personification of eternal beauty, purity and light. Thereafter I went to the little church almost every evening. When, on the first Sunday after my arrival in Saint Nolff, the bell rang for Mass, I took *Les Grands Initiés* by Edward Schuré under my arm, sat down in a shady place outside the village, and kept my Sunday in the open air. From this book, as also from Balzac's *Seraphita,* I received many religious impulses. There echo through its pages the plaintive longings of thousands of years. One seems to hear the *De Profundis* of the old pagan world. It is at the same time the cry of a high-minded man, who suffers terribly in the midst of a prosaic, shallow and spiritually impoverished age. Let us hear a little of what he says: " As far as we, poor, abandoned children are concerned, who believe that the Ideal is the only reality and the only truth in an ever-changing and ephemeral world; we who believe in the fulfilment of its promises, both in the present history of mankind and in that of the future world; we who know that this fulfilment is a necessity (because it is the reward of human brotherhood, as well as the explanation of the universe and the logic of God); we who are convinced that for us no other choice remains, let us proclaim this truth, as loud as possible. Let us try, through meditation and personal initiation, to make our way into the temple of eternal thoughts, in order there to arm ourselves with indestructible principles."

The book has, however, great defects. A childish credulity is apparent in many narrations. The continual mixing up of the eternal and the temporal produces an unpleasant effect. A foolish construction of history and violent and arbitrary interpretations of Scripture make the contents of the book suspicious. Hence it could not permanently satisfy me. It did not seem to me sufficiently simple, to be entirely true. It certainly raised me into lofty regions of thought, but left me there unfed. Theosophy also fails to make one permanently happy. It exaggerates the extent of human power. It does not reckon with the soul's need of grace, and it lacks the Sacraments of the Church. It is a halfway station for the better class of pagans, upon whose vision the light of perfect truth has not yet dawned, a temporary dwelling for the spiritually homeless, a fencing-school for religious dilettantism. If its devotees would employ only one half of the time and effort which they use to initiate themselves into the doctrines of Brahma and Buddha in gaining a deeper understanding of the Christian mysteries, what a splendid increase both in quantity and quality the Church would soon be able to rejoice over. For there is no doubt that among theosophists there are some rare spirits.

On the second Sunday, I sat in front of the inn, and read Schuré's book again. Everybody had gone to church. The singing of the choir mingled with the tones of the organ and the sounds of the cornet. It was so homelike and attractive! Within those walls people were celebrating holy mysteries, and dedicating themselves to their noblest task, that of praising God and praying to Him. There they were all united in one common purpose, while outside, I was sitting all alone, " like a solitary sparrow on the housetop " (Ps. ci.

[132]

8). Alone? No not quite alone, for in spirit I was in the church. Why was my body not there also?

On the third Sunday, having taken, unobserved, a prayer-book from a glass-case in the inn, I carried a chair into the church and seated myself among the men, just in front of the communion bench. I took part in all the ceremonies, kneeling and sitting down, like the others. I already knew how to make the sign of the cross and was not ashamed of doing so. Why should I be ashamed of it? Did it not recall the sacrificial death of Christ? During the sermon in the Breton dialect, of which I did not understand a word, I turned the leaves of my prayer-book. There I found all that I wanted to know, especially a precise explanation of the ritual of the Mass. In the offertory the bread was conse-crated, and after the priest's communion every one received a portion of it. The *Kyrie eleison, Gloria, Sanctus* and *Agnus Dei* were sung by all the people in Latin. The old priest celebrated and chanted with great dignity. I also prayed as best I could, and no one stared at me. I left the church with a heart filled with joy, and thenceforth went to Mass every Sunday and feast-day, and attended Vespers also frequently. Soon I could sing everything with the others, and this gave me great pleasure.

THERE were two priests in Saint Nolff, the rector and the vicar. Both were well-educated men and model priests. Each had his own dwelling and kept house for himself. I soon made their acquaintance, and whenever the vicar met me on a walk, he joined me. He was tall and strongly

[133]

built, yet slender rather than stout. From his full, sunburnt face looked out through his spectacles two kind and gentle eyes. In his expression there was visible a quiet melancholy. He was already rather advanced in years, yet still only a vicar. He stammered a little and could not chant the service well. On that account he was often passed over in clerical promotions, a fact which made the sensitive man suffer greatly. He told me how moved he was when he had seen me at church, and said that God certainly had great things in store for me. He assured me also that he prayed for me every day. Sometimes he took me by the hand silently, as if he wished by his priestly touch to banish from me all evil influences. I could not help laughing at such times and thought, " You will not capture me." And yet he finally did capture me after all. The warmth of his faith, his cordial manner and the ingenuousness of his nature had a very beneficial influence on me.

The rector was always very polite and friendly towards me, but he almost never touched upon religious subjects. One saw him seldom taking a distant walk, but usually only in front of the church or on the road to the railway station in conversation with passers-by, sometimes also with his rosary or Breviary in his hand.

Since no painter had ever been in Saint Nolff before me, every one was very cordial to me. They all had confidence in me. In a large, empty room for guests there soon hung a row of portraits of girls and children. On Sundays, before Mass, three or four young girls regularly sat on a bench, one or other of whom would be sketched. Meanwhile the peasants would come into the room, look at the pictures already finished, and were very glad when they recognized the faces represented there. "That's Marie Perrine, that's Marie Anne, that's Marie Louise," they cried. Almost all the girls of Saint Nolff bore the name of Marie. As a reward for sitting as a model, each one received a copy of her picture. The original I kept myself.

Thus the time passed little by little, and the day came when Ballin also arrived in Saint Nolff.

In reality I felt the appearance of my friend upon the scene to be a disturbance of my peaceful life. I felt so contented in my solitude, so happy on my way to the Catholic Faith. On the first Sunday after the arrival of Ballin I did not go to church. But in the course of the following week I made no more concealment of my inclination towards Catholicism, and on the second Sunday I once more went to Mass and Vespers.

The Dane was displeased with me, and brought forward all those prejudices against the Catholic Church which have become common property in all Protestant lands. "The veneration of saints is idolatry; in the Catholic Church pictures and statues are 'worshipped'; the Blessed Virgin is also 'worshipped'; the Pope is infallible; that is, he can commit no sins; the Church remits sins for money," etc. — all infamous perversions of the truth which have been disproved a hundred times, but which are still circulated as true statements even by otherwise honourable and highly educated people. And yet must not every thinking man say to himself: "It is impossible that the Catholic Church teaches such things, because if it did, it could never draw to itself men like Pascal, de Maistre, Frederick Schlegel, Brentano, Stolberg and hundreds of others. In fact, it would have already perished long ago, for whatever is built upon such errors cannot endure for two thousand years." But one does not *think,* when using such language; one only *affirms.*

Every time that Ballin attacked the Church, I defended it as well as I could, for I already loved it, even before I had perfectly grasped its doctrine, and before I had found in its bosom the plenitude of life. Moreover, I perceived in my friend the same unrest which had taken possession of me a year before in Huelgoat. Every morning he came to me in the same bad humour. He did not know what was the matter with him. "It is such curious weather today," he would say, "quite different from usual." He had no wish to work, and the end of it was always, "Come, let's take a walk."

I, however, wanted to work, and rarely yielded to his request. That made him angry, and his unrest drove him forth. He even made a journey to the peninsula of Quiberon, and returned in really better spirits. He promised himself much from a sojourn in Auray, a charming little city, distant only half an hour from Saint Nolff by rail. We should have the opportunity of visiting each other often.

One day Ballin brought me a "fearful piece of news."

"In two weeks," he said, "the Jesuits are coming here

[136]

to hold a mission." That was too much even for me. "My Lord!" I exclaimed, "when those celestial dragons come, we will get out, and come back again only when they have gone away." On Ascension Day the first Jesuit appeared, in order to announce to the population the coming of the mission. I did not go to Mass that day, because a Jesuit was to preach. We heard him outside "thundering." "Horrible," I said. "Horrible," repeated Ballin.

The mission was to be held in the week of Pentecost. I had heard much of the resort of pilgrims, Saint Anne of Auray, and I was told that thousands of them came thither from all parts of Brittany on the eve of Pentecost. It would be a fine opportunity to see the different national costumes. I had been tormenting myself in vain for several days over a small bit of work. "Perhaps I shall succeed there," I said to myself, "I'll go to Saint Anne of Auray, and stay there till the mission is over." And so it was. On the eve of Pentecost I went away, but Ballin still remained.

THE fifty days between Easter and Pentecost had already brought me very near to the Catholic Church. I knew now the principal points of its doctrine, and it was really only the subordinate questions which presented difficulties to me, as is almost always the case with converts. One such question, for example, was the credibility of the Mosaic account of the creation in the Book of Genesis, and another was the doctrine of original sin.

After having discovered that the book of Schuré, *Les Grands Initiés,* abounded in mere hypotheses, I determined to go myself to the sources of truth, and I read the New Testament very attentively. I did not for a moment doubt that I should find there unadulterated Christianity, and it was at once clear to me that the evangelists both loved the truth and wanted to tell the truth. One can feel this clearly, as one reads the text and no great knowledge of men is necessary to perceive that fact. When I now compared what I read with what the catechism teaches, I had to confess that they agreed excellently. It is true, I recoiled a little, when I found that the Catholic Church takes in their literal sense the words of Christ: "For my flesh is meat indeed; and my blood is drink indeed" (John vi. 56) and, "This is my body, this is my blood" (Mark xiv. 22, 24).

But finally I said to myself: "Why attribute to these words a figurative sense, if the oldest tradition of the Church accepted them literally? Is such a miracle impossible, if Jesus is truly the Son of God, true God and true man, as He repeatedly asserts of Himself and as the Apostles believed both before and after His death?" Gradually the whole doctrinal teaching of the Catholic Church appeared to me logical and reasonable, and therefore worthy of belief. Nevertheless I could not yet really believe. Or is it that I did not want to believe? Often the thought came to me: What! are you going to become a Catholic? Will you cease to be your own master? Would you like to remain forever chaste, even in thought? It is true, I did not consider it as an impossibility. But to be obliged to do this or that by the authority of the Church and to have to confess possible transgressions.

[138]

ONCE MORE IN BRITTANY

Some readers will perhaps ask me, "Did you never think of becoming a Calvinist or a Mennonite, like your family?" No; never for one moment. Outside the Catholic Church I had found too much sectarianism for me to want to seek my salvation there. It is possible also that the religious indifference of my relatives, as well as the coldness of the Protestant service, had repelled me. At all events, I said to myself: "If I become a Christian, I will become one thoroughly." And for me that meant to be a Catholic.

The question of religion had now occupied me for almost a year and a half. During this time I had changed my views continually and had been, as I have said, driven hither and thither by every wind of doctrine from whatever side it came. Evidently I had not yet found the right way, and the thought came to me: Can one really ever fight one's way to the acquisition of truth by one's own strength, or must not the eternal Truth come to our assistance and lead us to the truth? I had already seen somewhere a remark of this sort. Now I believed it, and I resolved, for the present, to read no more new books. In fact, I felt an excessive distrust of all reading and now, with the extreme confidence of youth, I expected to learn everything by a direct revelation from God.

I ARRIVED in Saint Anne of Auray in the forenoon. It is an insignificant village with no charm whatever. Only the place of pilgrimage is attractive. On the west side of a great square, bordered by trees, rises a large basilica; opposite this stands a gigantic altar, open on three sides, to which one ascends by high flights of steps. Here Mass is read to the pilgrims assembled in the square on holy days. Towards the north stands another sanctuary, and on the south side extends a row of houses. Of course, the usual shops with objects of devotion and tasteless manufactured goods are not wanting in the immediate neighbourhood of the church.

I put up at one of the numerous inns, unpacked my painting materials and, after lunch, began my little work. The weather was fine and warm. As often as I looked out of my window into the vivid sunshine of the street, I saw small groups of pilgrims approaching. I sketched the whole afternoon and was successful in my work. After the meagre dinner, at which, although it was a fast-day, they served me the left leg of a tough old rooster (the right leg of the same fowl I had eaten at noon), I went out into the church square. There many pilgrims had already ranged themselves in rows, with lighted candles in their hands. Soon the multitude, which must have numbered a thousand persons, set itself in motion, and went in procession around the great square, singing loudly. It was a wonderfully beautiful sight, this long line of pilgrims with lighted candles, passing slowly in the twilight underneath the tall, leafy trees. Beside me stood a bombastic Frenchman, one of the sort that is full of a hate which expresses itself in blasphemy. He was one of a type that is often met with, especially in Latin countries. He began in a loud voice to revile the pilgrims. Such a procession, he declared, was a stupidity, pure superstition, absolutely irrational, and moreover not even beautiful. What was there really to see in it? Nothing, simply nothing! Thus he shouted and blustered, evidently against his better sentiment. "You miserable blackguard," I thought and I ran to a woman who was selling candles, bought one and joined the pilgrim-train, chiefly in order to defy that blasphemer.

After the procession had made the round of the square, it turned behind the church into the courtyard of the boys' seminary, where the bishop of Vannes, who had come for the festival, was received with cheers and sacred songs. Then the people passed into the church, where a sacramental benediction took place. Finally, the program for the following day was read aloud: "From four o'clock in the morning opportunity for confession. At nine o'clock pontifical Mass."

I was in a strange state of mind. My mood was most serious, and I must have looked very pale. I trembled frequently. Perhaps I felt that I was standing at the parting of the ways, and that now my future was soon to be decided, even if I had yet no idea what a profoundly decisive event for the whole life the entry into the Catholic Church can be. An agonizing feeling of oppression came over me. "My God, let me see the truth; show me where it is to be found. My God, enlighten me; draw me to Thyself." Thus did I pray again and again. And when I returned to my room, I had to confess to myself anew: The Catholic Church has certainly a wonderful power over men.

On the following day, I rose rather late, yet came in good time to the pontifical Mass celebrated by the bishop of Vannes. The church was not very full. Evidently many pilgrims had already departed, after having confessed and received Holy Communion. I now saw a pontifical service for the first time, but scarcely recognized in it the usual Mass. I was still greatly agitated and prayed with fervour.

I also implored Saint Anne, that she would work a " little miracle," and obtain for me a sign, so that I could no more doubt the truth of the Catholic Church. All those books I had read had not helped me at all; they had only confused me more and more. When the pontifical service was ended, I left the church relieved, as if my prayer was to be answered. During the day I continued to paint and sketch on my little work. When, at the time for Vespers, I bought some refreshments in a confectioner's shop, opposite my inn, the woman said to me that her son, who lay ill of an incurable disease, had been very happy to watch me from his bed while I was at my work, and that this was a pleasant diversion for him. She hoped that I would remain there some days longer. This hope was not to be fulfilled. In the night from Monday to Tuesday I was so tormented by insects that I resolved to go away. But whither? There was nothing to do but to return to Saint Nolff. I said to myself: " After all, I don't care a straw for the Jesuits. Ballin will have gone away. My work is far enough advanced; there is not much more to do. So, in God's name, let's go back."

ONCE MORE IN BRITTANY

I<small>F</small>, in a previous chapter, I compared the striving of God to win the human soul to the effort of a young man to win the heart of the former playmate of his youth, the comparison was justified by the fact that often a conversion as well as a betrothal is preceded by the same ridiculous but poignant anxieties, a sign that love is in jeopardy. To the would-be convert as he progresses, come the wildest doubts, because his state of mind is so touchingly sensitive. Since he has the greatest reverence for everything religious, he is in constant fear of offending some one and giving cause for scandal, whenever he goes to church. He thinks he has clearly perceived that " good people " resent his taking holy water and crossing himself as they do, and they have good reason for it, for what has God to do with Belial? This feeling of humility is really a manifestation of the grace of God, but it is one which the devil tries to exploit for his own ends. If he cannot entice a man to commit evil deeds, he seeks at least to suggest a false notion of virtue. He tried this also in my case.

Scarcely had I arrived in Saint Anne of Auray, when all at once a frightful feeling of shame came over me, because I had been " so bold " as to attend Mass quite regularly in Saint Nolff. " You fool," I whispered to myself, " what have you in common with those good people there? Are you not ashamed to be such an intruder? What are you thinking of, to take holy water and to make the sign of the cross, and thus to dishonour things, which to others are sacred? "

I even came near sending a note of apology to the parish

priest of Saint Nolff. But, as I worked on, I grew more reasonable, and after the episode of the procession the temptation vanished, as if blown away.

EVERY ascent is fatiguing, including the ascent to the truth of revelation. It would be less so, if one had always a good guide. It seems, however, to be actually necessary that, at the commencement, the seeker after truth should be not only without guidance and obliged to discover the way himself but that he should be led astray by false opinions and inexact statements. It is as if, after long wanderings, a bold man should at last arrive in a fair land, where in the sun-illumined distance, not too far away, the peaceful peak of a high mountain beckoned him to come to it. It promises his soul, so eager to behold it closely, new and undreamed of horizons, and a wide view over countries never seen before. So one day he sets out joyously upon his way to it with knapsack and staff. But what happens? Is the mountain retreating? The wanderer has advanced for hours, and yet the peak is always just as far away. He turns back disappointed, and gives up the hope of ever standing on that tranquil height. Yet, after all, what would he do there on that summit? Is it not also beautiful here in the valley? Still, on sunny days, the mountain, the landmark of the country, rises clearly before his eyes, and lures the stranger thither with sweet promises. Now he starts out again, and this time better equipped. But in vain. Late in the evening he returns, after wandering the entire day. At first the mountain had seemed, as before, to retreat from him, then he lost sight of its beautiful summit, and other peaks pushed themselves into the foreground. And through what a frightful solitude his route had led him! He had met only a few herdsmen, who evidently did not trust the stranger, for they gave only evasive answers to his questions. One of them had even treated him threateningly, and told him to move on. Only one mysterious old man had responded to his inquiries, and understood the longing of his heart. Yet even he had admonished him to look for a guide. There was only one route, he said, to the peaceful mountain-crest, only one way, which many had already taken, after some one, divinely inspired, had pointed it out to them. He added that one should put perfect confidence in one's guide, if he seemed to be an honourable man. Then he had shown him his way back, and disappeared. The stranger will, however, have nothing to do with a guide. " What any one else can do, I can do," he thinks.

WHEN I arrived in Saint Nolff about noon, I found to my great surprise Ballin still there. " I have stayed on here in spite of the mission," he said; " one can stand it all right; it is even quite lively. Those who live at a distance remain all day in the village, where usually it is so lonesome; now one sees at least some people here." " Have you already heard a sermon? " I asked. " The thought had not occurred to me," replied Ballin, " but it would not be a bad idea for you to go and hear what the Jesuits say." I promised to do so, and on the same day kept my word.

In the principal church a sermon was preached in the

[145]

Breton dialect, but in the chapel of Saint Anne the sermon was in French. No one who understood the Breton language was allowed to go to the French sermons. Hence at the evening service, which I attended, there were only about thirty persons present. The Jesuit father, a short, compactly built man of forty years, intoned a chant and then began his sermon. It was a dry discourse on the subject of hell which, he said, one could escape only by means of an honest, contrite confession, if one had had the misfortune to fall into mortal sin. I hit it off, therefore, pretty well for the first time. I was not at all edified, but on the contrary angry and disappointed. Motives of fear had never been able to exert any special effect on me. Merely to escape punishment I would not have let myself be deterred from anything. Leave something undone from motives of magnanimity or generosity? Yes. But through a fear of punishment? Never! But yet my soul knew nothing of *holy fear*.

"Well, how was it?" asked Ballin sarcastically, when I returned. I did not wish to acknowledge all my disappointment, so I answered: "The Jesuit preached on hell. He wanted to scare those poor people to death, so that they would go to confession. I am not going to any more sermons. I've had enough of them."

"If only those damned Jesuits would leave here today!" said Ballin. That would certainly have been most agreeable to the devil also.

On Thursday evening, shortly after sunset, Ballin and I were standing before the house of the vicar. We were both

[146]

deeply impressed by the solemn beauty, which lay out-spread over the landscape. It was one of those awe-inspiring summer evenings, when nature, all aglow with a celestial splendour, seems to be sunk in ecstasy. Not a leaf moved, even the easily agitated poplar trees were still. The clock in the church tower struck the hour, and the reverberations of the bell prolonged themselves in lingering cadence, as they died away. Swallows with noisy twittering shot inde-fatigably through the golden air, and flying bats announced the coming night. Innumerable insects darted hither and thither and formed together a fine network floating in mid-air. "My God!" exclaimed Ballin, "how beautiful it is this evening!" Then he added suddenly, "Look! here comes a Jesuit towards us." "What can he want?" I asked. Already he stood near us. He was the one who had preached on hell. He greeted us amicably and began a conversation with us. Ballin spoke of the magnificent eve-ning. Then the Jesuit also surveyed the country and said, "Very beautiful." After we had exchanged a few phrases, I asked, "Do you sometimes go walking here?" The father replied, "Certainly." "May I accompany you the next time, if convenient?" I continued. "I shall be very glad to have you do so," answered the Jesuit, "I like to talk about art occasionally." "I would like to talk about something else," I said. The Jesuit smiled. We made an appointment for the following afternoon, after which he took his leave, for he had still to read his Breviary and the next day would again begin early for him, since at four o'clock he must already be in the church. I was horrified at the thought of such an

[147]

early hour. "To rise at half past three? Terrible!" How often later on was I myself to do the same.

How did it happen that the Jesuit father spoke to us? I learned this later. He had been alarmed to see us in the village and had asked the parish priest who we were. When he heard that we were painters, he had been much disturbed and said: "My dear rector, be on your guard! A short time ago we held a mission in a place where there were also two painters who turned the whole parish upside down." The rector answered him: "I cannot complain at all of these young gentlemen. One of them comes every Sunday to Mass, and in the evening also prays in the church, although he is not a Catholic, and the other seems to be also a thoroughly respectable person." Thereupon the Jesuit replied: "If that is the case, then I must speak with them both."

When, on the following day, I walked with the Jesuit father through the lovely countryside, I spoke of my struggle to arrive at faith, and asked him to enlighten me on some points. It is true, I did not do this with that humility and simplicity, which become a seeker after truth. I wanted to put the priest to the test, and therefore brought forth not only my own, but all sorts of difficulties as well. It pleased me also to make on him the impression of a well-read young man. The Jesuit father was not a learned man, but a simple missionary, whose whole line of thought proceeded from his positive belief, and who was thoroughly bewildered in the chaos of modern opinions. He said this quite frankly and from a feeling that for him to go more deeply into my difficulties could only increase them. He contented himself, therefore, with correcting some statements which I brought forward, and invited me to come soon to Vannes. He said there was a Jesuit college there and he would like to make me acquainted with some fathers who could remove my doubts better than he. It had been a long time since he had finished his studies, and he had therefore forgotten much. But one thing he would do, and that was to pray for me and to ask others to do so, as well as to write to me, and provide me with books. Finally he said to me further that it speaks well for the character of a young man, if he strives earnestly to acquire truth, and that this presupposed a purity of thought, which unfortunately is at present rare; a remark which flattered me very much. In general I was very well satisfied with my walk and my heart was lighter. I had at last spoken out my mind freely. Encouraged by the priest, I attended in the evening another sermon. This time it was not Father Le Texier (the name of my new-found friend), but another father who preached. He spoke on prayer, and indeed so beautifully that this time I was able to say to my friend Ballin, " The sermon was splendid, profound, and yet not over the heads of the people."

GOD *can* let us find the way to truth through the working of His grace alone, without any human coöperation, but usually we reach its resplendent heights only with the assistance of a guide. This guide must be a man who possesses an ardent love, which gives to him clear insight, and who does not hesitate under certain circumstances to be somewhat insistent and authoritative, for conversions can be easily too long drawn out. Here, too, the motto is applicable, "One must strike the iron while it is hot." Otherwise the convert runs the risk of becoming one of those, of whom the Apostle says that they are "ever learning, but never attaining to a knowledge of the truth." Such a guide Father Le Texier was to become for me. As a director of souls, of much experience, he encouraged what he found good in me, and was anxious to give free course to the line of development which my spiritual life had taken. In the beginning he wished to have me read various books, but when he saw my aversion to reading at that time, he limited himself to urging me to pray diligently, and said to me repeatedly: "From the moment that you pray and pray willingly, the truth will reveal itself to you ever more and more."

With my reason I was now constantly coming nearer to the Catholic Church, only, as I have said, I feared the obligations which I should have to assume, and I could not yet really believe. I told this to Father Le Texier, when I paid him a visit one day in Vannes. He was not at all surprised, and said quietly: "So long as you are not baptised, you cannot believe, as we Catholics do; for the supernatural virtue of faith is a grace, which we receive only in baptism. When you are once baptised, it will probably be with you, as it was with an American, to whose conversion one of my fellow-brothers contributed, and who was in almost the same state of mind as you. This man, before his baptism, made all kinds of objections, but after his baptism there

[150]

was no one more happy. All his difficulties had disappeared, and nothing was easier than to prepare him for his first Holy Communion."

These words went straight to my heart, for I had a secret longing for baptism. I hoped thereby to enter into a mystical relation with Christ and His Apostles, and I considered this Sacrament as an initiation into the Christian mysteries, which in a certain sense it is. In doing so, I thought of what I had read in Schuré's *Les Grands Initiés* concerning introduction and initiation into the Greek mysteries. Here again theosophy was for me a bridge. But even if I did desire to be baptised, I did not yet on that account desire to be a Catholic. To be baptised as a Protestant, however, I desired still less. So my longing remained unsatisfied. This exasperated me, and I often denounced this "cursed inclination to Catholicism, which leaves one no peace, and makes quiet work impossible." Ballin had gone away and established himself at Auray, where he found Rasetti with his wife and child. At first I was glad to be rid of him. Now I could again paint more quietly, and the discussions about religion were ended. But soon I could no more endure the solitude. The month of July had come, when the landscape is most monotonous, when the birds cease to sing, when the dust blows into one's eyes and the heat makes one always more indolent. In my heart, too, a strong reaction had set in against everything religious. I became restless, discontented, moody and idle. "This everlasting haggling with subtle distinctions must cease," I said to myself one day; "either you must become a Catholic, or not. In

[151]

the last analysis your piety is only a form of exaltation, a kind of sickness, which will pass away again, if you will only lead a gay life, as you did formerly. The proverb says that a painter must live joyously, drink much and fear nothing. It is true, Le Texier has promised to pay me a visit, and no doubt he means all right, but just for him I am not going to remain here." So, without sending any word to the father, or even saying whither I was going, I boarded the train for Quimperlé and walked from there to Pouldu, to spend a week again with Drahtmann in that inn of Marie Poupée, where life was always so full of fun. "There," I thought, "my wish to be a Catholic will soon disappear."

And in fact for the first few days it seemed as if I should never again listen to the tender admonition of God's grace. My friend Drahtmann, always glad to have a patient auditor, opened the floodgates of his eloquence and poured out upon me the long pent-up torrent of his philosophy of absolutism. He seemed fairly to revel in paradoxical thoughts. One should, he said, go to the furthest limit in everything; then only is a man a genuine artist. For the artist the commonplace moral limitations, which fetter the rest of mankind, do not exist. He has only one anxiety, and that is to create something beautiful.

Drahtmann's views indeed went, perhaps unconsciously to him, so far as to venerate art as a kind of divinity, of whom one thinks day and night, for whom one, occasionally at least, works oneself to death and suffers hunger, sleeplessness and self-torment, but a divinity who, in return

[152]

for this devotion, gives one *carte blanche* to indulge in every sort of dissipation, even in positive debaucheries, and in such vices as wear the appearance of virtue, as when one condemns the suppression of the passions as " suicide," dispenses borrowed money lavishly, without ever repaying it, spoils worthless men and dissolute women with presents and attentions, pardons a lack of character, and throws oneself away, instead of devoting oneself to others.

My friend located the moral significance of an action too exclusively in the sentiment which determines the motive of the action. He forgot that the good we do must be *well* done and for a worthy object. For such a greenhorn as I was in regard to ethics, it was not at all easy to distinguish between those apparent virtues and the real ones. Fortunately I chose for the most part, as moreover Drahtmann did also, instinctively, a worthy object for my sentiment, which was often excellent, and then the absolutist principles of my friend were of use to me. I have done many a good action, which is attributable to his influence.

With a cigar almost constantly in use and a bottle within reach, with the body well nourished, and for the most of the time in a recumbent position, we passed the days quite gaily. One day something evil came near happening. It was of an evening, and we were precisely engaged in a profound discussion, when a temptation came to us. It was, however, of too coarse a nature, and offended our aesthetic feeling. Hence we were saved from it. At last the hour came for me to take leave of Drahtmann and Marie Poupée, and to return to Saint Nolff.

[153]

YESTERDAYS OF AN ARTIST-MONK

WHEN I once more made my appearance in Saint Nolff, I was received most cordially. I was told that Father Le Texier had been there on July 27th and had asked about me. I pretended that I had had no notion of his coming. But, in the afternoon (it was Sunday), when I was taking a walk, shame and remorse overwhelmed me. I knew how little free time the father had, and therefore said to myself: " While he was concerned about you, you were sitting beside a bottle of wine and wasting your time — or was it not rather God who was concerned about you, while you had fled from Him ? "

Gradually a great longing for the Supreme Good again came over me, and a strong desire for what was sure and stable, and for a definite aim in life.

Father Le Texier had in his last letter indicated precisely what an adult who wished to be baptised must know and believe. He wrote me to go to the rector, if I still had to struggle with difficulties, and then at last we could quickly arrange everything in reference to my baptism.

But I did not go to the rector. I took up, instead, a book which the father had sent me. It was an explanation of the Catholic faith by Girodon. One of the good points of this volume is that it states exactly what the strict dogma of the Church is, and what is unanimously accepted by all theologians.

I was greatly surprised to see how much room for freedom of thought the Church leaves open in regard to many questions, and precisely those which had made difficulties for me, and I became better acquainted also with some teachers of the Church, particularly St. Augustine. As I put the book down, I said: "Taking everything into account, I can believe most readily what the Catholic Church teaches. All that I have elsewhere heard and read of religion demands ten times more faith than does the inexorably logical doctrine of Catholicism."

Is it, then, more difficult to believe in the incarnation of the Son of God, than in the pre-existence and incarnation of the soul and in its transmigration in the Buddhistic-Platonic sense, doctrines which I also once for a long time accepted and agreed to?

But even with this clear perception of the truth my vacillation did not cease. If one wishes to become a Catholic, other questions come into consideration besides those regarding the truth of the Catholic doctrine. Before all arises the inquiry: "What will your family, your superiors, your friends say to such a step? Will you not be disinherited?" I rightly thought that I need not fear any such step on the part of my parents, yet I felt that I should certainly cause them great sorrow if I adopted the Catholic faith with or without their knowledge. Yes, that I knew. How many conversions have been wrecked on the cliffs haunted by the fear of men. How many convictions of the truth have weakened in view of the cruel threat of social misery, if one should become Catholic! I personally had almost no fear of men (but unfortunately this was only because I was proud and despised the opinion of others), and my youthful optimism soon drove away the dark clouds of care concerning my daily bread. There remained only my anxiety concerning the displeasure I should give my parents. But I consoled myself with the thought: " In any event, if I do let myself be baptised, it is only a 'trial,' and for the present father and mother need not know anything about it. Besides, will it really come to that? "

I WROTE to Father Le Texier a letter of apology and said, among other things, that when he did not find me at home, I probably had made on him the impression of a sheep that wanted to escape from the care of the good shepherd. To this he replied, " No, I have rather the impression that the sheep was seeking the pasture of truth." Then very clearly and concisely he corrected various statements which I, more from ill humour than from conviction and driven by a spirit of contradiction, had asserted in my last letter, as a despairing final shot at the Catholic Church. In conclusion he wrote, " Your baptism could take place on August 26th."

Was I already decided, when I received this letter, or did it still need this slight additional impulse? Almost without a struggle, and with a " Well then, I'll make an end of the story," I made up my mind to go to Vannes and say to Father Le Texier that I was ready to be baptised. My attempt to drive away thoughts of conversion at Pouldu had failed pitiably. I found no other way of escape, and accordingly surrendered. To be sure, this took place at a time when all the grounds of probability known to me in favour of the truth of the Catholic Church offered to my reason sufficient certainty to allow me to make a decision, but I promised myself: "If I do not find my happiness in the Catholic Church, I will turn my back on it with the same determination with which I now wish to enter it."

A few hours later I was already in the bare, comfortless room of Father Le Texier. While I was standing near him by his table, he turned his eyes upon me and asked, "Well, have you already decided?" "Let us do it on the twenty-sixth," I answered immediately. The father sprang up joyfully from his chair. He had evidently not expected this reply. He congratulated me, and said that I need not concern myself about anything, as he would take all the necessary steps. I was only to prepare myself spiritually, and he would have special prayers said for me, that my baptism might bring me the perfect light.

Happy and contented, I returned to Saint Nolff. A passionate ardour filled my heart, and during the next three weeks I read diligently the books which Father Le Texier had recommended to me.

AND now I had to look about me for a godfather. I chose for this post of sponsor a young miller, named Jean Gachet, an amiable, fine-looking young man, who was pious and light-hearted. One evening, therefore, I went to see him. We had already met frequently and had become good friends. As usual he received me very cordially. We sat down side by side in the garden, a sweet, quiet place, and after we had talked for a few minutes on indifferent subjects, I said to him: "Jean, have you not often heard the people here in the village say that I would surely become a

Catholic? Is not that the general talk of the place?" "Oh, what an idea!" he cried; "but what will not people gossip about? Nonsense, nonsense! Don't pay any attention to it." "But, Jean," I continued, "suppose that what the people say is true, would you like in that event to be godfather at my baptism?" "*Sapristi, sapristi,*" exclaimed the fine young fellow, springing to his feet joyfully, "why, of course I would. Isn't that glorious? Ah! the Catholic religion is a wonderful religion. Monsieur Jean, this just delights me. Come into the house with me. We must empty a glass in honour of this. Mother, please give us at once some wine and glasses. To your good health, Monsieur Jean: here's to you."

And the next day the young miller went into the city and bought a beautifully bound prayer-book to give me on the occasion of my baptism.

When I had asked my future godfather, "Have you not often heard the people here in the village say that I would surely become a Catholic," it was merely a supposition on my part. As a matter of fact, I cannot sufficiently praise the delicate reticence of the inhabitants of Saint Nolff. I was observed at every step, my conversion formed their usual topic of conversation every day, and they waited impatiently for the moment of my baptism. Several times, in fact, a number of women had lingered in the church on Sunday after Vespers, thinking that I was then to be baptised. One rich, elderly spinster burned with a desire to be my godmother. Yet of all this I then knew nothing, and should never have known of it, if Jean Gachet had not told me later. After my baptism also people maintained towards me the same reticence, although they were all happy over it. The only perceptible difference was that they were even more cordial than before and that I was invited to all the weddings and festivities. One Sunday afternoon, however, a man, who was slightly intoxicated, came up to me, held out his hand and said stammeringly, " Monsieur Jean, don't you believe in the Blessed Virgin? " I naturally made him no answer and sent him away, yet it made me angry that the man had touched upon this delicate point.

I was not baptised in Saint Nolff, but by my express wish in the chapel of the Jesuit college in Vannes. I had retired thither two days before, in order to prepare myself quietly for my " illumination," as baptism was formerly called. The pupils were all absent on vacation, and the great house seemed completely deserted. I lived in the vacated room of a professor, the bare, soiled walls and tasteless furniture of which were repugnant to me. All the more, therefore, did the beautiful chapel of the college and the great garden with its park-like grounds give me satisfaction, and here for the most part I passed those wonderful hours of retirement. I was so happy to have finally come to a decision. And I looked forward with joyful expectation to the mysterious hour of my baptism.

The morning of the great day dawned. It was a Friday, August 26, 1892. I had to fast, for after my baptism I was to receive my first Holy Communion. The rector and my godfather, Jean Gachet, had come to Vannes by the first train, for it was not Father Le Texier, but the parish priest of Saint Nolff, who was to baptise me.

Since baptism is the door through which we pass to the other Sacraments, and since not only one's original sin but also all one's past sins are by that Sacrament effaced, I did not need to confess beforehand, which rendered my entry into the Catholic Church much easier.

Of the long baptismal ceremony I remember only a few details of secondary importance. The rector marked a cross upon my forehead and breast, and placed salt in my mouth, and I had to pray the "Our Father" several times, while kneeling. He also touched my ears with saliva, saying, *Ephpheta;* that is, "Open," and then touched my nostrils with the words, "For sweet perfume." After the baptism itself a white veil was laid about me, and a lighted candle was put into my hand. At this point some curious boys burst into the chapel, but with this exception everything passed off, as in a dream. After the baptism I felt exhausted, but entirely happy: *I believed.* My difficulties had vanished, as if swept away. The Holy Eucharist had suddenly acquired for me a great attraction, and I was happy to receive my first Holy Communion immediately after my baptism. Father Le Texier assumed the vestments for the Mass, and advanced towards the altar. Visibly moved, he recited with great feeling the words of the prayer at the foot of the steps, *Introibo* — "I will go in to the altar of God, to God, who giveth joy to my youth. I will give praise upon the harp, O God, my God" (Ps. xvii). During the Mass and after the Communion I thanked God

[160]

with fervid prayers. It seemed to me that I had gone through a severe illness, which had taught me much and deepened my character. I felt satisfied, improved and full of goodness and charity for my fellowmen. But I realised also the responsibility which I had assumed, and a slight reproof from the father for a word of self-complacency, which had escaped me shortly after the ceremony, warned me that I had ceased to be a pampered pupil on the road of instruction to faith. Jean Gachet was to be my godfather also at my confirmation, which took place on the following day; but when, owing to a misunderstanding, he did not appear at the appointed time, we went to look for him in the market place, for that day was a market-day in the town. After a long search we found him, and hastened to the designated church.

The hour agreed upon had, however, passed. The bishop stood already before the Communion rail, and was making an address. My attendants were terrified. " Monseigneur does not like to wait," said one. Father Le Texier, the rector of Saint Nolff, his vicar, my godfather and I knelt penitently down in the rear of the church, and only when the bishop had concluded his address, did we rise. The kneeling certainly had seemed very long. Then I received Holy Confirmation, together with two or three sunburnt men and the children of some strolling gipsies, who had been prepared by pious ladies for their first Holy Communion and Confirmation. After all, I belonged to such a company, for what was I but a strolling painter?

· After the ceremony we were all conducted into the palace

of the bishop, Monseigneur Jean Marie Bécel. A gipsy child recited a little poem with much grace, and received from the bishop a kiss on the forehead. To me the prelate gave a book of sermons, which he had delivered on various festal occasions in Saint Anne of Auray.

Now I was a Christian, armed with the weapons of faith and adorned with the gifts of the Holy Spirit. Not without pride, therefore, did I attend High Mass on the following day in Saint Nolff, no more as a stranger, but as a child of the house.

For the present I kept my conversion a secret even from my best friends. Not a single nabi was informed of it. In my letters the subject of religion was indeed often mentioned, and my parents remarked it, but they did not think it possible that I could become a Catholic. In the first days of September, that is, soon after my conversion, Ballin wrote me that he was reading with increasing interest the book by Girodon, which I had loaned him, explaining the doctrine of the Catholic Church. He said he could not always agree with the author, but that he found his arguments of great importance. The proofs of the existence of God did not, it is true, appeal to him at all and provoked him to contradiction, but the doctrine of the infallibility of the Church and of the Pope seemed to him perfectly logical. Only he asked himself whether such a gift was not better suited to angels than to human beings. Still he did not wish to express any further criticism until he should have read the whole book. He said he must certainly become acquainted with the writings of Saint Augustine, and that the quotations from this Church Father formed the finest passages in Girodon's work.

The next letter from Ballin informed me that he had procured the *Soliloquies* and the *Confessions* of Saint Augustine; that he was living in the utmost seclusion, without however being melancholy; and that though he was not painting anything for the present, he did not reproach himself on that account. He added that he was convinced that the studies, with which he was now occupied, would be of benefit to his art. Very striking were the following thoughts in his letter: "Only when one feels that everything good that one does proceeds from the faith of a believing soul, and that everything evil is felt to be in absolute contradiction with it, do the fruits of religion become abundant and sweet. Only simplicity in the faith and that complete devotion which manifests itself in sacrifice can, in my opinion, bring that renaissance in art, which we so ardently wish for. Why is the impression made upon us by a painting by Redon, in comparison with that produced by one by Raphael, doleful, morbid and unbalanced, and why is the impression of a picture by Gauguin distorted and exaggerated? Yet both these painters know the works of the great masters, seek honestly the truth, and are very clever. What they lack is, certainly, the immovable foundation of religion. Like us, those artists also take an interest in religion, but it needs perhaps several generations before what I feel now by a kind of intuition will become the most powerful sentiment of our souls."

[163]

In conclusion he wrote: "Let us strive still more to acquire this sublime religion. If we persistently seek it, God will give us the grace of faith and love, without which religion is only a kind of subordinate affair, without any real worth, when it is not a matter of fashion."

These words of my friend certainly surprised me, but I did not attach to them any special importance.

Some days later (it was a Sunday) Ballin paid me a visit and told me how he often went in Auray to the convent church of the Augustinian nuns, who sang very beautifully. Their voices were weak, it is true, probably because of the many penitential exercises which they imposed upon themselves, but they were very expressive.

When the bell for Vespers rang, Ballin said to me, "I will go with you today." This was really not very agreeable to me, for Ballin was a peculiar man, who had ways and customs of his own, and I feared that he might perhaps cause some scandal. But what was my astonishment to see him kneel down on a *prie-dieu,* his head in his hands, and assist with the greatest reverence at the service of Vespers.

I thought to myself: "My good man, what is the matter with you? It seems to me that one must pray for you." When the service was over, my friend left the church with the greatest composure and naturalness, and said, "That was nice, but you ought to hear the nuns in Auray sing." I promised him that I would soon return his visit. When I stood in Ballin's room a few days later, he said to me suddenly, "Jan, do you know what I have been often thinking lately? There will come a time that we shall both be Catholics." I gazed at him in astonishment and answered, "Do you know it then already?" "What should I know?" asked Ballin. "Well," I replied smiling, "I am already a Catholic; on August twenty-sixth I was baptised in Vannes."

Ballin remained for some time speechless; then he burst forth in reproaches. "You villain!" he cried, "why didn't you tell me something about it? Well, I will be baptised too, and that within the next few days." I asked him whether he had already received any clerical instruction, and when he replied in the negative, I said to him in a superior tone: "Do you think that it goes so smoothly as that? No, my friend, you must first study diligently and learn the catechism, or you will not be taken into the Church." "Nonsense," replied Ballin, "I know all that now. If I go to the parish priest tomorrow, he will baptise me the next day surely."

"We shall see," I muttered.

Then he talked of a great plan, which we had conceived on the Sunday evening when we had gone to Vespers together. We had sat then talking pleasantly of the great masters and their works. At last I said: "I should like so much to go once, if the opportunity offered, to Basel. In the museum there are most beautiful portraits by the younger Holbein. I have the feeling that my stay here has no more sense in it. What I would like best would be to make a journey to Basel across France on foot. Heavens! that would be fine. Will you go with me?" "To Basel?" answered

Ballin, "I would rather go to Italy." "Of course, I too," I exclaimed, "but I haven't money enough for that." "Let's go to Italy anyway," said Ballin decidedly. "Scrape up just a little more money, and I'll take care of the rest." That very evening I wrote to a friend in Holland asking him to lend me two hundred francs, and to my father requesting his permission to go to Italy. At first the latter made some objections, of which the principal was that cholera was raging there, but finally he yielded and without my having asked him sent me, besides my monthly allowance, two hundred francs more, very fortunately too for me, as my friend had excused himself, saying that he could not help me this time.

Towards evening we attended the service with benediction at the chapel of the Augustinian nuns. It was a small, poor little church. Above, on the right, near the *presbyterium,* was the choir of the sisters. Ballin acted like a child of the house. As I heard later, he had often been seen kneeling on the floor near the door, paying no attention to those about him. He was a man of great natural piety, full of ardour, a true disciple of Saint Augustine. At last there were signs of life in the choir. The Holy Sacrament was exposed, and the sisters sang *O Salutaris Hostia.* It was truly as if one were listening to voices from another world, a pure world completely isolated from terrestrial things. What they sang was really a salutation, a loving greeting to their divine Bridegroom, and at the same time an appeal to the world, which they had left, to repent and pray.

On the following day, Ballin went to the parish priest of Auray and declared that he wanted to become a Christian and to receive baptism as soon as possible. The priest, however, did not seem at all inclined to grant his request so quickly. " Why are you in such a hurry? " he asked. Ballin replied that he wanted to go to Italy with me in a short time, whereupon the priest answered: " If you were obliged to return to Protestant Denmark, I would admit you into the Church within a few days; but since you are going into another Catholic country, it is better that you should first be instructed in the faith there for some time. Remain for a few months longer a student of the catechism, as Saint Augustine was for a long while." Ballin acceded to this, and having told me of his conversation with the priest, he said, " Now nothing stands in the way of our journey; let us, therefore, start as soon as possible for beautiful Italy."

WHEN my entry into the Catholic Church became generally known (which did not occur at once, as will be seen), many sought to explain my conversion psychologically. Certain interpretations of my step were not exactly flattering to me. Some thought at the time (and I cannot blame them for it, since there were reasons enough for the supposition) that my conversion was only an " artist's whim." Others, I hope without foundation, connected it with a slight attack of religious mania, while others still were of the firm conviction that I had let myself be " caught by the priests."

One, with clearer insight, said that what had decided me to turn to religion was the need of setting over against nature a solid system of ideas, governed by its own laws, something external, which could serve as a guide to my tem-

[167]

perament, which was far too mercurial for the merely abstract. Then, when once the external form of the Catholic Church had been accepted the doctrine of the system had followed.

Another thought that, after having succeeded with much difficulty in becoming religious I had not in my joy waited for a further spiritual development, but had deposited my new-found treasure in the Catholic Church, as it were through fear of possibly losing it again. And finally many were of the opinion that I had become Catholic in order to satisfy my aesthetic needs, and that the beauty of the Catholic ritual had fascinated me.

What are we to conclude from these and similar attempts to explain my conduct? Some, especially the last three, no doubt allude to causes which had to do with my conversion, but one should not attribute too much importance to them. Opposed to them, on the other hand, were many other weighty reasons, which could have held me back from entering the Catholic Church. Perhaps I have not laid sufficient stress on these in my book, being too anxious to reveal very clearly my inclination to Catholicism, which runs like a red thread through my whole life. Hence I would like to add the following: From my very childhood I had an innate aversion to the Catholic Church. When we boys taunted a Catholic with being a " Roman Pope," we associated with this expression a real hatred. The " Spanish yoke," the "atrocities of the Inquisition " and Catholicism itself had become for me, through a one-sided instruction in history, synonymous ideas. I had also an

actually devilish aversion to " Mary, the Mother of Christ."
"Priestly domination" also was in our home a household
word. And the Hollander's passionate spirit of freedom
rebels against everything which appears to be an encroach-
ment on his self-determination.

It was no wonder, therefore, that many who had known
me from my earliest years did not attempt to explain my
conversion at all, but simply said, " It is incomprehensible."
They could not understand it, however, either because they
did not believe in a direct or an indirect intervention of
God in our destiny, or because they had not a sufficient acquaintance with the period of life which preceded my conversion to recognize it as an act of God's providence. Yet
so it actually was.

If the permanent transformation and improvement of
my whole life has not already proved that to them clearly,
I hope to have subsequently convinced some of them of it
by my narrative. One should believe the words of Christ:
" No man can come to me, except the Father, who hath
sent me, draw him " (John vi. 44).

Only because God drew me by His grace,* illuminated

---

* What I here designate as *grace* is that undeserved, supernatural aid
or gift which prepares within us in advance every work of salvation, and
accompanies and completes it. Grace has a transforming and uplifting power.
It works, if God so wills, with irresistible force, and yet without overpowering us. It reaches its aim in the most secret ways, draws everything
under its spell, and is able to make use, for the realisation of its plans, of all
the capacities and talents of the individual. For it in no way removes
from a man his natural powers, but rather develops and perfects them. St.
Thomas Aquinas teaches that " Grace perfects man's nature, not merely

[169]

my mind supernaturally and strengthened my will, did the events, which had brought me ever since my childhood into connection with Catholicism, finally acquire the power really to decide my destiny.

I entered the Catholic Church voluntarily, but the decision to enter it was brought about by God's gracious influence. In this way must my conversion be understood, if one takes into consideration the whole truth.

In the first part of my book I have endeavoured to discover and make clear the hidden ways of God's grace by describing what became for me, so to speak, a bridge to the Catholic Church. In the second part I shall now relate how from the young plant of faith, which I was after my baptism, I became a small tree, which God took from out the world and transplanted into the paradise of the cloister.

GREAT are the gifts which God confers upon the sinner on his way to conversion, but greater still are the blessings which the pardoned soul receives in baptism. God Himself enters into the soul of the neophyte and makes His abode in him, according to the words of the Apostle: " The love of God is poured forth in our hearts by the Holy Ghost, who is given to us " (Rom. v. 5).

This love of God does not, of course, remain unfruitful, but calls forth in the justified soul a special elevation and

---

the intellect and will, but also the inferior powers of the soul, which are subject to reason, so that the whole nature is brought back from weakness and disinclination into proper order, and strengthened in its moral activity."

improvement. Not merely occasional, so-called *actual,* graces (of which alone we have thus far spoken) are given to it, but there is established in it also an inward source of higher life, a new life-principle, the so-called *habitual* grace, a quality which is imparted by God to the soul permanently, and which makes it directly or indirectly capable of the noblest of life's activities — namely, a participation in the mysterious life of God, that is, in that perception and love, with which the three divine Persons know and love one another and are thereby inexpressibly happy in their divine eternally active existence. Here on earth this participation in the mysterious life of God is made possible through the " inspired virtues," first of all, through faith, hope and charity, which proceed from the *habitual* grace, as higher principles of action. Since this imparts to the soul an abiding spiritual elevation, it makes possible for the convert a permanent transformation of the whole life, which cannot possibly be produced by purely external, fortuitous impulses. It is true this lasting conversion requires a continual struggle, and it rarely happens that there are not relapses into sin. Usually it is only gradually that the power of grace grants to the convert the victory over his undisciplined inclinations to the world of creation. When, however, the spiritual eye has become purer, it acquires ever deeper insight into the world of revelation, and his faith grows stronger, his joy in virtue constantly increases, and finally the life with Christ and His Church becomes an indispensable need.

Not always, however, does a conversion follow this

course; and not always does the entry into the Catholic Church bring about a spiritual change and improvement. Christ speaks of conversions, the last state of which is worse than the first (Matt. xii. 45), and the Apostle Peter uses the figure of a dog which returns again to its own vomit, and of a sow which, after being washed, wallows once more in the mire (II Peter ii. 22). How can this be explained?

I have already remarked that grace does not take away man's nature with its endowments, but rather presupposes them. " Under the domination of the supernatural the laws of the natural life do not cease to exist; the work of man's creation, with its tasks and duties continues in the work of his redemption and supernatural elevation, and this is well. If God should hide all our mistakes and follies, and remove all the natural and social obstacles to good, the necessity of moral and spiritual self-discipline would disappear, and a moral quietism would establish itself in the soul, which is the opposite of genuine perfection and of likeness to God."

If now, in the case of converts and in general of most Catholics, the supernatural virtues, infused into the soul at baptism, do not arrive at their full development and in fact often come to no development at all, the reason for this lies in the defective state of the intellect, the will and the inferior powers of the soul of the individual. *Man must collaborate with grace,* if it is to lead him to spiritual freedom. Without the energetic effort of man's free will and without the intervention of the natural virtues, prudence, jus-

[172]

tice, fortitude, moderation etc., the supernatural powers and aptitudes cannot develop their beneficent activity.*

In many instances conversion comes too late. The propensity to sin has become so strong by reason of long continued habit that it always gains the upper hand. The imagination is thoroughly corrupt and the will extremely weak, and if the neophyte is not, at least in the beginning, protected from temptation, and is not disciplined with great wisdom, he remains the same poor creature he was before. Only a miracle of grace in the true sense of the word could in such a case cause a change, since God in this instance would have to supplement the natural powers by special graces, or stimulate them to action in an extraordinary way.

Hence every one asks himself, when he hears of a conversion, " Will he or she hold out? " I think one can answer the question definitely in the affirmative; first, if the convert has led a virtuous life before his conversion and entry into the Catholic Church, and has become a Catholic from profound conviction, and not merely in consequence of external circumstances or compulsion; secondly, if he feels a great need to penetrate more deeply into the mysteries of his faith, and thirdly, if the neophyte from the moment of his conversion, energetically contends with certain vices and shows great repentance after occasional relapses.

In the first case he will find again in the Catholic Church

* This truth Christ Himself portrayed clearly and strikingly in the parable of the sower (Luke viii. 4–15). Everywhere the same seed of grace and faith is sown, but, according to the different kinds of soil on which it falls, it has a different fate, and is either fruitful or worthless.

[173]

all that he formerly prized and loved and much more besides, which will be to him a source of continual surprise and joy. In the second and third cases the convert has found the right connection with the sources of supernatural power. " The truth shall set him free " (John viii. 32), the good will little by little drive away the evil, and the love of purity will prepare the way to a higher knowledge.

AFTER having explained in a general way the importance of the *natural* capacities and virtues for the activity of the *supernatural* virtues and impulses, in connection with which their curative, elevating and accumulative power must be always considered, we may very properly ask, What natural qualities and virtues did the grace of baptism find in me? If I dare to make a brief résumé of them, I do so, believing the words of the Apostle: " What have you which you have not received? " (I Cor. iv. 7), and also with gratitude to God, who gave me good parents.

I had, first of all, a sound mind, practical common sense, and versatile gifts, and furthermore a love of truth, simplicity and gentleness, enthusiasm for the beautiful, and joy in my art, which I at times pursued with great patience and tenacity. I was amiable in my behaviour and naturally cheerful, yet could be also serious, I was never a jester. Ingenuous, yet at the same time shrewd, I was quick to decide and prompt to act. I recovered from disappointments easily, and was in general an optimist. Excessive ambition and a desire to dominate did not form part of my character, yet I liked very much the work of organisation. Finally, I had a sensitive heart, without being susceptible.

It would be incorrect to conclude from this self-revelation that I possessed a purely sanguine temperament, even if many things might seem to indicate it. My temperament had at that time already a tendency to melancholy, and I have also something phlegmatic and choleric in my disposition.

But it is time now to go on with the story of my life.

ITALY: Florence and Rome

I wanted to end my sojourn in Saint Nolff worthily. Hence on the morning of my departure for Italy I went to Holy Communion. This third Communion in my life was exceedingly efficacious. I was in haste and made only a very short prayer of thanksgiving, but when I had come again to my room, the Sacrament once more cast its spell upon me and forced me to my knees. Converts are often at the beginning visited with such perceptible graces. God wishes to bind the still wavering soul to Himself. After taking leave of the rector, his vicar and my dear hosts, I went to the railway. Once more I looked from the train upon the blessed village, birthplace of my faith. Friends waved to me from many windows a cordial farewell, and with a grateful look I greeted for the last time the two little granite-gray, moss-covered churches, which a year before had so powerfully attracted me, as I travelled by.

In Auray I met again my friend Ballin, and our journey together across France began. During the forenoon the weather was somewhat misty, but we saw that the country in the neighbourhood of Nantes which abounds in streams had, with its beautiful groves of trees and attractive castles, a genuinely French character, rich, luxuriant and tasteful. As we travelled more to the east and south, the country became hilly, yet rather monotonous and dry.

Moreover, as the day advanced the sky became steadily brighter, and by evening was entirely clear. The mighty disk of the sun set fiery red, and then came night. We tried to sleep, but in vain. In the miserable French railway-car we were too much jolted about. A married couple, round as balls, who sat opposite to us, were more successful, for they leaned against each other.

On the following morning, we arrived at Lyons. We were in the best of spirits, even if we had not rested well.

Travel is for man a delight. It is so sweet to escape for a time from the regular round of domestic duties and, in the sense that one is a stranger in the country through which one is passing, to be *free*. Formerly every journeyman used to go on his travels, after he had, as an apprentice, served his master for years in affectionate submissiveness. That was indeed a happy time, which was not passed in haste and workingmen's disorders. A fortunate era, when the seriousness of old age was mellowed by the recollection of the joyful years of youthful wandering, and when the memory of all the countries, with their cities and villages, through which one had then travelled, wove a brilliant background for the stage of later life.

We visited in Lyons the museum and many noble churches, and strolled about the city the entire day. Then when evening came, we went again to the station and boarded the night-train, which was to convey us to Italy. At daybreak Ballin awakened me. " Jan," he exclaimed, " just look out of the window. My God, what a marvellous

[177]

country! " The train was passing through a wild, mountainous region. Such high mountains I had never seen. Clouds of mist hung about the summits, and much water dropped from the trees and purled in little brooks down from the heights. I was full of admiration, but this Alpine scenery did not seem to me to be the real Italy; it was too northern, damp and foggy. From Chambéry on we had been alone in the compartment, but now an Italian merchant came in, who spoke French well and gave us some information about this region. About eight o'clock in the morning we steamed into the railway station of Turin, where we had to change trains.

Our goal for the present was Florence, the city of the Medici. From Turin to Florence we had pleasant company. It consisted of two Florentine ladies and a French nun, a Little Sister of the Poor. The two ladies were returning from a business trip through France to their native city; the sister, hitherto stationed in Turin, was also travelling to Florence.

I can hardly recall pleasanter travelling companions than those Italian ladies. They were friendly, lively, cordial and quite unconventional in their behaviour, yet they knew how to combine with this true womanliness. The French nun seemed to want to edify us, but she did not succeed. In such things one must not " want." Her words betrayed a defective ascetic training, which affected me painfully. But for this one should not blame the little nun; she was doubtless a good little sister. But nuns on a journey, outside the cloister, are like geese out of water; they are not in their element. Like every one else, they must be observed in their own sphere of activity, if one would rightly estimate them.

In the north the joy of life is hidden in the cosy home; in Italy it descends laughingly from the blue sky upon a happy humanity, circulates freely under the brilliant sun or lingers in luxuriant gardens, where the grain ripens under heavy-laden orchards and the vines are entwined in garlands from tree to tree. It also lies outspread upon the deep blue sea, over which glide the swiftly moving ships with coloured sails; it manifests itself aloud in song, and gives itself expression in the dances of its gaily dressed children. And this joy of life is imparted also to the sons and daughters of the north, who tread the sunny soil of Italy. We drank it in with deep draughts, as the train passed alternately groves of olive trees and the blue sea, and as brightly tinted villas in the midst of fruitful gardens greeted us from the neighbouring hills, whose inmates seemed to call out to us travellers: "Come, you who live in so much haste and in the rush of business; come, rest with us and enjoy the happiness of this fair land, so blessed by God. Here also labour flourishes; behold our well-tilled fields and well-kept gardens. But here is also rest, which many of you scarcely know. Here Mary and Martha dwell together in harmony."

Yes, Bethany, where Jesus often spent the night, the Mount of Olives, where He mourned, the mountains of Judaea through which Mary hastened on her visit to Elizabeth, the fig tree, which at Christ's word withered, and much more besides from Holy Scripture, revealed themselves and found their explanation on our journey.

On the third evening after our departure we approached Florence, and it was already night when we arrived at the station of *Santa Maria Novella*. We took a carriage and drove to the *Casa Nardini,* a pension, which had been recommended to Ballin. We had no idea what artistic treasures we thus passed in the darkness. Florence seemed like any other city. But suddenly, flooded with electric light, the dazzling white-marble façade of the cathedral rose before us. The sight was enchanting. We uttered a cry of joy, and with thankful hearts made the sign of the cross.

The next morning at five o'clock we were aroused from sleep by a deep, solemn voice. It was that of the great bell in the cathedral tower, and it called to us: " Brethren, it is now the hour for us to rise from sleep; watch and pray " (Rom. xiii. 11; Matt. xxvi. 41). We listened to the deep vibrations with delight. Many a suffering invalid also may have rejoiced to hear it, to whom it brought the promise of release from a weary vigil of loneliness and pain.

How beautiful in the stillness of the night is the sound of different church-bells! Yet what wonderful audacity it requires deliberately to awaken those who sleep. Certainly only the Church should allow herself to do that. She has the right to do so, since she must always admonish us to watchfulness. Of course this pious disturber of the peace has been suppressed in many places, and instead of it we now must hear the hideous rattling and ringing of trams and the abominable honking of automobiles. Today we are not longer told to " watch and pray," but to " step lively and rush," for time is money and money is power, and power permits pleasure. But after all what is pleasure? Alas, one must continually ask that question, till finally one sees what the things, of which one is so proud, are really worth. And pleasure eventually breeds disgust. Is not that true? Yes, God be thanked, it is true; for that fact has brought many a sinner to his senses, and given to him again an appreciation of what it means to watch and pray.

ALMOST every one who travels through Italy for the first time receives his strongest impression, not from Venice, Rome or Naples, but from Florence. The city on the Arno is indebted for this power of impressiveness to the harmonious style of its monuments of art, which do not, like the art-treasures of Rome, have their origin in totally different epochs. Moreover they are not, like those of Rome, scattered about in all directions, but are arranged near one another in an almost unbroken series.

Florence in its art is a city eternally young. Within its walls the greatest men of Italy have passed the morning of their lives. There they completed their earliest works which were full of such great promise, and there they created a youthful art, which has remained still capable of development. It is this which has always so endeared Florence to young artists, who can educate themselves only by means of such art and it can become acquainted with it only here. Finally, Florence is the city of Beatrice and her companions, and the city wherein the Blessed Virgin and virginity have enjoyed the highest honour. Everything beautiful that Florence offers is youthful, budding, and still in process of growth. It is the city of youth.

When we took our first walks through Florence and its environs, we could hardly believe that we were so far from home. It did not seem to us that we were strangers there at all, and we felt as much in our element as a fish in water. In the midst of the flood of beauty which everywhere streamed out to meet us we moved with rapture. We found pleasure in everything, and poured out upon everything our kindly feelings; hence everything appeared to us lovable and beautiful. And without a trace of fatigue. Was it the soft air, or was it the fiery wine? We breathed so freely, we were in such high spirits, and we experienced such immense pleasure. Only before the different works of art did we become silent and serious, and called each other's attention to their beauty in whispers, with the mute longing in our hearts to make once something similar.

Although I was not a good pedestrian, I could not for the first week, walk about enough. Ballin was amazed at this, and had finally to give up going with me. Then alone, but wonderfully happy, I wandered through the environs of Florence. There were endless walks mostly between gardens enclosed by high walls. For a long while I saw nothing but their white-washed surfaces, over which looked down olive and fig trees, from which hung roses and climbing-plants, until suddenly a gateway permitted a distant view of the city of the Arno in the amphitheatre of the valley. Above the sea of houses rose the cupola and campanile of the *Duomo,* as well as the *Vecchio,* the municipal palace, with the high, slender tower of its front wall, and also the *Palazzo Pitti* and *Palazzo Strozzi.* And I went on and on with jubilation in my heart, and gazed and gazed, and feasted my eyes, and thought only of the joy which I experienced. For, in the midst of contemplation such as that, reasoning ceases.

After Ballin and I had spent a week in the *Casa Nardini,* we sought a cheaper pension, and found one in the *Via Fesulana,* named so probably because at the end of the long vista of this street one sees the hill of Fiesole, on the crest of which stand the seminary and the cloister of the Franciscans. We had gone out to seek a new abode in a pouring rain, and on this occasion saw much that was amusing. In making the arrangements Ballin was spokesman. He had learned Latin at school and knew at least the Italian numerals. Now and then he appeared to be speaking this language with tolerable fluency, only no one could understand him. He assented to all the conditions which the people made, and assured them usually that we would come again that evening, if we found nothing to suit us better. But hardly had the house-door closed behind us, when we seized each other by the arm, and laughed and laughed till we almost burst. " Again nothing," Ballin would then say, and on we went through the pouring rain. I still recall a visit made to the house of an opera-singer who, she told us, had just returned with her husband from an operatic tour in the Argentine. In the reception-room stood a grand piano, while on the walls hung great wreaths with broad coloured ribbons. Where had we seen this couple? All at once it came to us. In the *Fliegende Blätter* in a sketch of the famous Oberländer. We also entered the house of a ruined noble family, as well as the apartment of a lively Italian lady, who asked only eighty lire a month for board and lodging. We would have gladly taken this, but her numerous children and a lot of unattractive looking furniture, standing about, frightened us away. In the pension in the *Via Fesulana* we each paid one hundred lire a month, and for this obtained a bedroom and sitting-room in common, and good food. At the commencement of the 'nineties life was still cheap in Florence, and, in addition, the Italian rate of exchange was very low. For a hundred francs we then received one hundred and thirteen lire in Italian paper money, a substantial profit, which allowed us to go to a café daily and to smoke. With all that, however, our purses were almost always empty, when the end of the month came. Once we had on the twentieth only fifteen centesimi left. We deliberated a long time what we should do with them, and finally decided to smoke them up. It is much more decent, thought Ballin, to have nothing more, than to have only fifteen centesimi. We therefore bought a cheroot, cut it in halves, and watched with joyful hearts our last money disappear in smoke. The situation was romantic, but still it was horrible to live an entire week without tobacco, and we were destined to regret bitterly the fact that we had consumed thus our last centesimo. On the first of the month I received from my father a check for four hundred francs. We joyfully hastened to the banker; but, alas! a stamp of fifteen centesimi was wanting on the check. We had to go away, therefore, without the money. We then explained to our landlady the distress in which we found ourselves, and she laughingly gave us the three soldi; she had herself known such situations. We did not show ourselves again, however, the whole day, but ran about Florence and its environs until it had become night.

WEEKS went by and Ballin had not yet been baptised. In the pension, however, we both passed for believing Catholics. Every Sunday and holy day we went to High Mass in the neighbouring church of the Servites, the *Sanctissima Annunziata.* The service there was always very solemn. After the Servite Fathers had chanted *Tierce,* a polyphonic Mass was regularly celebrated with an instrumental accompaniment, a custom which originated in the time of the Hapsburg rulers. The solos were often of great beauty, even though the singers after the Italian style forced their voices too much.

My daily intercourse with Ballin was at first a disadvantage to my religious development. He had not yet the full grace of the Christian, and by reason of his fiery temperament was very much exposed to temptation. I therefore found in him no support, when a great temptation came to me also; on the contrary he precipitated my fall. For I did fall, after having made a long resistance. On that day I went to sleep without praying. The child goes out of his father's way, when he has done wrong. On the following

[185]

morning, however, Ballin and I were standing in the church of *Santa Croce,* in one of the side chapels which Giotto painted, at the right of the high altar. I was silently contemplating the scene from the life of John the Baptist, in which the daughter of Herodias dances before Herod, who sits with a gloomy expression at table with his guests. At the left a handsome youth plays on a violin, a wonderful bit of painting. Before this picture I was seized with deep remorse. It was as if Christ Himself tenderly reproached me with my sin, and yet so gently that I could only love Him for his gentleness. I found again words of prayer, words of repentance, words of love to God. I was saved. Yet I wanted to confess my sin that very day, and after lunch I disappeared, ran to *San Domenico* and went into the church of the cloister, for which Fra Angelico painted the great altar-picture, which I had so often admired in the Louvre. After a short prayer I climbed the steep path to Fiesole, and rang the bell at the door of the Jesuit monastery, where at that time the General of the Order still resided. I had received from the well-known Jesuit, Father du Lac, with whom I had become acquainted in the days of my preparation for baptism in Vannes, a letter of recommendation to a father, whose name I have forgotten. I was fortunate and found him at home. But it is always difficult to confess. I could not bring myself to tell the father precisely why I had come. It was only at the end of the call, when I was taking my leave, that I said I would come again soon to confess. The father did not, however, let me go and said, " Come, my young friend,

[186]

let us begin today." How gladly I consented. He led me to his poorly furnished room, where I made my confession. Up in the cathedral of Fiesole I made my thanksgiving and my penance. When I left the cathedral with a lighter heart, I thought. "How good it is, after all, to be a Catholic." Only I was ashamed to have received so light a penance from the father.

My fall was for both of us a good lesson, and we became more careful. We perceived little by little whose hand was in this plot, and who it was who wished to enslave us again, after we had become free through faith. But we had not yet found the way to that love of God which preserves us best from sin, and in fact excludes it.

A saint was to show us this way. It was Saint Francis of Assisi. Ballin discovered him. He had never abandoned his plan of being instructed and baptised, but did not know to whom to apply. Stimulated by what he had read of Lacordaire, he would have preferred to commit himself to the care of a Dominican, for he thought that they were the best theologians and that he needed an excellent one. But could he find one in Italy who spoke French? I must today reproach myself with having been of too little assistance to my friend in his conversion. I was far too much occupied with myself. I wanted to be, and felt that I was destined to be, a *somebody*.

While Ballin was copying some details of the frescoes in the *Cappella Spagnuola,* I sketched and painted in the gallery of the *Uffizi.* But one day, after lunch, Ballin wanted to paint my portrait. "Sit quietly, your head a little to the right," he said. I obeyed. After a few minutes he again admonished me, "But sit *still*." I lost my patience, and shouted back at him. Ballin stood up, threw down his sketching-board on the floor, took his hat and said, "Good day." I had not expected that. Night came, and Ballin did not return home. This made me uneasy. During the dinner, however, he appeared. He was in good spirits, gave me his hand, and said, "Excuse me, I was a little nervous this afternoon." Then he continued at once, "You would never guess where I have been." "Well?" I asked. "In a cloister," he said mysteriously, "in fact, in two cloisters." "By Jove," I exclaimed enthusiastically, "in one cloister, in fact in two cloisters?" The word *cloister* had always made an impression on me ever since my childhood, whenever I had heard it or read it. "Yes," continued Ballin, "and you must see one of them tomorrow. I have promised to go back there with you tomorrow afternoon." The other people rose from the table, but I remained sitting by my friend. And now he related to me how he had wandered about at random, and how his steps had led him to *San Domenico*. Suddenly the thought had occurred to him to ask for instruction for baptism there in the Dominican cloister. Yet they had not been very cordial in the matter. They had indeed listened to him, but had excused themselves, saying that for the moment there was no one in the cloister to take him in charge. "Apply to the Franciscans in Fiesole," they had said to him as he was leaving, "there are several fathers there who speak French." So, without reflecting about it long, he had climbed the hill of Fiesole. Up in the Franciscan cloister he had been received with the greatest cordiality. They at once declared themselves ready to assist him, and showed great interest in him. He had at first spoken with a Father Norbert, a celebrated preacher, then with an elderly father who had been a missionary in Egypt, and finally with a younger father from Naples. " Those fathers," he said, " have fine heads, and how beautiful it is up there. A veritable paradise. Their cells are very small; one can hardly turn round in them. Each father has a little writing-table, a chest for clothes, a bed with a sack of straw, a little oil-lamp and a book-rack. It is a subject for a picture, how the monk sits behind his little table and writes. From the small windows of the cells one looks down into the valley of the Arno, as far as Pistoja. Behind the cloister is a most romantic little forest of stone-pines. But you will see all that yourself tomorrow," concluded my friend.

Ballin then lit a cigarette and blew away its little clouds of smoke, quite lost in thought, and with the air of comfort, characteristic of a man who has just enjoyed a sumptuous repast.

THE next day the electric tram, which then still started from the *Piazza San Marco,* brought us to Fiesole. Whoever has made the ascent from Florence to the old Etruscan city on a sunny day and who from *San Domenico,* a sort of halfway station thither, has been borne upward into ever more enchanting regions of beauty, and who then upon the hill above, where the view is finest, has seated himself upon the bench, which an Englishman caused to be constructed there for his "brothers, the travellers and pilgrims," and thence has gazed upon the city of flowers garlanded with gardens, will never forget that day. It is doubtful if anything more beautiful than that view exists in the whole world.

I still remember an Italian who, on one such ascent was quite beside himself with astonishment and exclaimed continually, " *Che bellezza, che bellezza!* " (How beautiful, how beautiful!)

Having reached Fiesole, we first visited the old basilica, though I still had little appreciation in those days of its severe beauty; then we climbed to the top of the hill, where any further ascent is impossible, and stood before the door of the Franciscan cloister. Upon this portal, protected from the weather by a covering of glass, was attached the following characteristic Italian maxim:

Un Dio solo! Se mi è inemico, chi mi salverà?
Un'anima sola! Se la perdo, che sarà di me?
Il primo peccato? Può esser l'ultimo. Se lo fosse, sono già
    dannato!
E poi? E poi bisogna finalmente morire.

Only one God! if He is hostile to me, who will save me?
Only one soul! if I lose it, what will then become of me?
The first sin? It may be the last. If so, I am already lost.
And then? Then finally I must die.

[190]

ITALY: FLORENCE AND ROME

The Italian is often poorly instructed in his religion, but he usually knows a few such pithy maxims and wise sentences which contain the whole substance of faith. Thus he speaks willingly of "the God-Christ," of "Christ in the Holy Sacrament," of "the Lord," of "the Good Shepherd" and especially of the "Great Mother of God," and of the "Madonna." It is in her that he finds most easily a connection with the supernatural and the symbol of his best sentiments. The Italian is, it is true, quick tempered, but he is nevertheless naturally kind-hearted. *Ci vuole pazienza* (One must have patience) is his favourite expression, and in suffering he often carries this sentiment to the point of heroism. Thus he is saved after his own fashion, and frequently finds the path to sanctity.

AFTER we had read the maxim on the door, Ballin rang the bell. A deep, resonant tone, as powerful as the call of a man, resounded and gradually died away. For a long time nothing stirred. Behind the door all remained solemn and still. It was only after some minutes that we heard a clattering of sandals, which came nearer and nearer. A huge key was turned in the lock and a tall, vigorous, brown-robed brother stood before us. He had piercing eyes, suitable for a porter, which evidently knew how to distinguish between people, but which assumed at once a smiling expression, when they saw us. Ballin wanted to kiss the monk's hand, but he did not allow him to do so. Then we stood for a moment together and talked a little in broken sentences and with friendly gestures. But what our eyes saw

[191]

was characterized by so much tenderness and charm that we soon ceased to speak.

We stood in a narrow, covered corridor, which enclosed on three sides a small paved court-yard, the open roof of which was supported by little columns, which rested on a wall surrounding the court-yard to a height of about three feet. On the right, the corridor was interrupted by a low structure with numerous little windows of the cells in the second story. In the centre stood a well which appeared, however, to be out of use. One felt oneself, in this paradise of silence and peace, miles away from the world. A handsome cat sprang down, and coming to us rubbed herself caressingly against the robe of the barefooted porter. "Come," said the monk. We turned into a long passageway, on either side of which cells had been built into the walls. Before the last of these on the right we halted and knocked. "*Avanti*," cried a deep voice, and when we opened the door we saw Father Norbert, the preacher, sitting behind his writing-table, enveloped in a large mantle. He greeted us with the vivacity of the southerner, and asked us to be seated, one on the clothes-chest, the other on a chair. It was very cold in the cell, and yet how attractive. All the pieces of furniture and other objects were so near one another, the bed, the clothes-chest, the *prie-dieu,* the writing-table and the book-rack. We had hardly exchanged a few words, when the aged Father Placido and the young Father Giovacchino also came to greet us. Now it was literally no longer possible to move in the cell. The three fathers surveyed us wonderingly, and we them. We seemed to one an-

[192]

other such strange beings. They could hardly understand how two such modern men as we had ever found the way to the Catholic faith and we, for our part, were delighted with that spirit of cheerfulness, readiness to serve and cordiality, which animated these men. It was the spirit of the great " poor man of Assisi " which had been transmitted to his sons. We soon came to speak of their spiritual father, and informed ourselves about the rules and usages of the convent. Father Norbert loaned us a life of Saint Francis of Assisi by Father de Chérancé and also the *Fioretti*. After we had passed again through the cloister and had admired the little grove of cypresses, we returned to Florence on foot talking, of course, of what we had seen and heard in the monastery on the height.

THE great poor man of Assisi now became our spiritual father too. It was his wonderful life and example that first really initiated us into the essential character of Christianity. Saint Francis " systematized in us the spirit of love " and enflamed it. He taught us how transient are created things, and awakened in us enthusiasm for eternal blessings. He taught us humility, resignation and renunciation. He made us gentle and generous, and communicated to us his amiability and joy. We must have been good young fellows in those days of our first real zeal and love. I still remember how we sent photographs to all our friends, to the nabis, to Drahtmann and others, although we certainly were not rich. But we had economized, and so some money still remained above expenses. Ballin presented me with his white shirts, as he did not want to wear any more such articles of apparel, but only woolen and coloured shirts with a soft collar and narrow tie. He also gave up eating meat, and all this out of a love for simplicity. Sometimes, to his great amusement, I compared his meals to the food which Saint Francis collected by begging, a horrible mixture. Yet notwithstanding this, he still remained the *grand seigneur,* and desired absolutely that each of us should wear a large ring of mediaeval style. I objected decidedly to this, however, and called him a spendthrift. Thereupon he gave up the idea. But to another proposition of his I assented gladly. It was that we should offer up an expiatory sacrifice to the Madonna by Cimabue in *Santa Maria Novella* for having been removed (it is true, already many years before) from the high altar into a side chapel, where she was much admired but less venerated. We bought from a flower-dealer, to her great astonishment, her entire stock of chrysanthemums, and took them to the church. The altar, above which the picture of the Madonna hangs, had no altarcloths, but that suited us exactly, and we covered it with flowers, and prayed for a short time before the lovely picture. A Dominican brother approached and wanted to bring vases at once, in order to put the flowers in them, but that we would not allow. We thought it was so much more beautiful as it was. The brother let us have our way, but the next day the flowers had been forced into two large vases.

Another painting of the Madonna of which we were very fond hangs in *Santa Maria Maggiore,* over an altar at the left of the entrance. We rarely passed this church, without going in to venerate the picture. I subsequently made a copy of it for Ballin.

SOME days before Christmas, Ballin retired to the cloister at Fiesole, to prepare himself for his baptism under the instruction of Father Giovacchino. On Christmas Eve I was also there and with childlike simplicity and joy we celebrated for the first time, as believing Christians, the birth of our Lord.

The remembrance of Saint Francis, who loved this festival above all others, and the touching piety of his sons helped us over many a liturgical inadequacy and put us in the right frame of mind.

The aged Father Placido sang the midnight Mass. He continually cleared his throat and shouted fearfully. It was beautiful nevertheless. Our own piety held out against all that. The next day I returned to Fiesole, but Ballin remained. He was to receive baptism on the vigil of Epiphany.

The Tuscan province of the Franciscans has a hospice for their travelling brothers near the *Barriera della Quercia*. There I met Father Giovacchino and Ballin on the morning of the vigil of Epiphany.

My friend was sunk in profound pious reflection when I wished to greet him. He was very silent and serious, and quite absorbed in his own thoughts. He seemed to have passed the last few days in continual prayer. I scarcely recognized him any more. Ballin had found in Father Giovacchino an admirable instructor. This Franciscan was an able theologian, a lover of mysticism, and a good confessor and preacher. From his earliest youth he had been educated in the cloister, and had literally grown up in the robe and cowl. Such an education has certainly its defects, but if it turns out well, it gives to the man who receives it that assurance of attitude and action which one also finds in officers of high rank, who have as boys already worn the king's uniform. And as the latter become in every fibre of their being soldiers, so too the former become in every fibre of their being monks and priests, precisely because they are *absolutely what they claim to be,* and do not become ordinary routine-men, who are always unstable.

Father Giovacchino evinced great vivacity and cordiality, and had in his manners something of that " grand air " which the Spanish influence implanted in Naples.

The hour came when we had to break off our conversation, and go to the palace of the bishop of Florence, Prince Donato di San Clemente, who was to baptise my friend Ballin. He was a tall thin man, of a noble appearance, who received us with great affability. Soon we were standing in the ante-room of his private chapel. He put on the amice, the alb, the cincture and the stole, and the long ceremony of the baptism of an adult began. One occurrence has remained vividly in my memory. When the moment came for Ballin to go from the ante-room, where the first exorcisms had been spoken over him, into the chapel itself, to pronounce his confession of faith before the altar, he did not stand up, but dragged himself thither on his knees, which made an amusing and yet touching impression. He

[196]

uttered his confession of faith clearly and emphatically, while the bishop, bending towards him, listened attentively, to be sure that he said everything correctly. In the act of baptism itself I, as my friend's godfather, put my hand on his shoulder. Afterwards the bishop read the Mass, in the course of which Ballin received his first Holy Communion.

"How do you feel?" I asked Ballin, when we stood again in the street. "Overwhelmed," was his reply; and it will be remembered that I also had the same feeling after my baptism. "What shall we do today?" I inquired further. "Let us first order a bouquet for the bishop for tomorrow's festival," said Ballin, "and then go out into the country. I cannot sit down today at the table in the pension." The day was a long one. That night, before going to bed, Ballin knelt down reverently and prayed. Up to that time I had always said my prayers while lying in bed. He was much more thoroughly converted after his baptism than I after mine. We felt now like two brothers, who had been united to each other by a common fate.

WHENEVER Ballin related to me details about his stay in the Franciscan cloister at Fiesole, and told me of all that he had seen and heard there, he would conclude with the words: "We ought to spend a couple of months there; that would be something immense." One day we inquired in the cloister whether such a thing was quite impossible. We were told that only the General of the Order in Rome could grant the permission to do so. For a long time we had planned a journey to the Eternal City and hesitated now

[197]

no longer. We asked for a letter of introduction to the Father General and in the middle of January took leave of Florence. Before our departure, however, we had had ourselves inscribed in the Third Order of Saint Francis. On our way to Rome we stopped in Sienna, although we had already made the acquaintance of this wonderful city, as well as Pisa, Lucca and Pistoia, having paid visits to these art-centres from Florence. The mediaeval city of Sienna was entirely to our taste, pre-eminently on account of its art. The school of painting there has never wholly abandoned its original primitive character, and even there, where influences of the early renaissance are powerful, it remains true to its tradition and its lyric art, and never descends to naturalism. The Siennese painters, Duccio di Buoninsegna, Ambrogio Lorenzetti and Simone Martini were, with Giotto and Orcagna, the artists whom we liked best. No wonder. Their paintings were the result of the religious enthusiasm which the appearance of Saint Francis had called forth in Italy. We found again the spirit of our saintly father in these works of art, and that strong will which always seeks especially to seize and to realise the inner value of things, without caring much whether the external form in which this inner value manifests itself, reaches its highest expression. But we loved Sienna not only for its art, but also because the memory of two Saints, Saint Catherine and San Bernardino, is still so vivid there, and because the surroundings in which they both lived and worked have, so to speak, maintained themselves intact. When one passes through the streets of Sienna, one thinks

[198]

that he may meet at any moment the tall, spare figure of San Bernardino, and imagines that he sees approaching in the distance Saint Catherine, riding on a donkey and accompanied by two Dominicans, and that she has been again at the court of the Pope, and has once more conjured him to return to Rome and to give up his sojourn in Avignon. If one visits the house of this steadfast and suffering bride of Christ, one would like, in any one of its little corners where she was wont to pray, to bury oneself in her writings, in order, carried away by her love, to partake somewhat of that joy which she experienced in her interviews with God. Prayer comes to one easily in this little sanctuary, as also in the chapel, which is consecrated to Saint Catherine in the church of *San Domenico,* where Sodoma has painted such wonderfully beautiful frescoes in which her spirit is in ecstasy with God, as she sinks, fainting, in the arms of two nuns.

The head of the saint is truly of a supernatural beauty, a masterpiece of art, which has remained indelible in my memory.

Of course we visited in Sienna also the great Franciscan monastery which is situated a half-hour distant from the city, the so-called *Osservanza.* Father Giovacchino of Naples had given us a letter of recommendation to Father Frediano Gianini, at that time reader of theology. This father, who subsequently became custodian of the Holy Places in Palestine and then Apostolic Delegate of Syria, was, like Father Giovacchino, a Franciscan of profound theological knowledge. Like the latter, he had worn the

Franciscan robe from his earliest youth, and his character had developed most harmoniously. When I recall this priest and monk, then about thirty years of age, with his crown of raven-black hair around a massive, smoothly shaven head, with his dark, intelligent eyes, his aquiline nose and firm mouth, and especially when I think of the quiet self-assurance of this attractive, because perfectly harmonious, personality, I feel like crying out to the enemies of the Church and its convents in Italy: "You who are blind! when will you perceive that your most eminent men are ecclesiastics? When will you see that you in reality have reason to be proud of saints like the blessed Cottolengo (†·1842) and the blessed Don Bosco (+ 1888) of Papal figures such as Pius IX, Leo XIII, Pius X and Benedict XV, and of cardinals like Rampolla, Ferrari and Gasparri? When will you believe the assertion of us foreigners, that you possess in very many monasteries in your beautiful land delightful oases which for travellers are among the most comforting and reviving things that can be found in your midst? Cease, then, at last to fight among yourselves even if in order to possess so many eminent men and sacred places, you have to put up with a few difficulties."

I have preserved for Father Frediano a true attachment. With what love and patience he listened to us, when we, in our repeated visits, enthusiastically laid before him our plans for the future. The life of Saint Francis and that of his first companions haunted us continually, and our dearest dream was to lead a similar life as tertiaries in the world. It vexed us that we had not the right to wear the habit of the Order, as the tertiaries had done in the Middle Ages; for we thought that, dressed in the robe of the Franciscans, we should have an entirely different authority, as preachers of the truth, and at the same time a great protection against the temptations of the world. We wanted to convert all our friends, to whom priests and monks had now no chance of access. We were ready and willing to undergo any kind of trial, for example, that of " begging our way " on a long journey, or that of " painting our way "; that is to say, we were desirous of painting, in return for our food and lodging, pictures of the Madonna and the saints on the walls of the houses of the villages through which we passed. And we wished moreover to make the entire journey on foot. That may have made on Father Frediano a specially strong impression, for Italians have a dread of pedestrian tours. He encouraged us at all events, and did not find the idea a bad one. Our enthusiasm was also perfectly genuine, only we overrated our moral force, and did not see how much of a desire to talk at random and to wander about as tramps, lay hidden behind our plans. Gradually, however, a slight perception of our foolishness dawned upon us, for we caught ourselves several times speaking most eloquently of piety, the spirit of prayer, fasting and abstinence just when we were enjoying a dessert following a good dinner. This seemed even to us suspicious, and hence we became little by little more reasonable and modest.

One morning we started for Rome, and towards noon the magnificent dome of St. Peter's, the distinctive mark of the Eternal City, greeted us in the distance.

YESTERDAYS OF AN ARTIST-MONK

ROME is not a city for beginners in art. It has seldom cradled a great artist. Under its protection, however, the most gifted men have found the highest development of their ability and strength for their greatest achievements. Rome is the city for an artist of maturity, when vaguely perceptive, tentative and timid sensibility is no longer the only guide in his creative work, as it was in youth, but when, through a clear perception of the rules of form and a complete mastery of the means of artistic expression, he has either already overcome that condition of mind, or is trying to do so.

And what I say of artists applies also to those saints who have come in great numbers to Rome from other lands and cities. Here their sanctity has ripened into its fullest maturity and here also their powers have reached their full development. We have only to think of the saintly Didacus, John of God, Felix of Cantalizio, Philip Neri and so many others, all truly immortal. Many of them were, like the Roman Saint Benedict,* legislators for a numerous spiritual posterity worthy pupils of legislative Rome. For Rome is a law-giver, and therein lies her importance and her power. Rome is not content with mere ideal views, noble sentiments and suggestions. She insists on putting these into an external form, which has been perfectly completed. Above all, she insists on objectivity. People who have merely "good ideas" are not much esteemed there. Such people should go to Paris, where they can celebrate their

* It is true, St. Benedict was born in Nursia in the Province of Perugia, not far from Rome, but he came from an old Italian family, studied in Rome and was in spirit a thorough Roman.

successes of a day. So long as the new idea has not reached a *definite form,* it cannot make any impression on Rome. Until then she is satisfied with the good ideas of the past. Indeed her love of form goes so far that she prefers mechanical work and even rigidity to the "free and easy" and the formless. Rome is the "Eternal City." A theory that is still in a state of fermentation and, therefore, not destined to be permanent, she rejects and if it asserts itself too impudently condemns it. A dog that is too demonstrative must be restrained, even if in its joy it makes here and there some graceful bounds. Rome has in itself nothing narrow, small or provincial, but is truly a universal metropolis. The whole world finds itself at home there. Yet Rome is not at all of the type that can be called graceful, pretty, charming, ingenuous, intimate or childlike; it is rather full of dignity, noble, virile and mature. In fact it is the maturest city in the world.

It is in this way that I look upon Rome today, and I think that those who have dwelt there for a long time or have often visited it will agree with me. I understand now also very well why Rome at first did not especially please us. Some reasons for this I have already given, but the greatest of all was that we missed there too painfully the spirit and the monuments of the Middle Ages. That which had so appealed to us in the Franciscan ideal, the special stress laid upon the spiritual and personal, seemed to be regarded in Rome as of little importance. Moreover there was not in Rome a trace of Umbrian amiability, or of Florentine graciousness, but everything was classically cold

[203]

and pompous in a way that is unchristian. Only the mosaics of the antiquated basilicas spoke a language which we could understand. As for the rest — In the bitterness of our disappointment the huge clumsy angels which, near the entrance of St. Peter support the basin of holy water seemed the perfect embodiment of the Roman ideal of art. The paintings of Michelangelo in the Sistine chapel we admired, of course, but we preferred the frescoes of Botticelli, Perugino and Pinturicchio on the side walls of that famous chapel. The frescoes of Raphael in the *Stanze* pleased us, it is true, but those of Fra Angelico in the chapel of Nicholas V we considered much more beautiful in colour.

And such was, necessarily, the experience of two young artist-converts, to whom the ideal of the Franciscans was not only one of the noblest fruits of Christianity, but seemed to be its last and highest revelation.

We should perhaps have fallen into the errors of the Fraticelli, and condemned everything which did not go about in sackcloth, shabby and a little dirty, had not our holy Father Francis taught us a great reverence and love not only for the Church, but for its head and ministrants. That rendered us somewhat cautious in our estimate of things, and restrained us from many a sacrilegious judgment. And finally, although the general impression made upon us by Rome was a very disappointing one, on the other hand many individual objects there pleased us so much, that we too little by little came to love the Eternal City.

[204]

ITALY: FLORENCE AND ROME

We lodged in Rome in the *Via Capo le Case,* not far from the *Piazza di Spagna,* the distinctively foreign quarter. Our house adjoined almost directly a small convent-church, where I often attended early Mass and confessed regularly to an Italian priest, who spoke French and had been a missionary in Australia. We went frequently also to the little church of the Fathers of the Blessed Sacrament in the *Piazza San Claudio,* especially in the evening, for the benediction. The service was celebrated there with great reverence and liturgical seriousness, and the singing was excellent. In no other church in Rome have I found such an atmosphere of prayer, as among these fathers. The Nabi Paul B. (previously mentioned) had entered their Order, and was at that time making his novitiate in Brussels, whence he wrote me repeatedly. He did not, however, remain to make his profession, and soon after left the Catholic Church, was for a few years an itinerant Protestant preacher and finally became, as the solicitous and devoted father of a family, a travelling salesman for hardware and bicycles. My Parisian friends Sérusier and Denis, whenever I asked after him subsequently, spoke with the greatest respect of the love and self-sacrifice of this singular man, and this gives me reason to hope that, before his death, he will find his way again to the Church.

We usually took our meals in the little restaurant of Don Cesare in the *Via Felice,* a continuation of the *Via Sistina.* There we astonished the regular patrons of the establishment, among whom were some journalists and artists, by making no concealment of our religious sentiments. At table we made the sign of the cross before every one and during Lent (which was the first in our experience) we ate only farinaceous food. Sometimes at lunch there would appear in this restaurant artists' models, dressed in the national costume, and one of these beauties, the Roman Bibiana, I frequently sketched and painted. Rome is perhaps the only city where one finds truly beautiful and respectable models.

Ballin met many acquaintances at Rome, for every educated Dane wishes to have been there at least once in his life. The painter Carstens and the sculptor Thorwaldsen may have founded in Denmark this partiality for the Eternal City. Thus through Ballin I became acquainted with several Danes, and among others, the important writer Henrik Pontoppidan, who at the time was very much interested in Catholicism. We were also introduced to the novelist Juhanni Aho, a Finn, and spent some delightful evenings in the company of himself and wife, who was also a painter. Juhanni Aho was interested in everything. Indeed he was returning then from a corner of the world into which not much that was either old or new had yet penetrated. He was glad to have us talk to him of Saint Francis and sat for hours absorbed in reading the *Lives of the Fathers of the Desert*. Even if our conduct did not produce any other results, it is certain that almost all those who associated with us for any length of time became at least a little " infected " with Catholicism.

Like all pilgrims to Rome, Ballin and I visited the principal churches of the Eternal City and the catacombs, prayed

[206]

at the graves of the martyrs and inspected the museums and the Forum.

We had also the joy of seeing the Holy Father, Leo XIII, on the occasion of a canonisation, and while the Pope was carried past us, I bore on my tall shoulders a young negro seminarist, who otherwise would have seen nothing. At a Papal ceremony in St. Peter's a painter-convert, von Rhoden, a well-known figure in the story of the "Nazarenes," procured for us two good places. Unfortunately, however, even though it was then half an hour before the appointed time, we came too late to be admitted into the basilica, and could only enjoy watching the exit of the immense multitude of many thousands of people.

Pontoppidan and his wife were among them, and both were most enthusiastic over the ceremony. It must have been truly something inspiring. At the studio of the above named painter, von Rhoden, I saw for the first time some photographs of sketches made by the Benedictine artist-monks of Beuron. We paid no special attention to these photographs, however, and found the representations stiff and cold. There was wanting in them the Franciscan warmth of Giotto, and where we found this lacking, nothing could please us.

With a certain reverence we made a pilgrimage, near the Forum, to the monastery of *San Bonaventura,* which since then has been unable to escape the excavations of curious archeologists. In this monastery lived for many years the Danish painter-convert Kügler, known as Fra Pietro, and a Franciscan monk was able to tell us much about him

[207]

that was highly edifying, and showed us some of his paintings, which reminded one forcibly of those of Perugino.

We made repeated attempts also to secure an interview with the general of the Franciscan Order in the monastery of *Sant'Antonio* in the *Via Merulana,* and finally succeeded. With a smile this exalted dignitary gladly granted us permission to live for some time in the cloister at Fiesole, with the sole condition of leaving there a little sum for charity on our departure. The provincial, he said, could just as well have given us the permission, and it had not been really necessary to come on that account to Rome, to ask it of him. On dismissing us, he gave us his blessing, and we were very proud to have seen the successor of Saint Francis, and anticipated with joy the beautiful days which appeared to be awaiting us in the cloister at Fiesole.

Before I left Florence for Rome, I had informed my twin brother Erich of my entry into the Catholic Church. He received this news on the birthday of his first child, December 16, 1891. A remarkable coincidence. The tidings certainly affected him unpleasantly, though principally for external reasons; but finally he no doubt said, " Each one to his taste," for the Hollander is temperamentally so.

According to Dutch law, I had attained my majority on September 18, 1891, my twenty-third birthday. "From that time on you must be able to take care of yourselves," our father had impressed upon us twins, already as children, and the state of his finances at the beginning of the 'nineties compelled him to keep his word, out of consideration to our younger brothers and sisters. After repeated warnings he became serious in January, 1893, apparently under the impression of his New Year's accounts, and demanded of me exact information in regard to my plans for the future. He wanted to know what I thought of doing, so that I should make no more claims upon his purse. Now I could no longer conceal the fact of my conversion, for what I had in view was the natural consequence of it.

Being a Catholic and enthusiastic over the frescoes of Giotto and his school, I was firmly determined to devote myself to church-painting. I had, therefore, thought out the following plan, and said to myself: " Jan, you will make your first frescoes in the Franciscan cloister at Fiesole, and then go on from cloister to cloister, or from one village to another. So long as you ask for no money, but are content with food and lodging, you will no doubt find, well recommended as you are, plenty of work, as a painter in churches. Moreover, by selling a few studies, you can still earn a little pocket-money for tobacco and such things. Erich will send you his old clothes, which will fit you perfectly; some one will make you a present of a pair of shoes, and you can always borrow a fine book. *Mein Liebchen, was willst du noch mehr?* (My dear child, what more do you want?) Nothing, absolutely nothing. If you can only paint and pray a little and have something to eat and a place to sleep in, the world is welcome to the rest. If you go home for a little visit, then you will take a room near your father's bakery. There is plenty to eat there, bread, biscuits, honey-cakes, butter and lard, and milk to drink be-

[209]

sides. What more will you need? " In forming this plan, however, I was already counting on the possibility that I could, towards the end of my days, become a fixture in some cloister, and singularly enough, I thought in that connection not of a Franciscan but of a Carthusian monastery, although I had never yet seen one.

The letter in which I informed my father of my conversion and of my plans for the future could hardly have been more awkwardly expressed. Its tone was not at all suited to the seriousness of the situation, and I put myself by this epistle in a totally false light. Without of course wishing to do so, I nevertheless gave myself the appearance of having become a Catholic for purely material reasons and almost without any spiritual struggle, in order to have, among other advantages, the opportunity of decorating cloisters and village churches. It was certainly a difficult task to inform my father of my step, but my explanation of it, owing to the false notions that he had of the Catholic Church, must have made that step seem to him either terribly inconsiderate or absolutely mad.

I had thought it best to present in my letter the external advantages, since he would not know how to appreciate the spiritual ones, but in doing so I lowered myself in his estimation, a mistake which I had soon to repent of.

The reply of my parents to my letter was a prompt one. My father must have wept when he read of my conversion. His letter and that of my mother evinced also great sorrow, above all because they had been deceived by a beloved child, and were confronted now by an accomplished fact.

ITALY: FLORENCE AND ROME

Of much else that was written to me in the moment of that first excitement I need not speak. Certain less flattering expressions were quite comprehensible and in part also fully justified. Only it should be mentioned here that in my father's letter (and of course in that of my mother) there was not a word either of expulsion from the family or of disinheritance, or even of any cessation of further financial support. In a word, my whole family has remained kind and good to me all my life; but I felt that it was now time for me to earn my own bread.

THE general of the Franciscans had given us permission to reside in the cloister at Fiesole, and now we had a strong inclination to go thither. We did not, however, return to Florence by the same route, but by way of Assisi, for Ballin, who had taken the name "Francis" at his baptism, wanted to visit the grave of his new patron-saint. This little city gained for him subsequently great importance. In the year 1894 he spent several months there, together with his countryman, the poet Johannes Jörgensen, who has described this episode of his life so exquisitely in his *Book of Travels,* in which as in other books of Jörgensen, one learns all sort of things about my dear and faithful friend Mogens "Francis."

In Rome we had always remained somewhat like strangers, but at Assisi we felt ourselves again at home. Now we saw with our own eyes what we had already known from books. The little city, so closely identified with the history of Saint Francis, with its churches and sanctuaries, is an idyll in the midst of an idyllic landscape. For an admirer of the great poor man of Assisi the place is like a new and intensified revelation of his spirit. When one beholds the poverty and loveliness, united with the sweet seriousness, which dominate Assisi and the Umbrian plain, one understands how the fullness of all those qualities could dwell in a man who was born there. Here the theory of the influence of environment finds distinct confirmation. Assisi remains one of my most beautiful recollections. Whenever I think of Saint Francis, it rises before my mental vision, as the architectural expression of that personality so touchingly pure and divinely simple. Assisi is as perfectly suited to Saint Francis, as is its nest to every bird, which builds it in accordance with its natural instinct.

Since I am speaking of Assisi and Saint Francis, I must also think of his spiritual twin sister, Saint Clare, whose life was the purest incarnation of his ideals, and in whom he always found consolation and faith in his work, whenever anxiety about his spiritual sons oppressed him. To saints are applicable the words of Saint Paul that everything works for the good of the elect. The love which they cherish for their spiritual female friends or spiritual daughters remains all their life long perfectly controlled, because they love them entirely in the spirit of God, while the spiritual love of less perfect souls can easily degenerate and lead to every kind of questionable and evil action. What often causes others to fall creates in the saints a new flight towards their highest aim, which is union with God. In loving, they increase their power twofold, and are inspired to utter those words of instruction and admonition, which as the fruit of pure love strengthen and vivify for centuries the souls which thirst for God.

I remained only two days in Assisi, but I took away with me, in leaving it, a strength of consolation sufficient for my entire life.

GREAT graces must be gained by striving for them. We had counted on being received as guests in the cloister at Fiesole immediately, but for the present nothing came of it. We were told that the provincial also must give his consent to the plan. But he would come only after Easter, and therefore we must be patient until then. Accordingly we could do nothing else than seek for a temporary lodging in Florence. We found one in the house of an impoverished count in the *Via Taddeo*. And now a still greater disappointment followed. My friend Ballin was called back to his country to do his military service. This was indeed a blow. But he consoled himself soon with the thought of the joy that this would give his good parents, who were longingly awaiting the return of their only child. They had, it is true, received the news of his baptism with great sorrow, but also with much tenderness and liberality. God be thanked, however, we had something besides disappointments. A great and joyful surprise was also accorded us. Quite unexpectedly the Nabi Sérusier announced to us his approaching visit in Florence. Unfortunately, when he came, there was no room for him in our house, but we saw one another almost daily.

Soon after his arrival I told Sérusier that at the end of

[213]

August in the previous year I had been baptised and received into the Catholic Church. The nabi evinced both joy and surprise and congratulated me. Yet the step caused him, on the other hand, some embarrassment, for it was he who had laid the foundation of my religious views, and now I had landed in the Catholic Church which he had left, although I was acquainted with his theosophical opinions and indeed had shared them for a while. Did Sérusier at this time receive his first impulse towards the Church? At all events, ten years later, when I was in the first year of my priesthood, he found, while on a visit in Beuron, the way back to her fold. Some days later we were sitting at lunch, when Sérusier said to me suddenly, " I spoke with Edward Schuré yesterday of your conversion." " Has he been here? " I asked. " Yes," replied Sérusier, "but was only passing through." " Well, what did he think of it? " I inquired further. " Schuré was very much astonished," said my friend, " that his book *Les Grands Initiés* could have led any one to the Catholic Church (which, indeed, was claiming too much), and when we tried to explain your conversion, we came finally to the conclusion that after you had attained to a belief in God, you were impelled to come to a decision, and you then became a Catholic, in order, so to speak, to reward yourself for having found the way to God." " No," I answered, " the principal reason was that I wanted to come into a mystical communion and spiritual unity with Christ and His Apostles, and baptism was the means of doing so. The rest then came of itself." Sérusier was highly satisfied with this answer, which certainly suited him exactly, and he said to me: " It is too bad that Schuré has already left the city. He would have been delighted with what you have just said; it is exactly the idea of a nabi, yet we had not thought of that."

EASTER (April 2, 1893) had come and gone. Ballin had departed. Upon the hill of Fiesole we had taken leave of each other with a brotherly embrace. Sérusier and I lived together in the house of the poor count. The last days of Holy Week I had spent in fervent prayer and strict fasting. On Easter morning I went very early to Fiesole, having of course eaten nothing, in order to make my confession and receive Holy Communion in the cloister. Shortly before, having been heated by walking, I had caught a severe cold in the cool rooms of the convent, and since then had felt depressed and weak. My stomach also took its revenge for my penitential fasting during Lent and acted as if it were offended. Moreover the Franciscan provincial's permission to reside in the cloister at Fiesole had not yet come.

I was working then in the gallery of the *Uffizi* on a copy of the "Venus" of Botticelli, filling a commission given me by the Danish consul at Rome. My easel stood near that of a distinguished English lady, who was copying the same picture. She was the widow of the celebrated architect Clark. She made my acquaintance, was very kind to me, and invited me several times to her beautifully situated country-house not far from the *Porta Romana*. She also made me acquainted with Mr. Stanhope, the pre-Raphaelite, whom I visited repeatedly in his spacious studio in the city and once in his princely villa outside of Florence. It has always given me great pleasure to pass some hours or days in a richly and tastefully furnished house, but scarcely had I left it when I usually exclaimed, " Thank God, that all that rubbish does not belong to me! " What I still especially admire in Mrs. Clark is the dignity with which she enjoyed the nobler pleasures of life. She remains for me always the most perfect type of a gentlewoman.

Yet how differently the " eternal feminine " expresses itself in different races and nations. What folly it is to regard the woman of any one people as the model of womanhood. Only one can be designated as " the woman," and she is Mary, the Mother of Christ, the second Eve, the most perfect image of the goodness of God in the purely created order of beings. In her shines the pure white light of womanhood; in the others this white light is separated into one or another of its inherent colours. To her are applicable the words: " Many daughters have gathered together riches, but thou hast surpassed them all " (Prov. xxxi. 29).

I passed the Feast of the Ascension (May 11, 1893) with the Franciscans in Fiesole, and on that occasion finally received permission to reside in the cloister on the height. Sérusier returned to France. The harmonious beauty of Italy did not appeal to him. He preferred the severer beauty of Brittany. My landlord in the *Via Taddeo* was sorry to see me go, but in a niche of his dwelling I left a large picture of the Madonna and Child, my first mural painting.

IN THE FRANCISCAN CLOISTER

WHOEVER has been privileged to live for a long time in a well-ordered cloister will have learned from experience what a benefit it is for both his body and his soul. Without being obliged to bear the burdens of monastic life, he participates nevertheless in that reward which Christ promises to those who have left father and mother for His sake. Then surely, more than ever before, has the truth of the words come home to him: " How good and pleasant it is for brothers to dwell together in unity " (Ps. cxxxii. 1). He has learned there also the rare happiness of tasting the peace of solitude and the tranquillity of silence without, however, being tormented by an oppressive feeling of loneliness. How much easier it became for him to collect his thoughts, and to hold communion with God in that atmosphere of prayer which always prevails when the solemn praise of God is worthily sung by the monks in the choir in connection with the sacrifice of the Mass, as the central point in the worship of God. He has moreover been agreeably surprised to find in the cloister a large number of distinct personalities and a wealth of strongly marked, accomplished, and in themselves well-rounded characters. And was it not a long-wished-for happiness to be able to choose from a great number of priests one with whom one could quietly speak of the state of one's soul? There perhaps for the first time in his life no distrust has arisen in his mind, when a kindness has been shown him in a spirit of humble sub-mission. One has not sought in the least to edify him in the cloister by pious aphorisms and discourses, and for that very reason he has edified himself greatly, And when, at parting, he has gratefully pressed the hand of the father superior or that of the father appointed to receive strangers, he has felt a greater love for that Church which, in spite of the persecution and hatred of so many ages, has still been able to maintain its convents through the lapse of centuries.

THE Franciscan cloister of Fiesole is rather extensive, having been at different times enlarged. The little courtyard with its well forms the nucleus around which in a quadrangle the church and the original cloister are situated. At the time I was there, the little ancient cloister, which is now evacuated, and has been made accessible to travellers, in-cluding women, was the residence of the clerics, that is to say, of the brothers who are preparing themselves for the priesthood by the study of theology. To this little courtyard there is now joined a much larger one with decorative ar-cades and a simple well. This courtyard is enclosed on the southern side by the apartments of the clerics, on the west-ern side by the refectory and library, on the north by the steward's rooms and on the east by the tailor's shop and a large refectory for visitors. Above the steward's rooms and the dining-hall for guests is a second story with projecting galleries, which furnish access to a row of guest-rooms of the most primitive character.

IN THE FRANCISCAN CLOISTER

Here I was now located. My cell, therefore, faced the north, and from my window I had a magnificent view of the grove of cypresses and the sombre Apennines. *Monte Senario* rose, clearly defined, from the mountain-chain, with the mother-cloister of the Servites on its summit. The furniture of my room consisted of a large bed, almost as broad as it was long, a wash-stand, a *prie-dieu,* a small table and a straw-chair. The walls were white-washed and the floor was paved with red bricks. No one lived in this story except the porter of the cloister and myself. From the open passage-way before my cell I could sometimes discern a young monk behind the little window of a cell in the clerics' residence, but otherwise I at first saw very little of the cloister's community, except in the recreation hours, when the fathers and brothers assembled under my window, or took a walk through the little wood. But little by little I came into more intimate relations with them and was known as " Giovanni " or, as the clerics called me " Gianni," for whom perhaps today there is still preserved a friendly recollection high up on the hill of Fiesole.

As I have already said, our first acquaintances among the Franciscans were Fathers Norbert, Giovacchino and Placido. During my stay in Fiesole, however, I was to come into great intimacy only with the last. Father Norbert was always absent on mission-work, and Father Giovacchino was transferred to another convent. Father Placido, the " very reverend " as he was called, was at that time about sixty years old. Tall and stout, he resembled (if the comparison may be allowed me) a good-natured mastiff, which was capable, however, of growling and showing its teeth. The fundamental trait of his character was kind-heartedness and gaiety of disposition. How joyously he could laugh, the good man. He taught moral and pastoral theology in the episcopal seminary of Fiesole, and was a zealous confessor. The fatherly tone of his deep and rough, because always hoarse, voice inspired love and confidence. I can see him still as he would come up to the convent perspiring and panting, with a fiery-red head, and a handkerchief around his neck, so that the collar of his habit might not be wet through. He had had to make the steep ascent from the seminary to the cloister in the burning heat of the sun, and when he caught sight of me he would exclaim, " Jean, *comment ça va?* " (He liked to speak French with me). " Ah, what a heat! Jean, Jean, *Dio mio,* how hot it is! But up here it is good; here there is always air; but down below it is a veritable hell. Jean, in the cloister it is fine. I am so glad to be at home. *Au revoir,* Jean."

Father Placido was my confessor during the whole time that I lived in the cloister. One day, when I wanted to confess, he said to me in his deep voice, " Jean, come in here, you can make your confession in the choir." He seated himself in one of the lower choir-stalls, and I knelt before him. When he gave me absolution, he stretched out both his arms before him, laid his hands on my head and spoke the *Ego te absolvo* with such earnestness, fatherliness and feeling that I can never forget that moment, and indeed

[220]

can just as little forget the dear man himself, who now has been dead these many years.

WEEKS went by and I did not even once leave the cloister. I was so happy within its walls, what could I want to seek outside them? In the morning, when I awoke, the dear sun greeted me, and cast a brilliant ray of light through the opening in the almost closed shutters, and wove a golden mosaic on the whitewashed wall. Ah, how easy it was to get up in that always beautiful weather. What a delight, when scarcely dressed, to bathe in the cool, morning air. My toilet was soon made. The brother who was shoemaker to the community had loaned me a pair of old sandals. Socks or stockings I wore only on Sundays and holy days; otherwise I always went barefoot. A shirt, trousers, a belt and jacket formed the rest of my outfit. I did not need to shave, for ever since my first sojourn in Brittany I had worn a short beard. My room was put in order in a moment, after which I went into the church and served as ministrant. I often assisted thus at two or three, or even more Masses. Every time, after the holy consecration, I recited, as is the custom of the Franciscans, six "Our Fathers" with out-stretched arms. The visitors to the church wondered at this. Sometimes they asked who this young penitent was, and said, "Does he wish to become a saint?" For in the opinion of southerners to become a saint is equivalent to doing penance. For them a saint is one who, in his longing to become like Christ, fasts frequently, prays much, remains a long while in church, has a poor lodging, sleeps on the

[221]

floor, and lives on charity, a conception which is indeed one-sided, but is undoubtedly justified.

After serving at Mass, I went into the little breakfast-room. There, on a small fire of charcoal, stood a large tin-can of black coffee, and on the table were rows of cups in which the sugar had already been placed. Near them was a huge loaf of bread, baked from the grain which the lay-brothers had begged for in summer. I liked the taste of it, and more delicious bread I had never eaten in my life. If Father Placido also was taking his breakfast then, he would say to me in his rough voice: "Jean, take a second cup; you don't find things in the cloister as you are accustomed to have them at home, no milk, no cheese, nothing." And then, when he had finished, he would add, "Good-bye, Jean, I must go to the seminary and do my teaching."

The rest of the morning I usually spent in my room, where I sketched, painted or read. Outside before the little grove of cypresses, a tiny garden glowed in the burning sun. Above the dark tips of the funereal trees stood the Apennines with *Monte Senario* towering upward into the cloudless blue. In the fig trees before my window chirped enormous crickets, which it was a pleasure to hear. From the city came the sounds of happy children. Now and then I heard below in the courtyard, when some one was drawing water, the striking of the copper bucket on the side of the well and the rattling of the iron chain in the groaning and creaking windlass. Sometimes also a caterwauling reached my ear, if the porter, Brother Vitaliano was chastising his cat *Buscherati*.

IN THE FRANCISCAN CLOISTER

Shortly after eleven o'clock the bell in the tower summoned the fathers and the clerics to the choir. After half an hour one heard them going to the refectory, chanting a psalm. Soon after, I went to the church, in order to ring the bell for noon, a duty which had been assigned to me. With the bell-rope in my hand I waited till the cannon was fired below in Florence, which announced the hour of midday. Then immediately I made the hammer give three strokes, and prayed an *Ave Maria*. When I had done that three times, I rang the bell joyously and was always proud when, up there in the cloister, it sounded sooner than below in the campanile of the cathedral. When this pious work had been performed, I fetched from the kitchen my noonday meal, which the cook regularly placed ready for me on the range, and ate it alone in a little guest-room down on the ground-floor of the building occupied by the clerics. Only on great festival-days was I allowed to eat with the fathers in the refectory. It cost me at first some effort to adapt myself to Italian cooking, but it suited me admirably, and I soon recovered from the weakness caused by my fasting. I felt stronger and healthier than ever, and Father Placido was perfectly right when, surveying me with pride, he said: " Jean, you look much better than when you came: it is the simple food and the good air up here that does it."

While I sat at table, the postman came in regularly, a little old man, who every day brought the letters for the cloister from the post-office and received in return his dinner. He could neither read nor write, but he was able to make out which letters were addressed to me, and whenever he saw that he was not mistaken, he grinned with delight. After dinner, I sought, for the most part, the society of some fathers who were conversing in the great courtyard or in the garden. Then came the time for the siesta, the noon-day nap, which is universally customary in warm countries. In Rome one says: "In the summer between twelve and two only dogs and Englishmen go out walking." We indefatigable northerners want to make use of these hours also, and often tactlessly disturb the repose of more sensible men.

In Fiesole the church was closed during the siesta, and it was only after persistent knocking that one then opened the door, "because of his importunity" (Luke xi. 8). Brother Vitaliano's face, however, on such occasions did not wear a very cordial expression, and he did not show certain parts of the cloister. I generally rose from my siesta early, and took up a book or wrote a letter. In the course of the afternoon the brother at the gate sometimes called me, and begged me to conduct some foreigners through the building, for since I spoke French well and German and English passably, I could converse with most visitors. Some of these cast furtive glances at me while we were making the rounds, and shook their heads. From their faces I could read the words, "What kind of a queer fellow is that?" They could not reconcile my jovial humour, education and knowledge of the world with my apparent intention to become a monk; yet there I was, already barefoot and looking somewhat unkempt.

IN THE FRANCISCAN CLOISTER

THE guardian of a Franciscan convent seldom remains longer than three years in his official position, at least in the same cloister. Hence, in May, 1893, I found a different superior in Fiesole from the one who had received Ballin and myself with such genuine Franciscan cordiality whenever we paid a visit to the monastery. The new guardian made the impression of a severe man, on account of which I was at first a little afraid of him and preferred to avoid him. But since he was very kind and good to me, I speedily lost this shyness, yet never came into close relations with him. Alas, he had been attacked early in life by a grievous malady, and perhaps did not possess the strength entirely to overcome this affliction in his spiritual nature. Therefore his character had in it something listless and disillusioned, which seemed to me then, in my zeal as a convert, unpardonable. Experience has shown me that new converts are apt to be very severe in their judgments. Called at the eleventh hour into the vineyard, they are amazed, if their fellow-labourers, who have from early morning borne the heat of the day, are not as fresh and full of energy as they.

I must also mention the vice-superior of the house, Father Vicario, a model monk who, as sacristan, was always very much concerned about the ever-burning light before the tabernacle. Whenever he came into the church, he augmented a little the tiny flame, if its illuminating power had somewhat diminished. He was a man who always quietly went his own way and said little. Besides these, the cloister's family at that time numbered the two readers of the theological school, Father Giovanni Cristomo and Father Teo-

[225]

filo, also Father Stefano, who was always much occupied, since he was not only manager of the kitchen and cellar, but was organist as well, and Father Ottato, usually called *Il Monti,* Fathers Nicolò and Stanislaus, and finally Father Joseph Maria Lochmann, a German-Tyrolese. The other inmates of the cloister were lay-brothers and clerics. With these especially I became always more intimate. It is true, the students were not strictly allowed by the rules of the cloister to associate with the laity; but the monks shut their eyes, if they came upon me in company with them during the hours of recreation in the cypress-grove. I scarcely think that my sojourn in the cloister at Fiesole would have been for me so delightful and beneficial, if I had not had almost daily intercourse with those young clerics. Having grown up in the convent, they had all of them remained veritable children, in whom the kindly spirit of Saint Francis found congenial qualities, so that they had easily accommodated themselves to his manner of life. I should say that their most beautiful characteristic was *sincerity of heart,* that direct honesty of purpose, which one finds in a high degree in children and saints. They were perhaps already too mature to be capable of still further development, a danger which threatens every southerner in his youth. But do we not all endeavor consciously to become what we were already unconsciously in childhood, in other words, to " become as little children "?

Some of those clerics showed me a tenderness and attachment during our acquaintance such as I had nowhere previously found, and yet withal were so respectful that their affection never degenerated into silly sentimentality. The ascetic nature of their education in the cloister had taught them renunciation and self-mastery. They "possessed their souls in patience" (Luke xxi. 19), and however ardent their hearts were, they held them under control. Their respect laid restraint upon their love. There were, however, always exclamations of joy when I appeared during their period of recreation. Frequently we chatted together in some shady spot, and often they instructed me in regard to some question of faith. Then I would join them in their game of quoits, or went with them in search of berries or mushrooms, and sometimes they had to serve as models for my sketches. One comment was always on their lips: "Become a Carthusian, Gianni, become a Carthusian. You must not be a Franciscan. Being a Franciscan and being a painter do not harmonize well. We have no money, and the painter needs colours and canvas and many other things. All that cannot be begged for. Father David, who is also a painter, has a hard time of it. The Carthusians are rich. Become a Carthusian, Gianni." I am indebted to these dear comrades for much good, and they exerted a marked influence on my spiritual life. Their faith was so perfectly spontaneous and so devoid of any doubt, and their piety was so natural, and their love — the test of truth — was so beneficent that I was incited to an ever greater joy in my own faith; and when on my return home, my younger sister made the observation that I had become much more amiable, she paid thereby unconsciously a compliment to my dear clerics.

YESTERDAYS OF AN ARTIST-MONK

In the religious atmosphere of the convent my soul developed wonderfully. There began for me then a new life, the life with God. The *Confessions of Saint Augustine* and the *Life of Saint Teresa,* written by herself, introduced me into this life. I still remember into what a deeply religious state of mind these books led me, and to what heights of enthusiasm for God's service they raised me. I could not understand it at all, if I saw a father going about the cloister without some special occupation. In the library were all the works of Saint Augustine; why did he not read them? There was surely nothing sweeter and more useful than to do so. I sat in my cell pouring over the *Confessions,* and as I read I was astonished. The book was already so old, and yet so entirely modern. Had not, for example, the community life which Saint Augustine had planned to lead with his friends Romanianus, Nabridius, Alypius and Verecundus, been also our dream, the dream of the nabis, with Sérusier as superior? "But," says Saint Augustine, "when we asked ourselves whether the women, whom some of us had already married, and those whom others of us thought of marrying, would consent to this kind of life the whole plan which we had so beautifully elaborated fell to pieces and was discarded; and precisely so was it with us."

How different from mine was the struggle which Saint Augustine had to make, in order to attain to the truth. And what a fervid spirit of prayer still streams forth from that book, what acuteness of intellect, what warmth of heart. Often in my reading I would pause and reflect on

[228]

what I had read. After a while my thoughts grew nebulous and vanished. Yet I did not remain alone. It was not only the stillness, with its occasional noises, chants and sighs that then surrounded me. No, I was conscious of a Presence there, of some one who was about me and in me. If I rose and went away, that Presence accompanied me, and if I halted and stood still, it waited with me. It was perfectly natural then for me to pray, and how blissfully happy I felt.

"I was nourished at the breast of his consideration," and "I drank of delights overflowing from the abundance of his glory." He "brought upon me, as it were, a river of peace." I was "carried at the breast and caressed upon the knees" (Is. lvi. 11 etc.).

The time for that passionate devotion to God which follows every serious conversion had now come to me, the time for a devotional ardour, characterized both by blessed joys and also foolish anxieties, by wholehearted self-surrender yet by a timid withdrawal into oneself. New converts usually confound this passionate ardour with the true love of God. That is incorrect. What they think is pure love has in it still an element of self-love and is even influenced by the senses. Even if such converts assert that they are not seeking themselves but only God, and that they wish to be associated with Him alone and to live according to His will, in reality it is seldom so. For in their love of God they still love far too much the *joy of that love itself,* the heavenly consolation which it brings, and that upward flight of the spirit which often, for a moment, makes of them artists, masters of words, and geniuses, capable of expressing themselves in fervid prayers, sublime poetry and clever designs. At heart they are seeking in their service of God, before all else, that enrichment of the ego, of which Goethe's "Werther" says, "I appeared to be more than I was, because I was all that I could be." When one is in this state of mind everything depends upon good leadership. A good spiritual guide will know then how to turn to account this impulse to self-expansion. He will assist his pupil by aiding him to free himself from bad habits, and to acquire good ones; for virtue is, after all, nothing but the habit of doing right. If only the true love, which manifests itself in fulfilling God's commandments, would always increase together with the emotional, ardent love. Then the latter would be a most beautiful trait. For how edifying are new converts, when in that emotional state. With what profound earnestness they do everything. How divinely sincere and loyal they are. In the final analysis, does not the ardent form of love always precede the true love, even though the latter does not always succeed the former. And as the true love increases, does not the passionate love in many instances always remain? One sees this often in very happy marriages and also in the lives of ecstatic saints, in whom the excessive intensity, inherent in ardent love, becomes a precious quality, because "the measure of one's love to God is immeasurable." Then ardent love loses its character of self-love, for it no longer seeks itself, or any created being, but only the Creator, and no material element any longer adheres to it, since it has become purely spiritual.

One often sees that new converts read by preference the

writings of ecstatic saints, a fact which finds its explanation in what has just been said. For they find in these saints precisely that intensity of feeling which ardent love awakens in even the most apathetic and commonplace individuals. The fire and flame of the ecstatic and mystics correspond to the first fiery zeal with which the neophyte is filled.

Although I also read the mystics by preference, I studied with great diligence dogmatic works, such as *Le Christ de la Tradition* by Monsignor Landriot. I was delighted with this book, which initiated me into a profounder comprehension of the principal mysteries of Christianity, the Trinity, the Incarnation and the Eucharist. It was indeed for me a priceless piece of good fortune to be able to live thus undisturbed by the outer world, and to nourish my soul with quiet meditation, prayer and reading.

It was for me also a blissful period, that springtime of my first religious zeal, that season of intimate communion with the Divine Presence! I look back upon it always as on a time of spiritual betrothal, when love is already resplendent in bloom, yet must be cultivated through fidelity and patience to a growth that shall make it bring forth fruit, a fruit destined to remain long after the beautiful blossoms shall have fallen.

AUTUMN had come and gone. Fearful torrents of rain had driven away the summer heat. It was often terrifying when the accumulated thunder clouds from the north came rolling over the plain of the Arno and discharged their contents over the cloister; but these storms were of short

[231]

duration and the sun quickly shone again upon the freshened fields. The fig trees before my window had already lost their leaves, yet the cypresses and oaks still retained their dark-green vestments. In the evening it was already dark at an early hour. From the window in the corridor of the convent, which commanded a view of Florence far below, I could see one light succeed another in the city. Little by little the outlines of the buildings there would disappear, and finally only thousands of tiny, sparkling lights were visible, while the reflection of the city's illumination stood out in bold relief against the sky. I thought then of the people who were living down there in the "world." Few of them assuredly were at that moment thinking of God; yet some perhaps were doing so, and if so, then these too were little lights in the midst of dark masses. They were like the fire-flies, which in the south fly about in such numbers on sultry summer nights, and carry with them a scintillating little lamp, which in their flight through obscurity they cause to shine. Again and again there came to me the words of Saint Paul: "For you were heretofore darkness, but now light in the Lord. Walk, then, as children of the light" (Eph. v. 8).

Yes, that is what I desired to do and, walking thus, to become wholly light. But then also to let my light shine. One would listen to me, only if I had first become wholly light. Or would it be with me, as it is said of Christ in the little Flemish poem:

> *He thought they would all comprehend it,*
> *That radiant light in his eyes.*

[232]

IN THE FRANCISCAN CLOISTER

I often thought of Ballin and wrote to him frequently. He had become a soldier in the artillery and, since he was stationed in an island fortress, he had often to row vigorously and to stand as sentry day and night. I also often thought of my home, which I had not seen for a year and a half. It both attracted and repelled me. But when Ballin urged me to make, in the spring of the following year, a little exposition of my paintings and drawings in Copenhagen, and also invited me to pass some months in his parents' house, I determined to accept, but first to return to Holland and spend the winter with my family.

I HAD painted two frescoes in the cloister of Fiesole, one of which represented Saint Francis of Assisi, stretching out his arms above six clerics, in giving them his blessing. In this work Father Joseph Maria, the German-Tyrolese, rendered me some friendly services. He would himself gladly have become a painter, but destiny had not allowed him to do so. An ardent love for art had nevertheless remained in him, and he spoke to me repeatedly of the Benedictines of Beuron and of their methods. Those painter-monks, he said, had done splendid work in the cloister of *Monte Cassino,* and with one of them, Father Lucas Steiner, he had become acquainted in Tyrol. The real founders of the Beuron school of painting were, however, Father Desiderius Lenz and Father Gabriel Wüger.

As I have already said, I had seen in the studio of the painter von Rhoden in Rome some photographs made from the drawings of the painter-monks, but I did not then know that these were the same works of which Father Joseph spoke so enthusiastically. My curiosity to become acquainted with their productions constantly increased, and finally I wrote to the cloister at Seckau in Austria, which belonged to the Beuron community, and which Father Joseph knew. " The abbot will forward your letter," he said. I followed his advice. In my communication I explained the views about art which I held at that time, and begged the abbot to send me some reproductions of the works of the Beuron painters. Inside of eight days I received two answers to this letter, one from the abbot of Seckau, Dom Ildefons Schober, and one from Father Desiderius Lenz from the cloister of Maria Laach. In both letters some little pictures and photographs were enclosed. I now entered into a correspondence with Father Desiderius, and received much information from him about Beuron's principles of art and the technique of painting. He also invited me, on my return journey to Holland, to visit Beuron, which I gladly promised to do.

It was in the afternoon of a beautiful, warm day in November, 1893, that I descended the hill of Fiesole, in order, after making a few last calls in Florence, to betake myself to the railway station. I experienced the joyousness of a young man who, after a period of seclusion, can once more move about freely and start out in quest of what is unknown and new. There was in the air a blessed tranquillity, and over the landscape lay a vision of the sunny joy of life, while a quiet, happy activity seemed also to weave about it all a robe of peace.

[234]

IN THE FRANCISCAN CLOISTER

My stay with the Franciscans had given to me great spiritual steadfastness, and I now felt myself strong enough to fight the good fight in the world also. In fact, I was so entirely certain of what I wanted to do, that I now advanced with a degree of assurance, which would have been effrontery, had it not been accompanied by genuine naïveté. Even if I had become more serious and devout, I had not lost my former naturalness, vivacity and freshness, and therefore it was with great joy and confidence that I took in hand again my pilgrim-staff after five months of conventual solitude. My plan was to direct my steps first, through nothern Italy, to Germany, Holland and Denmark and then to return to Italy, to decorate the walls of the Tertiary Chapel of the Franciscan cloister of *San Salvatore al Monte,* magnificently situated on the left bank of the Arno near *San Miniato.*

In the evening of the same day, the train brought me to Milan, and on the following day, I travelled slowly onward, stopping a few hours in Chiasso, and going thence to Lugano, where I inspected the principal sights, after which I slept a couple of hours in the waiting-room of the station, and at ten o'clock in the evening once more boarded my train. There I soon fell asleep. When, however, we were passing through the tunnel of the Saint Gotthard, the noisy voices of my fellow-travellers awoke me. How gruesome is the time passed in a tunnel. Scarcely had the train again halted in the open air, when a young lad opened the door of the car. A driving snow-storm struck him in the face. " Brr! " he exclaimed and closed the door again with a bang. "What, snow?" I cried, *"snow?"* "Yes, snow," replied the youth; " up here it is bad." " Heavens! " I thought, " now one sees for the first time that it is November. Farewell to the south. Farewell to the sun." It grew cold in the car, and I began to shiver; but somewhere among the Swiss mountains, in gloomy, rainy weather, there was at last an opportunity to drink a cup of hot coffee at a railway station. " By the gods," I muttered, " how ugly these women are. Nature too seems here to be theatrical and artificial in its decoration; and what a strident contrast between the gigantic masses of the mountains and the Lilliputian chalets and tiny toy-trees in the valleys. Yet people travel hither from distant lands to look at them with astonishment at the command of Baedeker or Meyer. One can pardon that in young couples who are on their wedding journey, but sensible people ought to be wiser. O Italy, beautiful Italy," I sighed, " how I am going to miss you," and in a bad humour I resumed my seat in a third-class car.

BEURON

In Zürich I inquired where Beuron was situated, and learned that I must travel *via* Singen, Immendingen and Tuttlingen, and in all these places must change cars. From Zürich on the railway carriages were heated, and in fact, after leaving Schaffhausen, to such a degree that it was almost unendurable. I therefore opened a window. When the conductor came through, he addressed me roughly and shouted, "The window must be closed." I could not help laughing, and said to myself: "Now you have found out that you are in Germany. Well, discipline and obedience have also some good in them." I therefore quietly shut the window, but not without remarking to the conductor that for me it was much too hot. Thereafter, whenever he came through the car, he left the door open for a little while and then shut it with a slam. The Suabian loves a warm, cosy room, and is often afraid of ventilation.

After leaving Immendingen, our train skirted the youthful Danube. The landscape was bare, poor and abandoned. All life was confined to the houses. It may have been two o'clock when I arrived in Beuron. The place gave me the impression of absolute seclusion from the world. I found myself in a narrow valley, enclosed by thickly wooded mountains. It was with difficulty that the Danube could find an exit from it. Here winter still reigned supreme,

[237]

and the trees on the mountains were stiff with frost. One had the feeling of being frozen in, and of being obliged to hibernate here, far from the inhabited world. From the station one sees neither church nor cloister; only five or six scattered houses are located there. I asked a man, the only traveller who had alighted with me, where the convent was. "There, near the inn, around the corner," he replied. "Just go straight ahead, and you will soon see it." I went on. On the whitewashed wall of the inn was painted a Saint Joseph with the Child Jesus, the first sign of culture. And there before me now, stood the cloister, a three-storied structure with a high, brown roof. The entrance was a small, temple-like portal, built out from the cloister itself. Here I was greeted by a second painting, a Madonna and Child, flanked by Saints Peter and Paul, Maurus and Placidus. Before entering the convent I examined these figures attentively. The design was noble, but the expression of the faces was somewhat insipid. I rang. "Father Desiderius is absent," said the porter, "but he will return this evening. Come into the reception room, and I will call the father who receives strangers." He soon appeared, a distinguished personality, tall, thin, and with a little black cap on his white hair, and a fresh colour in his still youthful face. After we had exchanged a few words, he inquired amiably: "Do you wish to lodge here with us?" I had no more ardent wish than to do so. "Come with me, then," said the father; "unfortunately the guest-room is not heated, but I will have a fire made at once." He conducted me to a large vaulted room in the lower story, which made on me an agreeable impression. There was a carpet on the floor, and on the bed a white counterpane, and what especially struck me, lace-curtains hung before both windows. I had not seen any for months. The father retired, leaving me alone without having asked me whether I had lunched. That would have been the first thing that a Franciscan would have asked, I thought. But fortunately they had given me in Fiesole a half a loaf of bread to take with me, and this was now a godsend to me. After I had refreshed myself, I sat down beside the crackling stove, and began to doze. After about an hour the father returned, and invited me to attend Vespers, assuring me that in Beuron the service was very beautiful. "First, however," he said, "you ought to eat something; by the way," he added suddenly, "have you had any lunch?" When I replied in the negative, he clasped his hands in pity, hurried away and returned, accompanied by a brother bringing me coffee, bread, butter and eggs. "So, so," said the brother, "now please eat all you want." I lost no time in satisfying my hunger.

In the great church of the convent, a rococo structure of a not altogether successfully modernised style, I took my place on the bench reserved for guests. At the sound of a bell the black-robed monks filed into the choir two by two, in a long, long line. They went into the choir-stalls and, after crossing themselves, knelt down to pray. At a sign from the prior they all stood up and bowed very low for half a minute. Then began the service of the *Nones,* which precedes the Vespers. It was merely recited. At the *Gloria Patri, et Filio, et Spiritui Sancto,* at the conclusion of every psalm, the monks rose from their seats and made a profound inclination. All this proceeded with an almost military precision and regularity in perfect order. After *Nones* the monks bowed deeply, and remained so for a long time, and raised themselves only at a sign from the prior. The organ now began to sound. A father sang the *Deus, in adjutorium meum intende,* and all the others responded, *Domine, ad adjuvandum me festina.* Then a small and a large choir chanted alternately. I was very much surprised. These monks did not shout, but really sang. It was something quite new to me. Ever since I had been a Catholic I had heard for the most part only shouting. In the cathedrals of Italy, especially in Florence, it had sometimes been unendurable. Instead of singing, one heard a veritable howling, which by the powerful echo was increased tenfold, and never ceased. In my love for the Church I had gladly excused the ugly features of it which I encountered, but when I now heard how magnificent and beautiful the chant is, if it is well sung, I felt a veritable joy. It affected me, as it might some one who had suddenly discovered a new and noble characteristic in a dearly loved friend. At the conclusion of the Vespers, after the magnificent *Salve Regina* had been sung, the monks remained kneeling for some time in silent prayer; then rose at a signal from the prior, and left the choir two by two.

When I had re-entered my room, I seated myself again beside the stove. The solemn Vesper chants still rang for a long while in my ears. " Wonderfully beautiful, wonderfully beautiful," I kept repeating to myself. Night came, and I lighted the petroleum lamp. In Fiesole I had had only a little oil lamp. How homelike and comfortable it was now in my room. And how happy I felt. Such homelike comfort is to be found only in the north, where life is passed mostly within the house, not outside of it, as in the south. It is no wonder that Germans and Italians do not understand one another. Their fundamentally different kind of life, which is largely determined by climate, causes wholly different virtues and capabilities to come in them to maturity. What must the dachshund, for example, think of the antelope, and vice versa? Must they not seem to each other strange and ridiculous? "No seriousness," says the dackel of the antelope. "No agility," says the antelope of the dackel. Both make a good roast, it is said, yet need a special preparation suited to the animal. Exactly: everything lies in the preparation.

At about seven o'clock the guest-father conducted me to supper. In the vestibule of the dining-hall I was introduced to the prior, who welcomed me cordially. After the *Benedicite* had been said in unison, I looked shyly about me. I found myself in a very large and lofty hall, along the left side of which were highly placed windows with many disk-like panes. The fathers sat at oaken tables along the walls, with their cowls drawn over their heads; the lay-brothers were in the centre of the refectory. I myself sat at the upper end of the dining-hall near the abbot's private table and opposite to the prior and the oldest fathers. After the monk whose duty it was to read during the meal had read a sentence from the Rule of Saint Benedict, the prior gave a signal with a little hammer. The fathers then laid back their cowls, arranged their napkins and ate their soup. The meal proceeded in almost as orderly a manner as had the divine service in the church. The monks ate in silence with dignity and propriety. All unnecessary noise was avoided. The table-servants wore soft slippers. Spoons, forks and knives were handled with precaution by the monks in eating. I could understand every word of the reader. After the sentence from the Rule, he had read out the names of the Benedictine saints whose memory was to be celebrated on the following day, and thereupon the regular reading of the biography of Saint Fridolin was continued. He read slowly and distinctly, always in the same tone, but with much expression. From time to time he would make a long pause. The table-servants passed assiduously around, and carried away the empty plates and platters to the kitchen-window. The noise of spoons and forks gradually ceased entirely. Only the voice of the reader was heard. Most of the monks remained motionless, their hands under their scapulars. The prior cast a searching look through the great hall, and then rapped with his little wooden hammer. The reader stopped in the midst of a sentence, closed his book, descended from the reading-desk, advanced to the abbot's empty table, bowed deeply and chanted, *Tu autem, Domine, miserere nobis.* The monks replied, *Deo gratias,* rose and placed themselves in front of the tables to say grace. After this I left the hall, following the prior, the second in line. In the vestibule I was presented to Father Desiderius. He was a tall, stout old man, a genuine German, with prominent cheek-bones,

[242]

which were well bearded. In fact, his mouth and chin were entirely concealed by a long, white beard. Gray, questioning, searching eyes lay deep behind bushy eyebrows, and a noble nose was surmounted by a massive forehead. Father Desiderius, a very attractive and dominant personality, shook my hand heartily in both of his. All men of genius are in certain things awkward amateurs. They need assistants to help them carry out their plans. Hence they are always eagerly looking for helpers. Only the savage, like the animal, can save himself alone. We spoke that evening of insignificant matters, "kitchen and calf talk," as they say in Holland. Tired from my journey, I went to bed even earlier than the monks.

THE next day, at the suggestion of Father Desiderius, I visited the St. Maurus Chapel, the cradle of Beuron art. The weather was cold and foggy. After I had walked for half an hour beside the Danube without meeting a soul, the chapel suddenly loomed up before me out of the mist. It was built in the form of a temple. I had expected something entirely different, and my first thought was, "Why did they ever erect here such a Grecian structure as that?" For I was then still inclined always to speak ill of classicism, for had not all classicism hitherto led to academism?

Walking on a few steps I stood before the chapel. It consists of a square cella and an open portico, reached by a high flight of steps. The whole structure is covered by a pitched roof projecting considerably from the sides and sheltering thus a painted frieze. On the façade of the cella over the

[243]

entrance is enthroned in a circle, which is itself again enclosed in a square, a Madonna of more than life size with the Child Jesus. To the right and left of the square stand in long rectangles two monumental figures, those of Saint Benedict and Saint Scholastica. Underneath runs a frieze a metre in height, interrupted only by the opening for the door, and representing five monks and five nuns, bearing in uplifted hands their crowns of virtue. At first, as I contemplated the whole composition, I was filled rather with astonishment than with admiration. Only the high frieze representing the saints especially pleased me. I passed through the oaken door into the interior of the chapel. The further wall was entirely covered by a fresco portraying the Crucifixion. Against a deep blue background stand out in bold relief in subdued colours, Christ on the cross and six figures of more than life size. At the right, below the cross, stand in line the Mother of Christ, Saint Joseph and Saint Catharine; on the left, the holy evangelist John, John the Baptist and Saint Cecelia. Above the figures of the saints are depicted the symbols of the four evangelists. High on the side walls angels kneel in adoration, as they look in amazement at the work of redemption. Beneath the decorated altar of white marble lies, as if in a tomb, the statue of the holy Abbot Maurus, carved in the severest style, and on the wall of the chapel containing the door is painted the representation of his death, as he expired at the foot of the altar surrounded by his monks.

The painter has his own way of looking at works of art. Usually what interests him most is how they are made. On a sketch which Raphael sent to him Albrecht Dürer wrote: "In 1515 Raphael of Urbino, who is so highly honoured by the Pope, has made this nude figure and sent it to Albrecht Dürer in Nuremberg to show him his hand."

It is precisely the hand of the artist that the painter wishes to behold, and what inspires him with respect is to see the powerful of the earth make use of that hand, because the painter knows that after God's gift of genius the most beautiful thing is man's gift of a fine commission for its manifestation. Very seldom only is a painter so impressed by a work of art that it really moves him profoundly. But if he is thus genuinely moved, then he no longer asks how it was produced, but stands before it speechless, or utters a thanksgiving that God has given to men such power. I surveyed the frescoes of the Maurus Chapel a long while. I was not deeply moved by them, but I felt great respect for the hand that had produced anything so noble. A comparison between these paintings and those of Giotto, Duccio and Fra Angelico was natural, since I had just come from Italy. It seems to me that these artists had a still more harmonious style than the Beuron painter, but the frescoes of the Maurus Chapel had, nevertheless, one advantage — the beautiful proportions of the figures. Was this attributable to the principal of "measuring and dividing," of which Father Desiderius had repeatedly spoken to me in his letters? I resolved to learn something more of this subject, since I was now at the very source of information concerning it.

On my way homeward I looked back several times. Observed more attentively, the chapel after all suited the landscape very well, and in fact enlivened it wonderfully. In the midst of the infinite varieties of the vegetable world with its immense luxuriance of forms, this chapel, through the strict necessity and symmetry of its parts and its Doric simplicity, was the symbol of a lofty spirituality, to which its romantic surroundings contributed their share.

SHORTLY after returning from my visit to the Maurus Chapel I knocked at the cell which served as the studio of Father Desiderius. " *Ave,*" cried a friendly voice. " God greet you," I replied as I entered. " May I come in for a little while? " The noble old man was sitting behind a broad study-table, with his spectacles on the end of his nose. He stared over these glasses toward the door. " Ah, it is you, Mr. Verkade," he exclaimed, rising slightly from his chair; " come in and sit down." " Do I disturb you? " I asked; " you were reading." " One can always resume it," answered Father Desiderius; " the holy Scriptures are so beautiful, when one reads them from beginning to end, much more beautiful than if one takes up only separate passages. I have read them through already thirteen times. The Old Testament especially is very instructive for painters. It has so much in it that is majestic, and contains so much poetry."

I looked around his cell. On the great table lay all sorts of writing and drawing materials, photographs and designs, the five regular geometric figures in pasteboard, a box of water-colour paints, some books and other things, all arranged in a certain order. Among the books I noticed the *Divine Comedy,* the *Nocturnal Reflections* of St. Augustine, a well-worn Breviary, the *Messenger of Divine Love* by Saint Gertrude and the *Glories of Mary* by Saint Alphonso. On a shelf above a writing-desk, on which lay a package of sketches, stood several little figures in plaster, among which was a Madonna with Child, as slender as a column and of an unusual delicacy and dignity. On the wall hung coloured sketches and papers with geometrical figures; and also, within reach of the old father's hand, several port-folios. I asked Father Desiderius to tell me a little how he had acquired his peculiar style of art and how the Maurus Chapel had come into existence. The old monk stroked back from his lips his heavy moustaches and began:

"I came for the first time to Beuron on January 20, 1868, attracted thither by the Gregorian chant. I was then thirty-six years old and cherished great plans for the future. I regretted that modern art was completely given over to naturalism and had become merely an affair of individual fancy. For many years I had remained, in respect to nature's ever-changing phenomena, well-nigh hopelessly confused, till finally I came to see that a mere laborious copying of nature could never produce a work comparable to the art of antiquity. Hence I sought to penetrate more deeply into the secrets of the technique of the ancients. The works of the early Christian and Byzantine artists, as well as those of Giotto, had indeed taught me that geometry and division are the principal factors in the execution of art, but I found wanting in those artists the conscious and intelligent appli-cation of these indispensable means. In the old Christian and Byzantine craftsmen the principles of measuring and divid-

ing rest evidently only on a very old and now weak tradition, in following which Giotto had consulted only his own
feeling. The old Greek masters appear, however, to have
applied well-defined laws to this system of measurement
and division. What were those laws? A careful investigation
of the structure of plants and especially the study of old
Grecian vases then brought me many steps further and,
finally, while studying the forms of vases, I came upon the
monumental work of Lepsius on old Egyptian temple-
architecture. While reading this volume with the greatest
enthusiasm, it seemed to me that I had already seen those
works of art before. For my innate feeling for number,
symmetry, order and repose found in them for the first
time complete satisfaction, and also a religiosity, as I understood the term, an astonishing withdrawal of oneself into
the depths of one's own soul and a profound self-absorption
in the eternal mysteries.

"Before these works, so full of dominating force and
touching seriousness, it seemed to me that the Egyptians
possessed the secret of moving the soul of man, of controlling
his savage nature, and of awakening within him a mysterious awe. And in the application of this secret two means
seem to have been employed: first, logic, an inexorable
criticism, penetrating to the depths all that is of vital necessity; and secondly, the law of symmetry and the harmony
of dimensions. This idea, the harmony of dimensions,
brought me to the domain of music. And now suddenly
it became clear to me that, as music in melody and harmony
is based upon the relations of numbers, so also the mysterious

force of simple numerical proportions (arithmetically, 2:3, 3:4, 4:5, etc., and geometrically, $\sqrt{1:2}$, $\sqrt{2:3}$, $\sqrt{3:4}$, etc.) is met with in the classical temples and sculptures of antiquity. That is, in fact, the secret of their beauty.

"Now at last I had ascertained what was essential, and when I came to Beuron, it was my dream to elevate all modern art, and to lead it back, purified and perfected by measurment, from a state of individual weakness to one of classical beauty. Our modern artists do not, however, appear as yet to wish to consider the subject of measurement. Number is precisely something divine, and our age lacks that deep religiosity which is characteristic of primitive peoples. It seems incapable of offering to the grace of God an open heart. What is the aim of art today? What is its philosophy of the beautiful? Where is its strength, where is its light?"

It seemed to me that Father Desiderius overestimated the creative power of measurement, and laid too little weight on the necessity of creative imagination, which makes use of measurement and must first give form to it, if it is to come to success. I said nothing of this, however, and merely asked, "And how did the Maurus Chapel come to be built?" The old monk continued: "Well, on the second day of my stay in the valley of Beuron, I paid a visit to the Princess Catharine Hohenzollern, the founder of Beuron and my former sovereign, for I am of the principality of Hohenzollern, having been born in Haigerloch. I spoke with her of my artistic ideals and showed her some sketches, which I had brought with me. It would seem that God inspired me with the right words. At all events, she told me that she had made a vow to build a chapel in honour of Saint Maurus. It is true, the order for this had really been already given to another architect, but he had so many commissions to fill that he certainly would gladly withdraw. I was, she said, to make a plan for the chapel at once. I now secured a room in the cloister and took my meals at the guest-table in the refectory of the fathers. Three weeks later, I submitted to the princess a fine plan. Unfortunately it was rejected. It was too expensive. The princess had desired only a simple chapel. I wanted to go away at once, but I reflected and made within two days another plan which was accepted.

" In September, 1868, therefore in the same year, the rough mural work was finished. Then I went to Rome to my friend, Jacob Wüger,* on whose assistance I had reckoned in advance for the painting of the chapel. Wüger was three years older than I, and was really more of a designer than a painter. Ever since his childhood he had studied nature with the greatest reverence, always careful to observe in its portrayal thorough accuracy in form. He possessed a strongly marked sense of sincerity in form and expression, and had a wonderfully sharp eye for anatomical construction, and showed great perseverance in his work. Whenever he sat contemplating nature, his eyes were like those of an eagle which gazes fixedly at its prey, in order to seize it without fail. When working at a composition, he was the very picture of calmness and inward concentration. Then his sur-

* Born in 1829 at Steckborn, Canton Thurgau, Switzerland; died 1892 at Monte Cassino.

roundings no longer existed for him. The freshness of his feeling and the tenacity of his will made him capable of exceptional fineness in the working out of form. The cartoons were now drawn in Rome, and in May, 1869, we both went to Beuron, accompanied by a pupil of Wüger, Fridolin Steiner.*

"The work of painting now began. All the pictures were painted *al fresco* and in the simplest way, since we merely used water-colours, without adding to them any lime.

"In the summer of 1871 the decoration was completed, and on September fifth of that year the chapel was consecrated by the bishop. In that year also Wüger assumed the monastic habit in Beuron and entered the cloister as Brother Gabriel. Fridolin Steiner followed him soon after, as Brother Lucas, and last of all I also entered the Order, although I had been the first to come thither."

What Father Desiderius at that time did not tell me was that all the designs for the decoration of the Maurus Chapel had been drawn by him. Wüger found in his sketches a precious preparatory work which he knew how to appreciate. He did not remove from them the smallest line, but studied them with a magnifying glass. On the other hand Father Desiderius, for the technical execution of his designs, was dependent on the help of Wüger, even in the smallest details. At that time the two friends complemented each other admirably.

"Well, and what did people say of the chapel when it was finished?" I asked. "They criticised it in the strongest

* Born 1849 at Ingenbohl, Switzerland; died 1906 at Beuron.

language," replied Father Desiderius; "but the princess was satisfied and in the course of time invective has given place to praise. But come with me, the bell has just rung for supper."

In the evening, after the compline, I knelt beside two young monks at the altar of Saint Benedict and looked up at the picture of the great founder of the Order. I found it a dreadfully common painting, yet I continued to gaze at it, much as a child looks attentively at a stranger, asking itself, "Can you be my friend?" Then there recurred to me the face of Saint Francis, who until then had been my great spiritual ideal, and I found the picture of Saint Benedict still more ordinary and insipid. Nevertheless I did not cease to look at it and to think: "Can you be my father? For if I ever should become a monk, I should like to become one in Beuron."

ONE day the guest-father said to me: "Tomorrow we are to celebrate a great festival, that of Saint Martin, the patron and guardian of our cloister and our congregation. I am glad that you will have an opportunity to see how such a high festival is celebrated by us." "Saint Martin, the *Sinter Maarten* of my boyhood, can he be patron of Beuron?" I thought. "How remarkable." I tried to learn something about the saint, and the guest-father told me, among other things, the following: "Saint Martin of Tours is the first confessor, not a martyr, the anniversary of whose death was celebrated in the Church. One of his pupils, Sulpicius Severus, wrote his life, and his story was one of the most widely known lives of the saints from the time of its composition (about A.D. 450), on account of which the veneration of the holy bishop became universal and thousands of old churches and chapels were consecrated to him." I told him how, as children, on the eve of Saint Martin's day we used to go through the streets with hollow turnips, in each of which a little candle burned, or else with coloured lanterns, and how we sang songs in front of the houses of wealthy citizens, and I asked him where this usage could have originated. "On that point I can give you no information," he replied; "but wait a moment; there stands Father Wigbert, who must know all about it." In fact, this father with a certain solemnity of manner then related to me the following: "This custom, which is met with not only on the Rhine, but also in Scandinavia and Finland, seems to be a very interesting remnant of German antiquity. In old times the year was divided into two seasons, summer and winter. On Saint Martin's day the departure of summer and the coming of winter were celebrated. In doing so, fire was used, which was known among the people as a symbol of the illuminating and the warming sun, from which one had now to part. At the same time fire was a symbolical prophecy of the return of the sun after the coming winter. Perhaps also the fire of Saint Martin was regarded as a symbol of the domestic fire on the hearth, which, at the commencement of winter in our northern lands, is sometimes already of supreme importance. In any case, the singing before the doors of wealthy citizens had for its object the collection of fuel for the winter."

It evidently gave Father Wigbert pleasure to relate this, and he looked at us triumphantly as if to say, " Well, what do you think of that? " Then he bowed his head, recited the *Benedicite* and left us. The guest-father looked after his retreating figure and said slowly and accentuating every word, " Father Wigbert is a treasure-house of learning."

THE festival of Saint Martin passed off most brilliantly. During almost the entire day the praise of God resounded in the choir of the monks. Scarcely had the *Matins* and *Lauds* been sung at a very early hour, and hardly had the still Masses been read, when the black-robed monks stood again in the choir to recite the *Prime*. An hour later High Mass was celebrated. Amid the strains of solemn music from the organ the monks filed into the church. When they had arranged themselves in the choir-stalls, the ministrants passed by them in procession. At their head marched two acolytes, each of whom carried a candlestick with a burning candle. Two by two, six torch-bearers followed them and the master of ceremonies with the bearer of the censer and four precentors. Last of all came the officiating priest, the prior of the cloister, and near him were the deacon and sub-deacon, holding the border of his cope. When the procession had taken its place before the high altar, the master of ceremonies made a sign. All knelt, the monks in their choir-stalls, the prior, the deacon, the subdeacon, the four pre-centors, and the master of ceremonies on the lowest step of the altar, the others in their places near the altar itself.

They crossed themselves and continued for some time in silent prayer. The black-robed monks in the dark stalls formed a striking contrast to the priests and levites in their white and gold vestments before the richly decorated high altar. The organ-music grew softer and more solemn, and seemed itself to join in prayer.

At a signal from the sub-prior the cloister community rose. Those who were kneeling at the altar turned around, bowed to the monks in the choir-stalls and went to their places; the prior and his levites on the right of the altar passed to their seats before the credence table and the four precentors to the singers' desk in the choir. After the *Tierce* had been sung, the Solemn High Mass began. Once more all crossed themselves; the prior with the deacon and subdeacon recited the opening prayer at the foot of the altar, and the precentors sang the introit-antiphon:

Statuit ei Dominus testamentum pacis, et principem fecit eum; ut sit illi sacerdotii dignitas in aeternum.

The Lord made to him a covenant of peace and made him a prince, that the dignity of priesthood should be to him forever (Ps. cxxx).

The choral melody gave to these words unusual impressiveness. It began powerfully with the first word *Statuit*, continued in solemn recitative to the words *fecit eum*, and then, as if carried completely away with amazement, burst forth in joy in the words *sacerdotii dignitas* and finally died

[255]

away into the conclusion *in aeternum*. After the verse from the psalm:

Memento, Domine, David,	O Lord, remember David
et omnis mansuetudinis eius.	and all his weakness.

The choir of the monks repeated the introit-antiphon. The word *Statuit* resounded this time still more forcibly and the *sacerdotii dignitas* still more triumphantly. In the meantime the priest had ascended the steps and incensed the altar, during which ceremony the choir sang the

Kyrie eleison.	Lord, have mercy upon us!

Increasing and diminishing sounds of passionate entreaty rose and fell in alternate chanting to heaven. It was not the loud clamour of agonized souls, but the rapturous petition of the redeemed children of God, in which the joyful certainty of being surely heard by Him rang through the words.

When the *Kyrie eleison* had died away, the priest began the *Gloria*. Jubilation expressed itself in his tone, as he chanted *Gloria in excelsis Deo*. The precentors caught up the thrilling words and bore them onward, " Peace to men of good will." Then the monks joined in and sang exultantly, " We praise Thee "; in holy rivalry the precentors responded, " We glorify Thee "; the monks surpassed them in intensity with the words, " We adore Thee "; the others answered, " We glorify Thee "; and in more sustained tones they sang on in hallowed joy, " We give Thee thanks for

Thy great glory." Now the holy rivalry between the two choruses ceased, and the melody went on in a measured movement. " O Lord God, heavenly King, God, the Father almighty," sang the lesser choir. " O Lord Jesus Christ, the only begotten Son," the greater choir continued, almost like an echo. " O Lord God, Lamb of God, Son of the Father," answered the others in accelerated tempo. " Thou who takest away the sins of the world, have mercy on us. Thou who sittest at the right hand of the Father, have mercy on us," came then from the choirs antiphonally. And now began again the rivalry in praise of God, " For Thou alone art holy," sang the precentors rapturously. " Thou alone art the Lord," chanted joyously the choir of the monks. " Thou alone art the Lord, Jesus Christ," exultantly proclaimed the others. " Together with the Holy Ghost," was the reply, and at the highest pitch of enthusiasm the two choirs sang in unison, " In the glory of God the Father. Amen."

The celebrant, who during the chanting of the *Gloria* had remained seated with his levites, now again ascended the steps, kissed the altar, turned to the congregation and chanted:

Dominus vobiscum. The Lord be with you.

and the choir responded:

Et cum spirito tuo. And with thy spirit.

Then the priest stepped to the Missal at the right and intoned the prayer for the day:

Oremus. Deus, qui conspicis, quia ex nulla nostra virtute subsistimus; concede propitius, ut intercessione beati Martini, confessoris tui atque Pontificis, contra omnia adversa muniamur.

O God who seest that we exist by no power of our own, mercifully grant that by the intercession of blessed Martin, Thy confessor and bishop, we be strengthened against all adverse things.

Thereupon the subdeacon read aloud the Epistle:

"Behold a great priest, who in his days pleased God, and was found just. . . . There was not any found like to him, who kept the law of the Most High."

While now various ceremonies at the altar prepared the way for the reading of the Gospel, the precentors sang the gradual-psalm united with the *Alleluia*. "*Alleluia*," sang the precentors. "*Alleluia*," answered the monks. Then the former chanted:

Beatus vir sanctus Martinus, urbis Turonis Episcopus, requievit; quem susceperunt angeli, atque archangeli, throni, dominationes et virtutes. Alleluia.

The blessed man, Saint Martin, bishop of Tours, hath gone to rest, and angels, archangels, thrones, dominations and powers have received him. *Alleluia.*

When the final *Alleluia* had died away the deacon read aloud a portion of the Gospel referring to upright character, a theme well suited to Saint Martin: "No man lighteth a candle and putteth it in a hidden place, nor under a bushel, but upon a candlestick, that they that come in may see the

[258]

light. The light of thy body is thy eye. If thy eye be single, thy whole body will be lightsome; but if it be evil, thy body also will be darksome. Take heed, therefore, that the light which is in thee, be not darkness."

With the *Credo* the didactic portion of the Mass found its conclusion. The real sacrificial action now began. The monks had leaned back in their stalls, and the precentors chanted the offertory:

Veritas mea et misericordia mea cum ipso: et in nomine meo exaltabitur cornu ejus.

My truth and my mercy shall be with him; and in my name shall his horn be exalted.

Meanwhile the celebrant offered up the bread and the wine mingled with water, consecrating them to Almighty God, and withdrawing them thus from profane uses. And these offerings, which were destined to be transformed into the body and blood of Christ, and which on account of this sublime destiny became exalted and glorified, he now presented to God for himself, and "for all here present and for all faithful Christians, whether living or dead, that they may avail for him and for them to salvation, unto life everlasting." He prayed that God would grant them all to have part in the Godhead of Him who had vouchsafed to share our manhood — Jesus Christ. He offered these gifts in the spirit of humility and contrition of heart, and implored God with a solemn uplifting of his hands to bless this sacrifice.

When the precentors had sung the *Veritas mea,* the organ

[259]

took up the task of keeping the minds of the people at this high spiritual level. It had glorious tones, which rendered the solemn melodies, at first softly, then more loudly, and finally gently died away. It was as if one sat in a stately forest, entirely absorbed in thoughts. One hears the wind first coming from the distance, then passing over one, and finally sweeping on through the tops of the mighty trees. Or as if one were sitting on the seashore, gazing at the limitless ocean and listening to the rolling of many waters.

The bearer of the censer had approached the priest with open thurible, and soon there rose towards heaven fragrant clouds of incense. First the sacrificial offerings and the cross were incensed, then the whole altar, at which the priest and his deacon came and went.

The words which the celebrant speaks during this symbolic action I also reverently prayed with him:

Dirigatur, Domine, oratio mea, sicut incensum in conspectu tuo: elevatio manuum mearum sacrificium vespertinum.

Let my prayer be directed O Lord, as incense in thy sight; the lifting up of my hands as an evening sacrifice.

When the priest had incensed the altar, he handed the thurible to the deacon, who incensed first him and then the precentors and the monks, in order thereby to make plain that all those present were not merely participants in the sacrificial action, but were also themselves offerings through spiritual self-consecration. The organ encouraged the congregation to this self-consecration with inspiring harmonies, and it seemed as if before the eyes of the organist were floating the words, "God loveth a cheerful giver." I looked towards the altar. The priest washed his hands, continued a while in prayer, and then turned to the people with outstretched hands and said:

Orate fratres.   Brethren, pray.

As an experienced ministrant, I silently prayed the prescribed answer to this command:

Suscipiat Dominus sacrifi-   May the Lord receive this
cium de manibus tuis ad   sacrifice at thy hands, to the
laudem et gloriam nominis   praise and glory of His
sui, ad utilitatem quoque   name, to our own benefit
nostram, totiusque ecclesiae   and to that of all His holy
suae sanctae.   Church.

Then I saw that the deacon returned to the altar, incensed the subdeacon, and then was himself incensed by the bearer of the thurible.

Then, after the priest had addressed to the faithful the words, *Sursum corda* (Lift up your hearts), he almost immediately chanted the Preface, that solemn hymn of praise, which introduces the real action of the sacrifice:

Vere dignum et justum est,   It is truly meet and just,
aequum et salutare, nos tibi   right and profitable for us
semper et ubique gratias   at all times and in all places
agere: Domine sancte, Pater   to give thanks to Thee, O
omnipotens, aeterne Deus: Lord, the holy One, the
per Christum Dominum   Father almighty, the ever-

nostrum. Per quem majestatem tuam laudant angeli, adorant dominationes, tremunt potestates, coeli coelorumque virtutes, ac beata seraphim, socia exultatione concelebrant. Cum quibus et nostras voces, ut admitti jubeas deprecamur, supplici confessione dicentes: Sanctus, Sanctus, Sanctus Dominus Deus Sabaoth. Pleni sunt coeli et terra gloria tua: Hosanna in excelsis.

lasting God, through Christ our Lord, through whom the angels praise, the dominations adore, the powers, trembling with awe worship Thy majesty; which the forces of heaven, together with the blessed seraphim, joyfully to magnify. And do Thou command that it be permitted to join with them in confessing Thee and unceasingly to repeat: Holy, Holy, Holy, Lord God of hosts. The heavens and the earth are full of Thy glory. Hosanna in the highest.

The choir also now sang:

Sanctus, Sanctus, Sanctus. . . . Hosanna in excelsis,

Holy, Holy, Holy. . . . Hosanna in the highest,

and then the precentors and the monks sank on their knees and remained with bowed heads in the most profound contemplation. The torch-bearers who had left the choir with the censer-bearer, now returned with large burning candles, and knelt in a row before the altar. One felt that the Mass had reached its climax. The organ still sounded,

[262]

but only very softly, and ceased entirely when the little bell of the ministrant announced the holy transubstantiation. It became still in the church, absolutely still. In my Missal I followed the action at the altar. The celebrant, after the *Sanctus,* had raised his hands in supplication, and again presented the offerings; then had prayed for the whole Church and invoked the protection of God upon it, and said:

Quam oblationem tu, Deus, in omnibus, quaesumus, benedictam, adscriptam, ratam, rationabilem, acceptabilemque facere digneris; ut nobis corpus et sanguis fiat dilectissimi Filii tui, Domini nostri Jesu Christi.

And do Thou, O God, vouchsafe in all respects to bless, consecrate, and approve this our oblation, to perfect it and to render it well pleasing to Thyself, so that it may become for us the body and blood of Thy most beloved Son, Jesus Christ our Lord.

Then he bent over the offerings, and uttered over them the words of transubstantiation:

Hoc est enim corpus meum. Hic est enim calix sanguinis mei, novi et aeterni testamenti, mysterium fidei, qui pro vobis et pro multis effundetur in remissionem peccatorum.

For this is My body.
For this is the chalice of My blood, of the new and everlasting testament, the mystery of faith, which for you and for many shall be shed unto the remission of sins.

[263]

YESTERDAYS OF AN ARTIST-MONK

While the congregation of the faithful avoided making any noise, and seemed in fact to hold their breath, the organ began again to breathe softly a plaintive melody. It was a heavenly music which seemed to be wafted thither from a great distance. The celebrant raised aloft the sacred elements. The little Mass-bell sounded. The monks in the choir bowed profoundly, and the faithful also celebrated in awe the sacramental birth of the Incarnate God. The torch-bearers and the choir rose, and while the priest with lifted hands continued to pray, the monks chanted:

Benedictus qui venit in nomine Domini!
Hosanna in excelsis!

Blessed is He that cometh in the name of the Lord! Hosanna in the highest!

Then they turned, silently, towards the altar, where the priest, bowing profoundly, prayed:

Supplices te rogamus, omnipotens Deus; jube haec perferri per manus sancti angeli tui in sublime altare tuum, in conspectu divinae majestatis tuae; ut quotquot ex hac altaris participatione sacrosanctum Filii tui Corpus et Sanguinem sumpserimus, omni benedictione caelesti et gratia repleamur.

We humbly beseech Thee, almighty God, to command that these our offerings be borne by the hands of Thy holy angel, to Thine altar on high, in the presence of Thy divine majesty, that as many of us as shall receive the most sacred body and blood of Thy Son by partaking thereof from this

[264]

Per eundem Christum Dominum nostrum. Amen. altar may be filled with every heavenly blessing and grace. Through the same Christ our Lord. Amen.

Moreover he bore in mind the dead, and implored for them "a place of refreshment, light and peace," but for all those who were present he besought the communion of saints, and then chanted solemnly the *Pater Noster*. How touchingly the Lord's Prayer sounded from the altar, as if it were spoken by Himself. And how thrilling also sounded the *Agnus Dei*, which the choir now sang:

Agnus Dei, qui tollis peccata mundi, miserere nobis. Lamb of God, who takest away the sins of the world, have mercy on us.

While the monks were singing the *Agnus Dei*, the deacon received from the priest the kiss of peace. The deacon transmitted it to the precentors and the choir. Very reverently the monks embraced one another, and each gave to his neighbour in succession the kiss of peace. Before the deacon had returned to the altar, the little Mass-bell again sounded. The celebrant held the Sacred Host in his right hand and said:

Panem caelestem accipiam, et nomen Domini invocabo. I will take the bread of heaven and will call upon the name of the Lord.

[265]

Then three times he repeated aloud the words:

Domine, non sum dignus Lord I am not worthy
(then in a softer tone)
ut intres sub tectum meum; that Thou shouldst enter
sed tantum dic verbo, et under my roof; but only
sanabitur anima mea. say the word, and my soul
shall be healed.

Thereupon the priest received the communion, after he had crossed himself with the Sacred Host and the chalice, and had uttered the words:

Corpus . . . sanguis Dom- May the body . . . blood of
ini nostri Jesu Christi cus- our Lord Jesus Christ keep
todiat animam meam in my soul unto life everlast-
vitam aeternam. Amen. ing. Amen.

The celebration of the Mass had reached its conclusion. Joyfully the singers chanted the communion-verse:

Beatus servus, quem, cum Blessed is the servant whom,
venerit Dominus, invenerit when He cometh, his Lord
vigilantem; amen dico vo- shall find watching. Amen,
bis, super omnia bona sua I say to you, that He will
constituet eum. set him over all his goods.

Then followed the concluding prayer and the deacon sang the

Ite, missa est. Go, the Mass is finished.

[266]

BEURON

The priest then solemnly bestowed his blessing, and in conclusion read the opening verses of the Gospel of Saint John as far as the words, " And the Word was made flesh; " then with his assistants he passed out through the choir and the church into the sacristy, while the tones of the organ rang gloriously through the building.

As I walked out through the cloister after the High Mass, I met Father Ambrosius, the first precentor and librarian of the convent. He looked at me with a questioning glance, as if he would ask: " Well, how was it? " " The High Mass was uniquely beautiful," I said, " and you sang gloriously." The father smiled contentedly and said: " Yes, that chant, that wonderfully beautiful Gregorian chant! I have been singing it now for twenty years, and I am always discovering new beauties in its melodies. It is true, it requires a long time before our ears, which have become spoiled and pampered, can comprehend them, for the formation of melody is something different here from that which characterises modern music. But in the art of rendering a musical theme with many variations, and of changing it and reshaping it and enticing ever new harmonies from it, the Gregorian chant is unsurpassed. Is not an *Introitus* such as the one sung today, really a solemn, richly coloured overture, which by its opulence of tone and lofty inspiration announces the sublimity of the approaching mysteries? And what a Gradual or *Alleluia,* with its melodious jubilation! It thrills the heart of the singer, when such a composition greets his eyes with its undulating series of notes, which needs no text. He can then sing as joyously as a bird." And Father Ambrosius smacked his lips and passed his hand over his breast, like one who had just swallowed something delicious. "And such an Offertory," he continued, "with its long intervals, which bring with them such immensely bold curves. In that the precentors show their masterly ability, for that is food for men. It is no work for boys. Men must sing that."

"And how about women?" I asked timidly. "Women in the choir? A deeply rooted evil, especially among us in Germany; it is against all the rules of the Church; it is a scandalous procedure, a great abuse, an evil which can now be eradicated only with great difficulty. It is true, that the Church in the consecration of virgins puts the Breviary into the hands of the nuns, and they certainly have the duty assigned them of singing God's praise in the church. But have you ever heard nuns sing?"

"Certainly," I replied, "I have heard them in France, and it was wonderfully beautiful." "Yes, yes," replied Father Ambrosius, "for the first time, I grant you. Then one thinks one is hearing angels singing. But if one has to hear them continually for a month, one feels sometimes like jumping out of one's skin. It is so languishing, but, hush, hush!" and he tapped his mouth with his right hand; "this mouthpiece, this tongue of mine," he lamented, "I have been working at it all my life, but it will not improve. Now, mind you, remember I have said nothing, absolutely nothing; in fact, it is often very fine, there are exceptions."

[268]

BEURON

And Father Ambrosius went his way, shaking his head.
A monk whom I did not know and who from a little
distance had been listening to our conversation came to me,
smiling, and said: " Do not believe all that this lion of the
Gregorian chant says. In our country-parishes especially
women's voices in the church-choirs are indispensable, and
the singing of nuns is not so bad after all."

I PASSED many more hours in the cell of Father Desiderius.
Little by little he gave me an insight into the mysterious
power of the simplest numbers and geometrical proportions
in their application to art. He spoke also of his system
of treating the human form, and showed me a male and a
female figure of the finest proportions, revealing an impressive contrast. The male figure was full of strength and
dignity, the female figure full of tenderness and grace. A
geometrical construction formed the basis of both, and determined the principal proportions. The same was true of
a drawing of a head of Christ, which revealed a spirituality
of expression that filled me with astonishment.

" See," said Father Desiderius, " how the whole outline,
as well as the position of the eye and ear, etc. are determined
by construction, and how nothing has been left to chance.
The whole is achieved by the use of compass and rule. It
is true, much depends on how one uses those instruments.
The amount of reverence with which they are handled
determines the fineness of the drawing. I can see immediately, when some one merely makes a circle on a piece of
paper with a compass, whether he has the right kind of

feeling or not. Reverence is a decisive factor, both in art and in piety."

The disclosures of Father Desiderius on the subject of measurement made a profound impression on me. They promised also to be of use to me. In so far as we are obliged in this world to learn almost everything, we are weak creatures, but in so far as we are able to learn much, we are strong. Hence we are always searching for a lever which can multiply our powers a hundredfold. The geometrical construction appeared to be such a lever; and did it not furnish also a new basis for community work and for a tradition in art? For it still remained my dream not to be left merely to my own individual weak attempts, but to participate in the help and comfort to be found in effort and creation in the company of others. Was not that also the dream of the great Vincent van Gogh? How often he speaks of that in his letters? His deeply religious nature urged him on to the idea of confraternity, which was, moreover, the favourite notion of his century.

So I thought then and so I still think today; only I know now that in my case indolence had something to do with my enthusiasm for geometrical construction, measurement and number. In every man there lurks the trickster, who tries to achieve as much as possible with little exertion. We would all like to be magicians, and measurement seemed to me now to be not only a lever, but also a magician's wand.

But if the theories and sketches of Father Desiderius attracted me greatly, all the less could I become enthusiastic over certain creations of the Beuron school, which had

[270]

been produced between 1880 and 1890. In contrast to the first Beuron paintings, I found no longer any analogy between them and the works of modern art. The influence of measurement appeared with the lapse of time to have retired more and more into the background, while the influence of the style of the school of Cornelius and Kaulbach made itself always more strongly felt. But this was the only thing that did not please me there. Beuron, as a whole, was unusually harmonious and in good taste, and I had already at that time a sort of intuition that the Benedictine character receives its stamp through its life in and with its liturgy. That happy blending of deep seriousness and un-clouded joyousness, that simple directness combined with meditativeness, that high measure of decorum, joined with great vivacity, must be peculiar to monks who daily under the eyes of the Most High enact a drama of the noblest sort — namely the liturgy, a drama, in which soul, intellect and sentiment solemnly celebrate all the high and holy festivals, and in which all the arts served it as handmaids, and are fully justified.

A VISIT TO MY HOME

On the festival day of Saint Gertrude, November 17, I left Beuron for my home. I wanted to be there on the twentieth, the birthday of my father. I remember of this journey the circumstance that in the Church of Mary in Stuttgart I saw the work of Beuron artists in the stations of the cross, but was unable to feel any enthusiasm for these paintings. In Cologne the youngsters in the streets called after me, "Look, look, there's a foreigner!" I had to laugh at their combination of timidity and impudence. In travelling through Holland the numerous and for the most part recently built little Catholic churches in the villages seemed to greet me with joy. I was in high spirits. For the first time I was about to see my home again, as a believing Christian and Catholic. I thought of my family with more tenderness than ever before. I had not seen them for so long. More than twenty months. And in Italy I had learned to love.

The stretch between Amsterdam and Haarlem, where my father had, during my absence, fixed his residence, I travelled over in a crowded second-class railway carriage. Until then I had been almost always alone, but now, whether I liked it or not, I had to listen to the uncouth, coarse chatter of some good Holland bourgeois. Their conversation, which was carried on in extremely boisterous tones, appeared to me horribly vulgar. Speaking a foreign language has the advantage of making one strive to find the right expression, instead of breaking out in all sorts of old commonplace phrases. Moreover, stupidities never sound so foolish in any language as in one's own. During that half-hour I actually suffered. At last the train came to a halt. I was in Haarlem. "Good-bye, gentlemen, much pleasure!" exclaimed a passenger who got out of the train with me. "Yes, yes, much pleasure," I murmured sarcastically, "it has been charming. The next time may your mouths be frozen up tight."

On the station platform I looked about to see if any one had come to meet me. Yes, there was my sister, two years younger than myself, accompanied by a friend. "Good day, Jan, and how are you? You look very much like a foreigner. Brother Edward has been very ill, came near dying. Appendicitis. But he is out of danger now." Then the girls went on chattering about all sorts of occurrences. They seemed to have no idea what a solemn moment this was for me, when I was coming home again after an entire revolution had taken place in my life. The new residence of my father was near the station, and we were soon standing before the house. Full of joy, my mother came to me and embraced me, but unfortunately my father was not at home. He had promised his friends in Amsterdam to go to the club there, and my telegram had arrived too late for him to cancel his engagement. I entered the sitting-room, where all the cosiness of home at once encircled me. Even though the room itself was a different one, nevertheless everything was as before, the carpet on the floor, the long curtains at the windows, the pictures on the walls.

And yet I stood there feeling suddenly transported into an atmosphere which had become strange to me, the atmosphere of the bourgeois life, rooted so firmly in old Holland traditions. I felt as if I were in a little town protected by high walls and broad moats, yet by reason of that very fact also a narrowly confined one.

It seemed to me that I should suffocate. My good mother was anxious about me at once. "Bina will bring you something to eat immediately," she said. Her Martha-like activity drove me to despair. Had nothing happened, then, in the last twenty months? My sister and her friend, both young, pretty and blooming, looked at me and laughed. They had not yet perceived how deeply I was moved. I suddenly felt myself frightfully alone in my parents' house, which had itself remained unchanged. The thought occurred to me: "How many things may have been conjectured about me in this room. Great heavens! and all of them incorrect." I became terribly depressed and looked about me for help. There stood my mother. I took her in my arms and sobbed, "Mother, mother!" I could say no more. The two girls quickly left the room. My mother had also tears in her eyes, and said, "Only be calm, my dear boy; you must take a rest." I still shed tears for a moment longer. Then Bina, the servant, came with my supper. Mother seated herself behind the tea-service. The tea-kettle began to hum, and the cat lying on the sofa purred audibly.

It had really been a critical time for my brother Edward

and he was not yet allowed, my mother said, to eat anything solid. Mother had not been able for some time to read anything, except the diary of the Brothers Goncourt, the pages of which she had skimmed through. About ten o'clock my father arrived. I went to meet him when I heard him at the house-door. He received me cordially, and not a word was spoken that evening about my change of faith.

WHEN I recall the two months which I spent in Holland in the second year after my baptism, I think of those poor *babus,* the little Malay girls whom Hollanders, living on the island of Java sometimes take with them on a visit to their European home. The poor little creatures are tormented by an indescribable homesickness. Silent, obliging, patient and friendly, they have with it all something laughable about them. They come in much too solemnly in their narrow, gaily coloured *sarongs* and their bright tunics. Also if they ingenuously ask or relate something in their broken Dutch one cannot repress a smile. Now I was feeling as strange as a *babu* although in my own country. In the midst of the everlasting fog there came to me an immense longing for sunny Italy. I perceived very clearly that I appeared to others ridiculous and that I bored them. Indeed I must have sometimes been insupportable. New converts and lovers are often so. They have something about them that is so immature, exaggerated and childish. They are like the man in the Gospel who sells all that he hath in order to buy a field in which he knows that a great treasure lies hidden, only they have not yet found the

[275]

whole treasure. All that they have acquired before, even what is good, they consider useless and throw away, without already fully possessing what is new and better. They are at the same time poorer and richer than before. Their poverty, however, reveals itself clearly, while their riches for the most part remain concealed. That is the tragic side of conversions.

To my artist-friends I preached Father Desiderius' gospel of measurement, but I did little painting. Moreover, I had no studio, not even my own room, where I could work. On the other hand, I fulfilled my religious duties most scrupulously.

I must mention one dear trait of my mother. Sometimes she would wake me early, so that I should not be too late for Mass. She also said repeatedly that I should keep up my acquaintance with Beuron and Father Desiderius, since this could perhaps be very useful to me. Mother thought only of one thing, the happiness of her children. The idea that she herself might suffer if I should finally enter the cloister, never occurred to her. Her love clarified her power of insight, and made of her a prophetess.

During Advent I observed strict abstinence. I neither drank any spirits nor smoked during that time. Nor did I now ever go to the theatre or anything of the kind. I still remember what remorse I felt when I allowed myself one day to go with a friend of my youth to dine in a very expensive restaurant. On one occasion I had a discussion with my father about religion. But he regretted it afterwards. He thought that to try to convince a new convert of his error was like trying to make a Negro white. According to what my sister told me, my father had looked forward to my reappearance in the family circle with great anxiety. "How much unnecessary trouble we have created for ourselves!" she said; "and what have we not had to listen to for the last six months. And, after all, you have become much nicer than you were before." Of course, I spent some days with my twin brother in our native city, Zaandam. My sister-in-law showed me with pride her first child. Notwithstanding my great resemblance to my brother, the baby began to cry, when I wanted to take him in my arms. My father's business, with the assistance of my brother, was now very prosperous and promising.

I did not remain long in Holland. My practical common sense saw, though not without great disappointment, that for the present there was nothing for me to do there. Moreover, Ballin was urging me to come to Copenhagen. So on February 2, 1894, I took leave of my family and went *via* Hamburg and Kiel to Copenhagen, where I arrived in the forenoon of the following day.

COPENHAGEN

How happy Ballin and I were to see each other again. He brought me at once to his mother, who received me with the greatest cordiality. During my three months' stay under her hospitable roof I came to recognize in her the model of a noble, orthodox Jewess. Very intelligent, lively, yet at the same time serious, she was besides a woman of strong character. For eighteen years she had had to keep to her bed almost constantly, until she finally was able to overcome her illness both intellectually and physically. At lunch I also became acquainted with Ballin's father, a thoroughly good man, although easily irritated. Both were deeply attached to each other, and Mogens was their only child.

Already in the first days of my sojourn there we held a consultation about a " Jan Verkade exposition." I had brought with me a number of small paintings and all my sketches. Ballin was the right man to conduct such an enterprise in the way to success. He was really a friend in need who, moreover, was almost always fortunate when he undertook anything for others. The subjects to be exhibited were carefully selected. There were about forty drawings, mostly studies of heads made in Brittany, and twenty small paintings, including portraits, landscapes and still life. I had glass cut for the drawings and framed them

[278]

myself with a narrow strip of dark paper. For the paintings I had the frames made. In the *Bredgade* Ballin found a suitable hall to exhibit them. The owner charged me nothing directly for the rent, but was to get his pay from the admission fees. He was even willing to provide a catalogue, for which I drew a title page. Then I painted a picture for advertising purposes, which represented the seated figure of a girl of Brittany. This bore in large letters the words:

" Jan Verkade's Exhibition."

The pictures were hung. They did not make a bad impression, but the walls were still somewhat bare. Ballin found a way out of the difficulty. In the same house where the exhibition was to be made was a shop in which Iceland embroideries were sold, and my friend thought they would form a fine decoration to the hall. At first the owner was unwilling to loan her wares. But when she had seen the " famous painter " Jan Verkade, of whom Ballin had spoken to her in enthusiastic terms, she hesitated no longer. I looked, she said, very much like her deceased husband.

A nephew of my friend, who was the owner of a large nursery, loaned us some ornamental trees and potted plants. These were tastefully arranged, and now the exposition-hall looked really charming.

When we began to prepare the catalogue, Mogens said: " Jan, there is just one thing to be borne in mind. If you want to sell anything, you must not ask too high prices."

I let him make them, and Ballin marked the prices on each picture. This varied between ten and fifty crowns for the drawings and between fifty and two hundred crowns for the paintings. On the evening before the opening we sent out about one hundred and fifty catalogues and invitations to well-known art-lovers and relatives of my friend. On the following afternoon about half-past one o'clock we went in high spirits to the *Bredgade*. The weather was unfortunately very rainy. "Of course there will be scarcely any one there," said Ballin; "it is too early. Moreover the thing must be first spoken of in the newspapers." But he was mistaken. To our amazement there were already many visitors, in spite of the dreadful weather. There was actually a crowd in the little hall. We went in. A whisper ran through the assembly: "There he is; that is Verkade." They stared at me from all sides, but I maintained my composure, greeted a few acquaintances and spoke French, German, English and Italian promiscuously. This evidently made an impression. A girl student asked Ballin: "What does Mr. Verkade speak least well?" "English," he answered. "Good," said the girl, "then I will speak English with him."

The opening day of my exhibition was also a brilliant financial success. With serious faces several gentlemen hastened to the bureau, and soon the attendant appeared with the welcome little label, "Sold," which he fastened to some of the drawings. By three o'clock nine drawings and one painting had been bought. It grew dark and the visitors retired. Ballin invited some gentlemen and ladies of his acquaintance to celebrate the success. About ten in number, we went first into a great furnishing house, where I purchased a new hat, and then made our way to a confectioner's shop. Needless to say, I was the one to treat the crowd.

The success of the exhibition continued. Several more drawings and the dearest of the paintings found purchasers, and almost all the larger newspapers dedicated long articles to the " Holland painter, Jan Verkade."

I had come to Copenhagen at just the right time. In Denmark also symbolism, synthesism and traditionalism, of which we were the ardent apostles, had just found a foothold, and my modest beginnings possessed at that time all the attractive power of the new. Today they would scarcely be noticed any more.

In the domain of religion also we introduced many new ideas, and what lent emphasis to our words was the bold acknowledgment of our faith. That two men, who were thoroughly modern in manners and education, should advocate, with all their energy, tradition and objectivity in religion and art, and this in Copenhagen, where realistic and naturalistic tendencies reigned supreme, produced, especially in the artistic world, a sensation. It even had a decisive effect on the subsequent spiritual life of the writer Johannes Jörgensen, who was universally praised as the most eminent and talented among the young poets of his day. One rainy evening we met him on a bridge. Ballin introduced me. His exterior had nothing poetical about it. He even had a tormented and ill-humoured look. After this first meeting, however, we saw each other frequently and soon became friends. He asked me to make some illustrations for his review *Taarnet*. Nothing could have been

[281]

more welcome, and so the February number contained some drawings from my hand. The consequence was that my name became always better known in Copenhagen.

MANY an artist on account of his want of success has first become discouraged, and finally lost confidence in himself, although a little applause and appreciation from his fellow men would have been for him an incitement to do the best that was in him. To others, however, success has proved a hindrance for the very reason (to mention only one of many reasons) that with the hour of success he loses the quiet and reflection which are so indispensable to the artist. The latter proved itself true in my own experience. On arriving in Copenhagen, I had said to Ballin: "Mogens, Lent will soon be here. We wish of course to keep it faithfully." My friend gave me an evasive reply. He probably saw in advance that this plan could not be realised. The good will indeed was not wanting, but circumstances were stronger than we were. Almost every day brought some new distraction and new pleasure. Through the exhibition of my paintings I had become known to a number of agreeable and talented people, with some of whom I passed many delightful hours. Before my conversion nothing would have been more welcome to me, but in this stage of my spiritual evolution such a lively intercourse with the great world brought about a conflict in my soul, which made me at times profoundly unhappy. I was, spiritually, still a young plant, or rather a tree, which had recently been transplanted into another soil. I had not as yet put

[282]

forth deep roots and therefore needed to be still diligently watered. Those distractions, however, produced in me a great aridity. It is true, I did not really fear the loss of my spiritual life, for I remained steadfast in the faith, but I was fearful of bringing forth little or no fruit. Often I seemed to myself a traitor, and this feeling of unfaithfulness came over me, one day especially, with overwhelming force. The evening before Ballin and I had formed part of a company of gentlemen. Almost all the invited guests were artists. The reader must picture to himself one of those banquets of the civic guards, painted by Franz Hals, to form an idea of what went on that evening. Towards midnight those refined Danes had become the hale and hearty Northmen of antiquity who with red faces, arm in arm, sang the old songs uproariously. We came home about two o'clock in the morning. I sat down on the edge of my bed. Ballin seated himself near me. "Great heavens!" he exclaimed, "how idiotic all that was." "Yes, perfectly idiotic," I replied. "I am tired to death," said Ballin. "And I can scarcely stand on my legs from weariness," I added; "this has been again a fearful day. In the morning one goes to Mass, and then comes home two hours after midnight. And now we must still say our prayers before going to sleep. Tomorrow again no work will be done. And in this way we are approaching Easter. Quick! Put out the light, that we may hide ourselves in the darkness." "Well," replied Ballin, "it is of no use to exaggerate it. We have not yet sunk to the level described in Baudelaire's *Examen de Minuit*. It is true, one item applies to us: ' We have drunk without thirst and eaten without hunger.' It is disgusting, disgusting." We both nodded our heads. Then my friend rose slowly and said with a yawn: "By the gods, I'm tired. Good night, Jan, till tomorrow."

When I was alone, I threw myself on my knees and tried to unite again the thread of my life with heaven, but the next morning there was still in my soul a gnawing feeling of dissatisfaction with my real self which would not leave me. In the afternoon I felt impelled to go into the church, where I remained a long while. I was entirely alone with the Blessed Sacrament. Again I tried to come into intimate communion with the supremely High, supremely Best and supremely Beautiful and to regain my lost peace of mind. It was not in vain. The peace of God descended on me, as it were, drop by drop, until it gradually pervaded my entire being. I was again free; and with a thankful heart I felt the longing to abandon myself entirely to God, and to offer up to Him my freedom, in order to remain free. With the greatest earnestness I now begged Him to show me the place where He wanted me to serve Him. Then I went to the Jesuit Father Esser, and made my confession. Thus even during my stay in Copenhagen my plans for entering a monastery slowly ripened. The possibility of doing so, with which I had already reckoned for a long time, became now little by little a necessity of my soul. I did not yet, however, form a positive resolution to do so. For the time being I adhered to my former plan of first going again to Beuron and then to Italy. God would then indicate to me the place in which He wished to have me.

[284]

COPENHAGEN

Even if the perception of my weakness and faithlessness caused me sometimes hours of sadness, I was not on that account in general an unhappy man. On the contrary, Ballin and I were the very embodiment of joyousness, and it was precisely this that made such a deep impression on Johannes Jörgensen. For he was not happy, although always longing for happiness. He had now come to the conviction that the truth can never make one unhappy, and hence that unhappiness is an infallible indication of some error of the intellect. The question for him was, therefore, "Are these two happy men, Ballin and Verkade, in possession of the truth?" On Palm Sunday we went to see him. I brought him a consecrated palm branch and said, smiling, "Here, take this. It will bring you happiness." I really did not attach much importance to these words, but subsequently Jörgensen told me what a profound impression they then made on him, for he was at that time seeking for happiness earnestly.

On March twenty-fifth Ballin and I celebrated our second Easter festival as Catholics. We had during Holy Week lived in great retirement and had taken part in the Church's functions during the last days with loving comprehension of their significance. We felt it to be a special cause for happiness and we were able to assist at divine service with the little Catholic community of Copenhagen in the pretty church of Saint Ansgar. The meetings there had in them something fraternal, and one experienced in them a strong feeling of solidarity. After the Resurrection Mass on Easter,

[285]

we took refuge in the beautiful forests in the vicinity of Copenhagen. Some bushes were already green, and the beech trees had put forth their reddish-violet buds into the cold grey air. We talked of Italy and Saint Francis of Assisi, of his sons in Fiesole and of Father Giovacchino and Father Placido. We called to mind again Sienna with San Bernardino and Saint Catharine, and endeavoured thus to warm ourselves a little. For, to tell the truth, we missed painfully in this excellent but frigid north the Catholic atmosphere of southern lands. And only to think that formerly up here in the north there were also abbeys and chapels and wayside crosses. But the Reformation had swept away all that, and so gradually that the people did not at all realise how little by little Lutheranism had taken the place of Catholicism.

"How beautiful it may be today in Beuron," I said. "Mogens, you too must see that place some time. If you go to Italy again this year, you must stop at Beuron on the way. Perhaps I shall still be there, and we will travel on to Italy together."

"I would like to have Jörgensen go with us," said my friend; "he seems to have come to a standstill, and needs absolutely to be stimulated. Maybe I can procure for him the money for the journey. I have already thought of getting up a lottery of pictures for his benefit. You certainly will gladly contribute a couple of paintings for it, won't you?"

Thus it was that, on that Easter day, a plan was formed which was destined for the most part to be realised, as

[286]

one can read in Jörgensen's *Book of Travels,* already mentioned.

I remained for almost the whole month of April in Ballin's house, and during this time I painted, among other things, a large fresco* in the atelier of my friend "Francesco" Mogens. For a long while I remained undecided whether I should travel to Beuron and Italy *via* Holland or Berlin. At last I chose the route by way of Berlin, which I did not yet know.

ONE Thursday morning, April 26, 1894, I left Copenhagen, and travelled first by rail across the islands of Seeland and Falster and then by steamer to Warnemünde, the picturesque little city on the Baltic. Thence I once more took a train and journeyed by way of Rostock and Neu-Strelitz to Berlin. The trip through Mecklenburg pleased me exceedingly. The weather was beautiful and full of pleasing

* At this point, when the name of my dear friend is mentioned for the last time, I must pay to him still a brief tribute, for unfortunately an early death has already removed him from this earth. In 1894 he spent some time in Assisi with Jörgensen. In the autumn of that year he was ill almost unto death, but by a miracle recovered. On January 26, 1899, he married a Danish lady of French origin, Marguérite d'Auchamp. About that time he founded an atelier for artistic bronzes which has produced some very beautiful things. Five children were born to him, but his wife died at the age of thirty-four on April 8, 1907. Ballin never recovered from this terrible blow. He gave up his business and devoted himself only to the education of his children, and to the welfare of the Catholic Church in Denmark. Soon after Christmas, 1913, he fell ill and died a very edifying death on January 27, 1914, at the age of forty-two. His eldest son, whom Ballin named after his friend, "Jan," has become a priest. A second son, Bengt, died in 1923 as an Oblate in the order of Saint Benedict in the monastery of Clairvaux in Luxemburg. A third son is studying for the priesthood.

changes; the trees were beginning to burst into leaf and flower, and it was all a vision of vivid green, rose, mellow-white and blue. One frequently saw recruits, spick and span in appearance, going through their manoeuvres with enthusiasm. They fitted well into the fresh landscape and the hurrying clouds.

Quite another picture did Berlin present when I arrived there about ten o'clock in the evening. There the life of a great city, which had at last become disgusting to me in Copenhagen, confronted me again. Hence I did not enter the Prussian capital with a joyous heart, as I once entered Paris, but unwillingly and with a feeling of repulsion. I surveyed everything therefore with a prejudiced eye, and it was not surprising that I did not comprehend Berlin. Some one has rightly said of the Prussian capital: "The inmost soul of this gigantic picture of life known as 'Berlin' does not reveal itself to the casual glance. The development of a true comprehension of Berlin is particularly dependent on an intimate personal acquaintance with the leading men of the different spheres of activity controlled by this powerful dynamo of work and vitality." I could easily have become acquainted with the most influential circles of Berlin through the instrumentality of the painter Leistikow, whom I had come to know in Copenhagen. But I did not want to. I was so happy to be at last entirely alone. Moreover I was still too sensitive and weak from the powerful impression made by God upon my soul, not to be scandalized and shocked by certain influences. I still remember how disgusted I was, in a popular restaurant, to see women drinking beer out of enormous glasses, to hear an automatic pianola in a shop of musical instruments rattling off mechanically the finest masterpieces, and to behold a woman making a frightful scene with her faithless husband in the public street. All this depressed me. True, the museums were magnificent, and the *Tiergarten* was beautiful, but nowhere could one find a *Notre Dame* or even a little old chapel, where one could pray, dream and seek repose for his soul. At all events I found none. And so I could endure only one day of Berlin, and twenty-four hours after my arrival I took the night-train for Munich, where I arrived about eleven o'clock on the morning of the twenty-eighth. A copious spring rain was streaming down, but I was glad of it, and glad to hear the robins singing with joy. Yet a French woman, in the very presence of the splendid fragments of the temple of Aegina in the *Glyptothek*, asked where the "beautiful things" in Munich were, and complainingly said, " *Ce que j'en ai pour mes coups de parapluie.*"

Life in Munich seemed to me more genial and the spiritual atmosphere warmer than in Berlin. At least I could sit there in a cathedral and gaze at the beautiful old decoration of the sanctuary. In the restaurants too the waitresses served one with an almost motherly solicitude, and in the hotel *Zum schönen Rosengarten* I obtained a good room with breakfast for only one mark and eighty pfennigs a day. Ah, the good old times! I remained in Munich two days longer than in the Prussian capital, and this was destined to be the last time that I should ever go about in a great city again, as my own master. What pleased me also immensely in Munich was its silence, and I fully recovered there my good spirits and was happy. As I wished to partake of Holy Communion on Sunday, I went on Saturday evening into the cathedral to make my confession. When I had prepared myself, I saw a priest just slipping into his confessional. He was a giant in stature and very stout. The natural man in me protested: "I will not go to him; he is much too fat for me." But my supernatural self replied at once: "It is precisely to him that you must go; you must not, in a priest, first look for the *man*. Now you have an opportunity to exercise your faith." I obeyed that spiritual voice, and it was fortunate for me that I did so; for never had I found in an unknown priest so much comprehension and kind-heartedness as in this confessor.

After I had, on Monday, once more visited the *Glyptothek* and had contemplated for a long while the impressive fragments of Aegina and the imposing statue of Apollo with the harp, I left at one o'clock in the afternoon by way of Augsburg, Ulm and Sigmaringen for Beuron. From Ulm on the train dragged interminably and stopped at every little Suabian village. But I did not find it at all tedious; new landscapes continually delighted my eyes and my heart was full of the thought of the beautiful cloistered life in Beuron, upon which I was soon to enter.

BEURON, THE NEW HOME

Soon after the train had passed the picturesque castle of the Hohenzollerns at Sigmaringen, it stopped again. A Benedictine priest entered and seated himself in my compartment. He was already known to me, Father Ambrosius, the precentor and librarian of the Beuron cloister. I went to him and took his hand, but as I raised it to my lips, he unintentionally struck his hard knuckles against my teeth so violently that the latter bled. "These monks ought to be more considerate," I thought. "One wishes after all to honour in them only the priest." The train continued its course along the Danube, save when it shortened the route by rushing noisily through a tunnel. The valley grew continually narrower, the mountains, overgrown with pines and beeches, and characterised by fantastically-shaped limestone cliffs, became ever loftier, and the whole landscape always more romantic.

Nature appeared very backward in its growth. In the extreme north on the island of Seeland, the beeches had long since budded, while here only a few bushes were becoming green. The father's thoughts seemed to be continually occupied with the May services in honour of Mary, which were to commence that evening. He was arriving just in time, he said, to chant a hymn to the Blessed Virgin. At the cloister Father Ambrosius consigned me to the care of the brother who acted as porter, and hurried away. The guest-father soon appeared, welcomed me cordially, and conducted me again for the present to the cell of Saint Fridolin, reserved for guests.

On the following day I paid my respects to Father Desiderius and the others whom I knew. The reverend father prior (the abbot was still absent) gave me permission to make a long sojourn with them and a little cell in the new refectory building was assigned to me, where I at once began work upon a drawing of the Madonna and Child, which I wanted to paint in fresco in the corridor where I lodged.

A great Benedictine cloister is a little world in itself, a world inhabited only by men, but in which also woman's care is not entirely lacking, since many women lend or consecrate their useful powers to its service, a world where many talents have mutually to bear and forbear, so that they may remain preserved from onesidedness and come to a harmonious development; a world in which the vocation to the solemn praise of God is regarded as a high distinction, and where ministration to others in imitation of Christ is an honour and a mode of " walking in the light," a world with its own laws which to those who observe them bring the peace and mercy of God, a world which can be a source of strength for all who seek for union with it, a fountain of consolation for the afflicted, a means of encouragement for the dejected, a refreshment for souls that are parched and withered and a stimulant for those who are eagerly advancing in the way of the spirit; yet also a world in which " the devil goeth about like a roaring lion seeking whom he may devour " (I Peter v. 8), and which on that account can also be the scene of the greatest scandals in accordance with the old proverb, *Corruptio optimi pessima.*

In Beuron an entirely different view from that in Fiesole unrolled itself before my eyes whenever I looked out of the window of my cell. While at Fiesole I had surveyed the little vegetable garden and the diminutive grove of cypresses, in Beuron my gaze fell upon the dairy-farm of the cloister, which has now been transformed into a garden for guests. Morning and evening the " dear animals " so tenderly cared for left the stable in order to quench their thirst at the reservoir. The oxen and cows walked thither deliberately, while the calves leaped about and played. The horses and cattle were harnessed and unharnessed by the brothers. The red-bearded Brother Marian, the head-steward, ran busily hither and thither and gave brief, energetic orders. I could not help laughing when I saw him, for already on my first visit I had heard of his slight appreciation of painters who could not be utilized for anything, not even to drive a cart of manure. The stalwart brother forgot in his zeal that one can be somewhat conceited also even in such achievements as his own.

I could also see from my window the small but powerful Brother Ernst, whose forge was in the corner of the courtyard at the left. All the peasants in the neighbourhood brought their horses to him, for in forging the iron and putting on the shoes he was a master. The continual hammering disturbed me a little, it is true, but it was a sound which belonged to country life, and told of industry and energy. Several times a day the brother who served the community as tailor passed through the courtyard in order to heat his flatiron at the kitchen fire, and at all times but especially towards evening I saw monks waiting about the little well-house, reciting quietly their rosary, till their turn came to obtain water for drinking or ablution.

How happy I felt to be again in the cloister. At four o'clock in the morning the house-bell gave the signal to rise. Then I would hear the watchman going from cell to cell, and calling out the words *Benedicamus Domino*. At my door, however, he did not pause. Five minutes later, the bell in the church-tower sounded. Ten minutes later, it rang again, but this time accompanied by several others. Then all remained quiet. In the church the *Matins* had begun. Usually I went quietly to sleep again, and sometimes did not even wake at all. But about five o'clock, or at the latest half-past five, I also rose. After I had heard a Mass, I went, if the weather were good, into the garden, and made a little meditation. Even if the sun had already risen long before, it still remained at that time hidden behind the rocky heights. Over the Danube hung usually a white cloud. Sometimes one could see crows on the wing vanish into this cloud and then suddenly emerge from it again. The trees, proud of their newly awakened productive life, raised aloft their branches laden with buds, as if conscious of their mission. Pearls of dew glittered on the grass. It seemed as if every blade bore a tiny white flower. Rustic noises now began to break the morning's stillness. Finches warbled, titmice whistled, garden warblers chirped, starlings sang in flute-like notes and the cuckoo called. Nature then resembled a child who has just waked from a happy sleep, and who from his cradle gives a shout of joy from a pure love of life. And as such a child quickly frees itself from coverings and wrappings, lifts its little arms and legs into the air and tries to rise, so everywhere the buds had burst their wrappings and the long retarded growth unfolded itself in all directions. My meditation also was a kind of self-development, an upward growth beneath the radiant light of divine illumination, a gradual unfolding of myself. For as the cloister-garden day by day exhaled ever more abundantly the still, prophetic spirit of infinite hopes, so in the midst of its ever-increasing floral beauty there arose within me the intimation of a new springtime of the soul, which I was steadily approaching.

Now that I was actually living in the midst of the cloister-family, I was especially impressed by the fact of how much praying went on there. Not only did prayer and labour alternate regularly, but also during work prayer did not cease, at least when the mode of work permitted it. How often in the daytime I would hear the voices of the brothers in the kitchen, as they recited prayers. And how diligently the work went on, not only among the lay-brothers, but also among the fathers. The monks seemed not to lose a single minute. If one met them in the corridors, they always passed one at a rapid pace, pushing back their cowls and bowing; and if a solitary monk went into the garden for a breath of air, one always saw him with the rosary or a book in his hand. It was for me almost too severe. I should have liked it better if the monks had occupied themselves more with the flowers, the birds and the white clouds. "It is genuinely German to seek all one's salvation in books," I said to myself involuntarily. "Just look at that man with his big spectacles. The blind finch! Does he see nothing else but what he finds in volumes?"

But I quickly banished such irreverent thoughts. Although the cloister-community numbered then already one hundred and fifty members, it was sometimes as still as a mouse in the building. It is true, in the upper passage-ways long strips of coco-matting deadened the noise of footsteps, and the rules of silence exercised there also their beneficent influence. It was only when the monks streamed in from all sides, after the *Angelus* at noon, to the common table, that one saw how great their number really was. After the meal, however, the rule of silence was relaxed, and there ensued an hour for recreation, during which fathers, clerics and novices formed groups by themselves. A general recreation for all was a very rare occurrence. The master of the novices invited me sometimes to join his pupils. He was a Prince Radziwill by birth and had been a deputy to the Reichstag, a man who had seen and read much and, therefore, could relate many things. Unfortunately he was blind in one eye, a fact of which the novices sometimes took advantage, notwithstanding their respect for him. As the recreation of the novices was held in common, and as their master was always present, there was no opportunity for me to make the intimate acquaintance of any individual members; but I always enjoyed their simple, youthful gaiety.

I felt, moreover, in Beuron no great need of personal intercourse. What attracted me here was the Benedictine *life* in all its phases, the Benedictine *family,* the Benedictine *state.* When one observes a colony of ants, one is indeed astonished at the marvellous performances of the individuals, but one's admiration is principally evoked by the spirit of solidarity which dominates these thousands of insects, and by the great idea to which they all instinctively submit. " Here a higher will is at work," one says to oneself. And it was this which I felt so strongly in Beuron. Here a number of deeply religious men have realised a divine plan, not by instinct, but by an enlightened will, and here God's spirit has found willing instruments. It is on this account that so many pilgrims stream hither constantly, especially on Sundays and holy days. They do not come to Beuron because of certain celebrated monks, but because of the cloister itself. They come because from this place emanates a wealth of spiritual stimulus and consolation which can issue only from united forces. They come to Beuron, as to an oasis, where living waters flow and sweet fruits ripen upon stately palms, and to a home of spiritual joy.

It was, then, clear to me in advance that it would be folly to wish to enter Beuron, in order to perfect oneself, as an eminent savant or artist. That should never be the principal motive. But was it not natural for me to prefer to become a monk at Beuron rather than elsewhere since, from the first, the cultivation of art had been most intimately connected with its spiritual development and appeared to be absolutely necessary to the cloister's organic development?

At Beuron the taste of the fathers was already formed. My fresco, which was already finished in that month of May, did not displease them, although it recalled forcibly the works of the Italian primitives. A series of sketches made by Father Desiderius, which had never been completed, had recently shown me also more than ever the great value of his efforts. I found in those sketches promises, which had been thus far only partially fulfilled, possibilities of beauty which far surpassed the artistic value of the latest productions of the school. Was it not a noble aim to wish to cooperate in the realisation of these possibilities? Why then was I still hesitating? Was I not after all already a Benedictine at heart? I loved the distinctive habit of the monks and the serenity and dignity of their appearance; I loved the solemnity of their divine services, the rhythmical prayers of the choir and the beautiful Gregorian chant. I loved their natural, spontaneous manners, combined as they were with dignity and indeed nobility; I loved the discipline which controlled their work in silence and in prayer. In fact, there was scarcely one monastic custom here which I did not esteem highly. Moreover, I had no need to be anxious on the score of health, lest I should not be able to endure the convent's rule of life. The food was good and abundant, in accordance with the Order's *Rules:* " Weak constitutions should be taken into consideration. Whoever needs less, let him thank God and not be downcast. And whoever needs more, let him humiliate himself because of his weakness and not be elated on account of this tender consideration." Could one desire more? Sacrifices must of course be made, but what condition of life does not demand them? A good monk makes them willingly. Accordingly I said to myself: " After all, even if it is strict in the Abbey of St. Martin, you will be able in the choir to give vent to your feelings and sing yourself out." That comforted me.

These reflections gradually strengthened my determination to enter the cloister. The thought that, if I should become a monk, I should be freed from many cares, threw, I willingly confess, a certain weight into the scales; but the decisive influence was something quite different. I had been reading in a review the history of the founding by Benedictine monks of the Odilian mission in Africa. It was the story of a goodly number of young men and women who, full of hope and courage, laid down their lives in overcoming the preliminary obstacles always connected with such an undertaking. Most of them after long years of preparation died there within a few months. Some even suffered martyrdom. Their work consisted of little more than death. As predestined, sacrificial victims, they disappeared, engulfed in the foundations of the mission.

The reading of this story filled me with contrition. " What have I ever done," I asked myself, " through love of God or for the good of others? " Now some one was calling, " Help us! " Ought I to assist them? I hastened to

[299]

Father Ambrosius, who had become my confessor. When I told him of the impression made upon me by what I had just read, he was exasperated. "That is the usual trick of the devil," he said, "to bring inexperienced souls to ruin. He urges them to choose an aim in life beyond their powers, with the result that they miss entirely their real vocation." Then he added curtly: "I do not think that your way to heaven lies through Africa. Try to discover the will of God." When he dismissed me, I had the feeling of an extravagantly demonstrative dog that has received a kick. I was much depressed, yet said to myself, "Good, you deserved it." In the depths of my soul I still had some misgivings, but on its surface there was jubilation.

I went into the garden. It was becoming always more luxuriant and lovely. The lilacs were in bloom and sent forth a delicious perfume. A few wagtails tripped gaily over the newly sown garden-beds; swallows flew between me and a little sun-lit cloud; a flock of ambitious crows contended for a place high up on the cross of the church, while others with more modest aspirations ranged themselves in close proximity along the ridge of the church-roof. But these, as at a given signal, would sometimes whirl aloft again with noisy cries, describe an extensive circle through the air in regular rank and file, and then resume their former places.

I thought of what Father Ambrosius had said, and also of what he had not said, at least aloud. Had he not really meant, "*You are stupid. Why don't you remain here?*" And had he not expressed thus what I myself had been

[300]

thinking for a long time? Strangely enough, I did not then
bother my head at all with doubts of not being accepted at
Beuron. I was conceited and foolish enough to think that
the monks could make use of me directly, at least as a choir-
singer of the Order, and without any further consecration.
Of becoming a *priest* I had not as yet thought. I did not
know Latin, and Father Desiderius was only a subdeacon.
From that day on I resolved to remain in Beuron, but I
spoke of this to no one. It was only a week later, after my
confession, that I informed Father Ambrosius of my intention. He fully approved of it and promised to present my
request to the father prior. Two days later, I sat confront-
ing the latter in his cell. Although hardly forty years old,
he impressed me as being a thoroughly serious, conscien-
tious and spiritually mature man. His appearance was,
however, not in the least gloomy. He had evidently never
desecrated his purity of soul, and this gave to him a charm
which made his manner kind and genial. He seemed to
hate intensely all frivolity and superficiality. Twice during
our interview the word *braggart* fell from his lips. He informed himself about my age, the extent of my education
and my family relations, and asked whether I had perhaps
incurred debts or promised to marry any one. When I was
able to reassure him on both these points, he said: " The
venerable archabbot will return to Beuron, after his long
absence, in about a fortnight. Have patience until then. I
would not, if I were you, be too precipitate. For the present
apply yourself with all your energy to the study of Latin,
for a knowledge of that language is an indispensable condi-

[301]

tion for acceptance in the novitiate. That means that you must be a child again." I replied that this would be no heavy burden, and took my leave of him. Father Ambrosius provided me with a Latin grammar, and the time passed rapidly, as I studied my *mensa, mensae,* and *amo, amas, amat.*

ONE beautiful June morning the news spread through the cloister that the father archabbot would return that day. In fact, I saw him that evening at supper. When I entered the refectory, this man of sixty-six years already stood behind the abbot's table at the end of the hall. He seemed in profound meditation. His hands were beneath his scapular, over which fell a cross of gold suspended from a golden chain. When all the monks were standing in their places he raised his eyes for a moment and then recited the *Benedicite* in a voice somewhat singular in tone but characterised by something unusually distinguished and spiritual. During the meal I could not get a good look at him, for though he was seated before me, it was in such a position that I could discern him only in profile. He was small in stature, powerfully built and gave one the impression of asceticism. Neither extremely slow nor extremely hasty in his demeanour, he wore a lofty air of serenity, which apparently proceeded from a profound conception of his rank, and gave to his movements something consecrated. He finished his meal sooner than most of his sons, and while his gaze wandered thoughtfully here and there, his right hand trifled absentmindedly with the small hammer which lay near him on the table. He uttered the prayer of thanksgiving as if he felt deeply every word. When I was leaving the refectory in the company of the guest-father, I said to him, "One sees at once that an abbot is after all something different from a prior." "I am glad that you feel that," he replied.

On the vigil of Saint John the Baptist, the archabbot sent for me to come to him. He was seated at his writing table, near the window, and invited me to take a chair at his right beside the table. He looked at me in a friendly and gentle manner, and then asked me several questions: "How long have you been here? Does it please you to be with us? You have, I believe, been in Italy and are a convert, and you had never been baptised previously. Why was that? But it is so outside the Church. First one dogma is denied, then another, and finally only private opinions are taught. Do you thank God every day? When God once begins to give, He does not usually stop very soon." At last I ventured to say, "I would like to ask you whether you will receive me in the cloister." Yet, as I uttered the words, I was suddenly conscious that my liberty was now at stake, and my pride revolted at the thought that I was making myself dependent on the Yes or No of another. It must be thus with a young man who asks for the hand of his future wife.

The archabbot replied: "When any one asks me to accept him here, I endeavour to keep free from any thought of self, and to try to discover the will of God. I have the feeling that God wishes to have you here. Therefore I accept you

[303]

and give you my blessing." I knelt down. The archabbot rose and said, as he blessed me: "*Benedictio Dei omnipotentis Patris et Filii et Spiritus Sancti.*" Then he added, "Now go to the master and ask him what you must do in order to become a good novice."

Whenever one makes a sacrifice, one is apt at first to say or feel something stupid, such as, "Well, I've done it now," but later comes the immense joy inherent in every sacrifice, when it is all transfigured and glorified. On winged feet I ran, with no thought of monastic conventionalities, to the cell of the novice-master. I knocked, but received no answer. Then only did I observe that a little tablet, fastened to the door, contained the words, "Returning soon." I stepped to the open window opposite the door of the cell, to wait in its deep embrasure for the coming of the master. I gazed thence down into the sun-illumined garden. There nature wore a tranquil robe of green. It no longer resembled a blooming bride, crowned with flowers, but rather a young mother in sober vestments, wearing but one, but a very precious, ornament. Along all the paths on high and slender stalks were blooming many lovely roses, white and red, but the most beautiful of all, in the very heart of the garden, grew about the Cross.